THE PRACTICAL GUIDE TO
LOCAL AREA NETWORKS

THE PRACTICAL GUIDE TO
LOCAL AREA NETWORKS

Rowland Archer

Osborne **McGraw-Hill**
Berkeley, California

Osborne **McGraw-Hill**
2600 Tenth Street
Berkeley, California 94710
U.S.A.

For information on translations and book distributors outside of the U.S.A., please write to Osborne **McGraw-Hill** at the above address.

A complete list of trademarks appears on page 280.

THE PRACTICAL GUIDE TO LOCAL AREA NETWORKS

  34567890 DODO 898

ISBN 0-07-881190-2

Cynthia Hudson, Acquisitions Editor
Lyn Cordell, Project Editor
Nancy Leahong, Text Design
Yashi Okita, Cover Design

To my wife Lizbeth and
my daughter Elyse

CONTENTS

ACKNOWLEDGMENTS

The author gratefully acknowledges the expert assistance of all the editors at Osborne/McGraw-Hill, especially Mark Haas, who planted the idea of writing this book; Cindy Hudson, who made things happen; Jean Stein, who directed the editing process; and Paul Hoffman, who turned my sometimes jumbled thoughts into solid prose.

The assistance of the network vendors in loaning their equipment for review is acknowledged as the cornerstone of this book's concreteness and substantial insight into the use of personal computer networks. Special thanks to Keith Grigoletto of 3Com Corporation, Jill Rollinson of Corvus Systems, Inc., Craig Burton of Novell, Inc., and Rowland Day of Orchid Technology.

Finally, sincere thanks are due to my associates, my wife, and my daughter for their patience and unfailing encouragement while this work was in progress.

PREFACE

Since the late 1970s, personal computer networks have made the significant transition from the development laboratory to the real world. Initially considered a research curiosity, they soon became a technology in search of a problem. The first commercial products were considered playthings for the high-tech avant-garde, and the industry was characterized as lacking in standards and in the total-solution approach that would result in mass sales.

Today, the situation has changed considerably. Most of the early problems with PC networks have been hammered out, and the applications software that makes a network useful is now available. The IBM PC family of computers in particular has spawned a large number of local area network products. Many PC users have decided that the time has come to investigate networking, and many are seriously considering installing a network.

This book treats the subject of networks at the levels of potential purchaser, installer, manager, and user. It assumes that you are reasonably familiar with the setup and use of IBM PCs, but do not necessarily know programming.

Chapter 1 explains what a network is and gives a brief history of personal computer networks. In Chapter 2, the benefits and costs of a local area network are explored, to help you decide whether to purchase one. Chapter 3 outlines the factors that should influence your selection, should you decide that a PC network is appropriate for you. Chapter 4 examines in detail the planning and installation of a network, and includes a discussion of how much hardware and software to buy. Chapter 5, which closes the first half of the book, tells you how to use a network to run both existing applications and new ones that take advantage of the special features a network offers.

The second half of the book is devoted to detailed discussions of five popular networks. These chapters give a clear picture of what it is like to install and use each system. The contrasts between the different networks reveal the variety of features available, so that you can decide which are important to you.

Networking is a rapidly growing and exciting aspect of personal-computer use. It can enhance the performance of existing computers and open up new applications impossible to implement with standalone PCs. If you need to evaluate what a network can do for you, or if you simply want to know more about PC networks, this book will help you achieve your goal.

I

LOCAL AREA NETWORKS: WHAT THEY ARE AND HOW TO USE THEM

1

WHAT IS A LOCAL AREA NETWORK?

All personal computer local area networks (LANs) have at least one thing in common: they connect personal computers (PCs) together. Most PC LANs connect computers that are located in a single building, within a few thousand feet of one another; hence the term "local area" networks.

Sharing is the common function of all networks; the sharing may be of information or hardware. Information sharing takes place when one computer user shares a message, program, or data file with another network user. Hardware sharing occurs when two or more LAN users make use of the same piece of computer equipment, such as a hard disk drive or a printer. Early PC LANs were weakest in information sharing and strongest in hardware sharing; modern PC networks have much greater information-sharing ability. As a result, PC LANs have become valuable solutions for applications that require a group of PC users to access the same data or pass information around.

To better understand the information-sharing ability of LANs, consider the way you work in a PC environment in which there is no network. Suppose you need to send a memo to several coworkers. You type it into your PC, print out several copies, and drop the copies in the interoffice mail system. If that system is fast, your coworkers may get the memo that day, but more likely they won't receive it until the next day at the earliest.

With a PC LAN and a type of software package called *electronic mail*, you can type the memo and "mail" it to those of your coworkers who are connected to the network: you give the software a command and the memo will be available on their PCs; they can read it on the screen, save it on disk, or send you an electronic reply. All this takes place very quickly and with no generation of paper copies.

1

Suppose further that you and another PC user in your department are working on a joint project. Each of you is developing part of a large spreadsheet model to forecast the sale of precious metals over the next six months. Without a network, you must keep passing disks back and forth, updating each other with the latest versions of your work. If a LAN connected your PCs together, you could simply copy the files over the LAN to each other's disk. Even better, you could keep only one copy of the file and access it across the LAN.

Some kinds of information sharing are impossible without a multiuser system or LAN. If two or more computer users need to read and modify some common information at the same time, passing floppy disks around simply won't do. This need for simultaneous data manipulation arises all the time in the business world. For example, if two salespeople use their own terminals to check and modify inventory to reflect sales, they must share the same inventory data. They can do this with a LAN because the inventory file can be kept on one computer. Using their LAN-connected computers, both salespeople can access the data one after the other.

As previously mentioned, the other major use of a LAN is hardware sharing, the use of a piece of computer hardware by many PC users. The LAN provides a connection between each PC and the shared hardware, and software lets each PC user access the shared hardware as if it were connected directly to that user's PC. For example, a LAN can make a 30-megabyte hard disk drive act like six 5-megabyte drives, one for each of six PCs on a network. These same six LAN users may also share a network printer. If one user tries to print something before another user is finished, the LAN saves the data to be printed out and prints it later, when the first user is done.

COMPONENTS OF A LAN

PC LANs have three components: workstations, servers, and a connection between them. Both hardware and software are associated with each of these components. (Workstations and servers are also referred to as the *nodes* of a network, a term that comes from the mathematical study of graph theory. In a network, a node is a device at the junction of two cables or at the end of one cable.)

Workstations

You use workstations to interact with the network. In most cases, a *workstation* is simply a microcomputer, such as an IBM PC, PC XT, or PC AT.

(Most of the examples in this book are drawn from LANs for the IBM PC.) However, even a network composed primarily of IBM PCs may contain some special-purpose workstations. Many people are finding uses for high-quality computer-generated graphics in their work, and a common special-purpose workstation is one dedicated to providing such graphics.

You can think of workstation hardware as consisting of two parts, as shown in Figure 1-1. The PC is just like that used in a single-user environment; the network interface is unique to the LAN environment. For an IBM PC, the network interface is usually a dedicated circuit board or part of a multifunction circuit board that plugs into one of the PC's expansion slots. The network connection is a cable leading to another network node.

The workstation software is shown in the block diagram in Figure 1-2. A workstation PC has the same software as a single-user PC: applications software, such as a spreadsheet or accounting package, and the disk operating system used to manage the PC hardware (called PC-DOS by IBM and MS-DOS by many makers of IBM PC-compatibles). But in addition, sitting between your applications and the systems software, LAN workstation PCs contain network software, which makes the connection between the applications and the network. Network software looks for requests that should be handled by the network and sends them to it, while passing other requests on to the PC systems software. A workstation's network software also monitors the network by looking for messages destined for that workstation, reading those messages, and taking appropriate action as necessary.

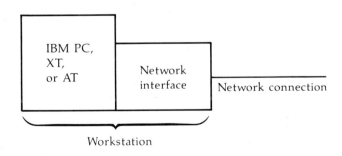

Figure 1-1.   Workstation hardware block diagram

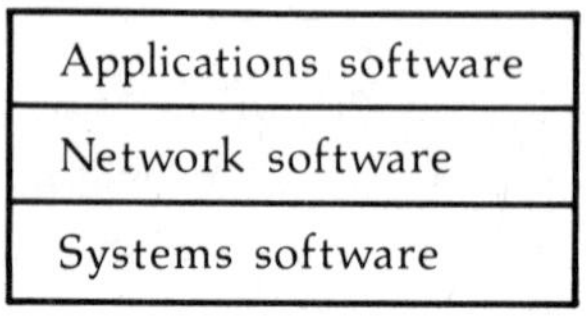

Applications software
Network software
Systems software

Figure 1-2.   Workstation software block diagram

Servers

A *server* is a computer that provides services to the workstations on the network, such as disk storage, access to a printer, disk backup, or access to a public network (such as Telenet or Tymnet) or to the corporate mini-computer or mainframe. The servers from some vendors provide multiple functions while the servers from other vendors offer only one type of network service.

With respect to its hardware, a server may be a specialized computer built specifically to do a given task, or it may be a general-purpose micro-computer such as the IBM PC, PC XT, or PC AT. Specialized servers can often provide faster response than a general-purpose computer, since they are designed to serve a network. On the other hand, many LANs allow general-purpose computers used as servers to double as workstations, which a specialized server cannot do.

Most servers — especially those based on PCs — run standard PC systems software plus special networking software. The PC systems software controls the server's hardware; the networking software provides a connection to the network and manages the sharing of the server's hardware by the network workstations. The sharing functions that are usually provided include:

- Dividing resources among the workstations, such as by making a single hard disk act as if it were several small hard disks, one for each workstation.

- Controlling sequential access to a piece of hardware that can be used by only one workstation at a time, such as by saving information destined for a printer until it is free to print it.

- Keeping information secure so that only authorized workstation users can read or modify it after supplying the correct password.

- Providing programming functions that applications software can use to control simultaneous access to the same file by many users.

- Managing the stored information about the network users, such as who has network access privileges and who owns or controls network resources.

The server software is an extremely important component with major impact on the capabilities and usability of a network.

Connections

The backbone of a LAN is the system that connects the workstations and servers together. This system is a combination of cables and special-purpose hardware. A printed circuit card called a *network transceiver* or *network interface card* is used to hook each PC workstation or server to the network. The cable that connects things together is usually a wire, although some LANs use optical fibers. The three most important characteristics of the connection component of a network are the type of cable used (wire or fiber), the way the cable is routed between server and workstation, and the nature of the electrical message traffic over the cable.

PC networks use many different cables; some even use more than one kind. The most common types of network cables are described by the general terms coaxial and twisted-pair. Coaxial cable consists of a center lead surrounded by inner and outer insulation sleeves, which are separated by a conductive shield. (This is the type of cable commonly used in cable TV hookups.) Twisted-pair consists of two insulated wires twisted together and covered by a common insulating sleeve. Some types of twisted-pair cable also incorporate a conductive shield around the twisted wires.

The way a network cable is run between workstations and servers — that is, its physical layout — is called its *topology*. The three most common topologies are the bus, ring, and star. In a *bus* topology, a single cable runs past all the network nodes, connecting to each either directly or through a short *drop cable* that runs from it to the node. In a *ring* topology, a cable is run from one PC to the next like a bus, but the two ends of the cable are connected together. In a *star* topology individual cables run from the server to each workstation. There are other variations on these wiring schemes, sometimes combining two, such as the bus and the star.

The form in which messages are passed along the network wire and the way a single network cable is shared by multiple nodes are described as the network protocols. There used to be heated debate among computer network engineers as to what was the best protocol, but it is now clear that there is room for more than one. The tradeoffs of the various approaches are well understood, and commercially useful implementations of several different protocols are available.

HISTORY

In the mid to late 1970s, local area networks were more a topic of discussion and development in research labs than they were commercial products. There were some exceptions, among the more prominent being Datapoint's ARCnet, a minicomputer network that today boasts a large installed user base and for which other vendors have made many adaptations into PC LANs. Also available around the same time was IBM's SNA (Systems Network Architecture). SNA is not a local area network, however; rather, it is IBM's large-scale computer communications architecture, serving such functions as connecting many large mainframe computers together with thousands of terminals. SNA is widespread and important enough that many PC LAN vendors offer ways to interconnect with it.

Prior to the PC's introduction in 1981, LANs started getting more and more attention, due largely to the efforts of Digital Equipment Corp., Intel Corp., and Xerox Corp., which combined resources to develop the Ethernet LAN. Ethernet has evolved considerably since then, and many commercial implementations of Ethernet are available today. In fact, IBM is one of the few major computer hardware vendors that does not offer a network based on it.

Corvus introduced Omninet in 1981, largely as a means of sharing a hard disk among several microcomputers. The IBM PC was not among them at first, although it is supported today. Also in 1981 the newly founded Novell Corp. delivered its NetWare network systems software (originally called ShareNet), which it has since adapted to dozens of different networks. Nestar was one of the first vendors to provide a LAN for the IBM PC, announcing their PLAN network in 1982.

There was a great deal of activity on the networking scene in 1983. Dozens of IBM PC networks were introduced, including 3COM's EtherSeries, an Ethernet-compatible system. The diversity of systems being delivered that year made it apparent that networking standards were needed to control the proliferation of incompatible hardware and software and encourage orderly growth in the industry. IBM announced a LAN cabling scheme without announcing a networking product, postponing announcement of the latter for some two years. The wiring scheme is called the *token-ring* wiring standard, referring to the low-level communications protocol used by the network. IBM gave their customers instructions on how to install the network cable so they would be ready when the complete network became available.

In 1984, IBM introduced its PC Network product, which was not based on the token-ring cabling. The IBM PC Network uses hardware from Sytek, an outside manufacturer, and software from IBM and Microsoft Corp. The Microsoft software, MS-DOS 3.1, has been adopted by a growing number of other network vendors, and it appears to be establishing a de facto standard for network programmers.

In October 1985 IBM fulfilled its promise to introduce a LAN product based on the token-ring, when it announced a series of hardware products that connect PCs together. In coming years IBM is expected to link most of its present and future hardware together by means of the token-ring network.

STANDARDS

There has been much committee activity directed to establishing formal standards in the networking world. Despite many useful results, conditions have not yet evolved to the point where you can easily buy a workstation from one vendor, a disk server from a second, and a print server from a third without first doing some very careful checking for compatibility. It is important to understand what the standards committees have and have not done, partly to become familiar with the jargon of networking and partly so you won't think you can buy network components and plug them together as easily as hi-fi components.

The most important work on LAN standards is being done by two organizations: ISO, the International Standards Organization; and IEEE, the Institute for Electrical and Electronic Engineers. ISO has published an almost universally accepted model for describing networking systems. Known as the *Open Systems Interconnect* (or OSI) model, it describes the general pieces that a network should contain. Each piece is slowly evolving into one or more standards, starting with the lowest levels. It is analogous to a committee's deciding that a house will be built from a foundation — wood framing, plumbing, wiring, a roof, and the like — and then looking at each piece in turn and refining it: the foundation will be poured concrete, wiring will be 110 volts or 220 volts, pipes will be 1" or 2" in diameter, and so forth.

International Standards Organization

The OSI model, illustrated in Figure 1-3, consists of seven layers. The layers represent both the hardware and software of a LAN, including servers, workstations, and connections. The same layers are used to describe the hardware and software in a workstation or a server. The lowest layers are the best defined and contain some real standards, such as RS-232C for asynchronous communications (familiar to most microcomputer users as the "serial port"). The upper layers are the least defined, and represent the interface to applications using the LAN.

Layer 1, the physical, is the lowest layer. It represents the network connection: the cables and hardware interfaces to the workstations and servers on the LAN. This layer describes mechanical connectors, electrical impedances, frequencies, and voltages. Compatibility at this layer is vital.

Layer 2, the data link, defines how information is put onto the LAN and how transmission errors are detected. If your applications program wants to send the word "hello" to the print server, that word needs to be packaged so that the LAN will know to send it to a particular print server. This data includes some information that will help the layer 2 software on the print server determine that an error has occurred; that, for example, it has gotten the word "jello" instead of "hello."

Layer 3, network, addresses the routing and relaying of information from one network to another. If you need to send mail to someone on another LAN, software at this layer needs to determine how to find that other LAN. This layer also guarantees that if one workstation sends another workstation two messages in a row, the first message seen will be the first one sent.

Layer 4, transport, contains the logic needed in order to split a long message into pieces of the size that the lower layers can handle. It also reassembles the smaller pieces into the original message at the other end of the wire. Layer 4 is also responsible for reliably transmitting information from one network node to another. For example, if an error is detected by layer 2, layer 4 must request the sender to send the message over again.

Layer 5, session, handles the connection of two network nodes for the purpose of exchanging data. If a session is disrupted, this layer is respon-

Layer 7:	Application
Layer 6:	Presentation
Layer 5:	Session
Layer 4:	Transport
Layer 3:	Network
Layer 2:	Data link
Layer 1:	Physical

Figure 1-3.   The OSI Open Systems Interconnect model

sible for restarting the session when the disrupting influence is gone. For example, say a user is sending 20 data files to another and the network fails after only 10 are transmitted; once the network is working again, proper session control will restart the transmission where it left off.

Layer 6, presentation, addresses such issues as the way data is displayed on the workstation monitor and translation between character sets used by a workstation and those used for data transmission.

Layer 7, application, provides an interface for applications programs using the network. In layer 7 reside the programs that *use* the network, rather than programs that *make up* the network.

Some detailed standards have already been published for the first two layers. Some industry standards exist for layers 3 and 4. One is SNA from IBM, and another is TCP/IP, the Transmission Control Protocol/Internet Protocol used by the United States Department of Defense. Xerox Corp.'s XNS (Xerox Network Systems) protocol is a third, and it is used in a large number of PC LANs.

Layer 5 is the layer implemented by IBM's NETBIOS, a software interface provided on the IBM PC Network and the token-ring network. NETBIOS is becoming a de facto standard; many PC LAN vendors have committed to providing it so that network systems programmers can write software that will run on many different LANs with little or no change.

The last two layers, 6 and 7, are not governed by any significant standards. The lack of a complete set of official standards for all the layers is the reason that network components from one vendor may not work with components from another vendor, even though both are, for example, "Ethernet compatible." Since both are designed for Ethernet, it is very unlikely that either will "go up in smoke" when connected to the same Ethernet cable, but there is no guarantee that one vendor's workstation will work with another vendor's print server.

IEEE 802 Standards Committee

The Institute for Electrical and Electronic Engineers has a standards committee, known as the 802 committee, that has published several standards for networks. These standards conform to the OSI model just described. It is important to realize that "IEEE 802" represents several standards, each evolving from separate subcommittees.

The early work on Ethernet was picked up by the IEEE 802 committee and resulted in the IEEE 802.3 published standard. Even though there now is a published standard for Ethernet, there is still some confusion on the subject. The IEEE 802.3 standard differs from the original Ethernet system jointly developed by Xerox, Digital Equipment Corp., and Intel, and the 802.3 version is sometimes called "Ethernet II." Nevertheless, most vendors are committing to the 802.3 standard. To add to the confusion, there is growing interest in another system called "Cheapernet," which is compatible with Ethernet II at many levels but uses less-expensive wiring and transceiver cards to reduce the cost of installing a LAN.

Another IEEE 802 subcommittee, 802.4, has published a standard based on Datapoint's token-passing ARCnet. IBM has been active in the 802.5 subcommittee, and the IBM token-ring network product conforms to the 802.5 standard.

Although there is still much work to be done in the area of networking standards, good progress is being made and the industry seems to be realizing the value of adhering to standards. As you will see later in this book, several combinations of published and de facto standards are evolving that can provide a good foundation for multivendor support of a single network installation.

2

SHOULD YOU BUY A LOCAL AREA NETWORK?

Although LAN sales are steadily increasing, many potential users are postponing the purchase of a LAN because of confusion over network applications, benefits, and standards. LAN hardware and software are rapidly maturing, and many of these early concerns are being addressed. Still, a LAN is not the only or the best solution for everyone, and you need to measure your requirements against LAN costs and capabilities. Multi-user systems offer many of the same benefits as a network, and many such systems can even be combined with networks. This chapter provides you with a framework for analyzing your own needs in order to make this important decision.

USES OF A NETWORK

Before you can decide whether to install a network, you need to understand how networks are used and how the various ways of using them satisfy your requirements. Most network installations fit into one of two categories: the first is a dedicated application system on which most users run the same set of programs; the second consists of communication between personal computer users who each use their PCs for individual functions. Users of a dedicated system tend to view the PCs and the network as a single appliance, while users of the second kind of installation may be more interested in learning technical details and experimenting with different applications packages. Each of the two kinds of installations meets a somewhat different set of needs, and it is worth understanding these.

The Dedicated System

A dedicated network application is usually one in which sharing of information is a critical requirement. The main implementation choice is between a multiuser system and a network. For example, you may be installing PCs in a classroom laboratory in which it is mandatory that the teacher and students be able to send information back and forth immediately. In a business situation, more than one employee at a time may need to enter invoices into accounts payable, or two sales clerks may need immediate access to inventory figures. In these instances, the users only need to run programs that are provided by the computer installer (who is often an outside consultant); no further demands are made on the system. In this case, the system configuration may remain fairly static and require little managing.

The hardware you choose for a dedicated installation may be less expensive than that intended for networked PC users. For example, your applications may all run from the network disk drives, allowing diskless PCs to be used as workstations. The pattern of use of the network itself may be more constant and predictable, allowing its peak needs to be handled with fewer server hardware components. Hard disk usage is easier to estimate and control, since the number and size of software applications are fixed and the data storage space needed is a function of business activity.

A dedicated system at a given site may be either a totally new installation of PCs or an enhancement to an existing PC installation. Each of these cases has a different set of problems that you should consider before installing a network. If you are designing a new PC installation, you have a chance to select a complete set of applications on the basis of their ability to share information over a network. This should result in consistent use of the network and good control over data. The negative side to an all-new installation is the larger number of new hardware components and software programs to install, get working, and train people to use.

If you are considering adding networking capability to a group of PCs already running dedicated applications, you need to decide whether to install networked versions of the existing applications or to try to convert the system over to new applications. In both cases, you not only must train people to use the new network software, you also must consider how you will get the old data converted for the new applications. Even using network versions of old applications introduces new questions of security and controlling access by multiple users to the same file.

Communication Between PC Users

The second category of useful network application is for a group of PC users who want to share hardware and information. This class of users may be working in small businesses and using PCs for a variety of word processing and accounting chores; they may want to add a fast printer that everyone can use, or set up a new accounting system that smoothly integrates functions previously done separately. Or such users may be managers in a medium-to-large corporation; they may be doing project management and financial analysis and would like to be able to send electronic mail or directly import information from the corporate mainframe. They may be programmers developing software on PCs and want to share common subroutines or control source code updates on a large project that many programmers are coding in parallel.

This group of users is likely to be using many applications, and their needs are usually much less predictable and controllable than those of dedicated applications users. Consequently, the job of network cost estimation is more difficult, and the ongoing management of the network is more challenging. Fortunately, there is usually at least one knowledgeable user at such a site who can handle the network management job.

Most such users are already experienced, productive PC users who must perceive a network as enhancing their productivity or they will reject it. They may be used to having their own machines, having total control over the way they are used, and having no need to share them with others. A network introduces a new requirement for cooperation. If the network was poorly chosen or installed and slows things down instead of providing benefits to the users, you will be faced with an unpleasant situation: thousands of dollars worth of unused networking hardware and an uncooperative group of users. If you find yourself in such a situation, review the information presented in this book on installing and using a network. It may turn out that the system you selected is suitable to your needs, and can be made efficient and productive through some simple configuration modifications that better balance the use of the network. If you still have problems, consider enlisting the help of an experienced consultant who can provide references of successful installations. Sometimes the initial setup is better done with the aid of an experienced hand.

BENEFITS OF A NETWORK

Like most investments, a network should be assessed on the basis of costs and benefits. Table 2-1 lists some of the costs and benefits of a network. Your list will no doubt include items not listed and omit items that don't apply in your case.

The obvious items of major expense are the network hardware and software. You can do a rough analysis without a specific network vendor in mind, but you should repeat it once your choice is narrowed to one or two vendors. People's time is also a factor, not only during the installation and training period, but also over the long term, because you will need a network manager: the person in charge of the network, responsible for

Table 2-1.   Some network costs and benefits

Costs	Benefits
Hardware	Financial
Workstations	Shared hardware
Additional memory	Improved hardware use
Additional disk storage	Increased productivity
Network connection board	Organizational
Cables	Improved communications
Servers	Increased sharing
Disk servers	Data consistency
Print servers	Backup control
Gateways	People
Other servers	Access to better hardware
Software	Sharing managed by system
Workstations and Servers	
DOS upgrade	
System software	
Network applications	
People	
Installation time	
Network management time	
End user training	

allocating its resources and authorizing people to use its various parts. For a small- to moderate-size network that doesn't change much, the network manager's job may be minimal and can probably be absorbed as a part-time activity by a knowledgeable user. In a large installation with many servers and a constantly changing user community, this job grows in significance and may become quite time-consuming.

Some of the benefits of a LAN are concrete, such as the savings in hardware costs achieved by having many users share one piece of hardware instead of each using a separate device. Your present hardware may also be better used, since different people will probably want to use it at different times, keeping it in use more often than when it was dedicated to a single user. Network applications like electronic mail can boost organizational communications, with beneficial results: increasing the amount of program and data sharing reduces redundant individual efforts; presenting the same file to many users at once provides a consistent picture of organizational data; assigning the responsibility for backing up data to a single person increases the likelihood that that vital function will be regularly performed.

After you build the cost/benefit list that is correct for you, you must quantify each category the best you can. You will find help with many of the common costs and benefits in this book. Some of the other benefits, such as increased control over backups and data security, are difficult to quantify.

The analysis takes a different form if you know that your needs cannot be met by establishing communications among isolated personal computers but instead require a network or a multiuser computer system—as, for example, when real-time access to data must be shared. In this case, the cost/benefit analysis can still be done, but the conclusion is a foregone one. Your application needs change the terms of the question. It is no longer a question of whether or not to use a network, but of whether to select a network or a multiuser system. You should do a cost/benefit analysis for each selection and compare them. Multiuser computers and networks are discussed later in the chapter.

Sharing Hardware

One of the most tangible benefits of a LAN is that it requires fewer peripherals per user than a stand-alone PC environment, since LAN users can share hardware. A worksheet like the one shown in Table 2-2 can be helpful in balancing the cost of installing a LAN against the savings in

Table 2-2.   Peripheral sharing cost analysis

Peripheral	Unit cost	Number needed w/o LAN	Cost without LAN	Number needed with LAN	Cost with LAN
Laser printer	$ 3500	2	$ 7000	1	$ 3500
10 MB disk	800	10	8000		
30 MB disk	1500			3	4500
10 MB tape	1000	10	10000		
60 MB tape	2500			1	2500
Peripheral cost without a LAN			$25000		
Peripheral cost with a LAN					$10,500
LAN peripheral cost savings					$14,500

shared peripherals. In this example, an installation containing 10 PCs is under consideration. Without a network, each PC needs a 10-megabyte hard disk and a 10-megabyte tape drive for backups. The two laser printers will be shared by the 10 users, introducing some operational difficulties since the printers are directly accessible from only 2 of the 10 PCs.

If a LAN is used, the same productive efficiency can be obtained from one laser printer, three 30-megabyte hard disks, and one 60-megabyte tape drive for backup. This setup represents a savings of $14,500 in the cost of peripherals. If the LAN costs $800 per workstation and $7000 for a network server, the $15,000 apparent LAN cost is reduced to $500 by the peripheral cost savings, and now all users can access the laser printer without leaving their PCs.

If, on the other hand, your hardware needs are considerably less—for example, you don't need a hard disk and you need only a $400 dot matrix printer per PC—savings from peripheral sharing won't justify the cost of a network.

A consideration that is separate from peripheral cost savings but perhaps equally important is the operational benefits of sharing hardware on a LAN. More convenient access to shared hardware may mean higher productivity. For example, in the absence of a LAN a user may copy a file to a floppy disk and carry it to the PC attached to the laser printer, interrupting the work of the person who normally uses that PC; then both people wait while the printing is done. By contrast, each LAN user has access to the printer as if it were connected to his or her own PC. It is easier to make sure your hard disk backups are done when the whole network can be backed up on a single drive than when 10 people must remember to do their own individual backups on separate drives.

Having fewer devices may lower maintenance costs. In the preceding example, 10 disk drives in a stand-alone configuration are replaced by 3 on a LAN, 10 tape drives by 1, and 2 printers by 1. This reduction from 22 devices to only 5 may sufficiently reduce maintenance costs to easily cover the last $500 of initial LAN cost figured in that example. There is, however, the consideration that having fewer devices increases the number of people who depend on each device. A failure of, say, the one network printer means *nobody* can print until it is fixed. However, having fewer devices to cover by a maintenance contract may enable you to justify a higher-cost contract with faster guaranteed repair time, reducing the loss of productivity from hardware problems.

Sharing hardware helps to justify the installation of faster, more-expensive peripherals on the grounds that the additional speed can increase productivity. But that increase may be offset by the increased number of users sharing the device, which in some situations may mean that users spend more time being unproductive while waiting their turn. Whether fewer, faster devices mean a net gain, loss, or neither depends on your particular patterns of use.

Every installation must be analyzed in its own context, since there are an infinite number of possible variations. Of course, before you can do such an analysis you need to know how to estimate the number of peripherals required with and without a LAN. The rest of this book provides much information on this process, especially the section in Chapter 4 on planning a PC network.

Sharing Information

Information sharing is less tangible than hardware sharing but in many cases may be more important. Business was transacted and people communicated before there were personal computer networks, so obviously there are other ways to get the job done. A network should offer some improvement over the system it replaces, provide a new service that saves time or money, or so enhance the work environment as to increase productivity and efficiency. Your job is to determine what that improvement, innovation, or enhancement is and how to measure it.

At this point in your decision-making process you perform a *payback analysis*. You need to understand what information is transferred today in your present system, how much the information transfer costs, and what the benefits of such transfers are. You then need to answer each of these same questions assuming a network is available. The term *information transfer* is used in a very general sense to mean any use of the network (since what networks basically do is transfer information). You need to factor your own circumstances in and use the right unit of measurement for your case.

The cost of transferring information in a network should exclude initial network purchase and installation costs, and should consist solely of the operating cost   the cost of running the network to transfer information. The benefits minus the cost of each transaction represent the profit or loss. If the network figure represents a higher profit or lower loss, then that increment times the number of transactions per year represents the net benefit of having a LAN each year. Divide the cost of purchasing and installing the LAN by this yearly benefit and you get a rough estimate of the network's payback period measured in years. If you found a savings from sharing hardware on a LAN, subtract this savings from the purchase cost of the LAN before entering the cost in the preceding equation. Of course, this estimate is unadjusted for depreciation or investment tax credits; if you need to increase its accuracy in these or other areas you should consult an accountant.

You may find it difficult to quantify the costs and benefits of information transfers. Don't be discouraged—just going through this exercise forces you to think about your business or organization in a new way that is beneficial if you decide not to purchase a network, and is of fundamental importance if you do. Analyzing information flow can help you see better ways to do things and uncover wasteful or redundant movement of data, be it on paper or electronic media. Consider the following potential improvements:

- Time saved trying to reach people on the phone if electronic mail is available as an alternative.

- Increased sales possible if clerks can handle more people through faster computer response.

- Improved control of your business if data can be gathered in real time from many control points and analyzed at any moment.

- Protection from losses if data is stored centrally where it can be kept secure and backed up.

This book contains many more examples of data transfer on a network, and you should think about the cases that apply to you and build your list as you read.

Table 2-3 gives a simple example of a payback analysis, continuing with the network installation described previously. In this case, it has been determined that the 10 employees in this department currently make an average of 10 phone calls a day, 250 days a year, or 2500 phone calls per year. These phone calls cost an average of $2.00 each, or $5000 per year. It was further determined that half of the phone calls made were completed successfully the first time, and the other half represent "call backs"— one or more repeated attempts. This estimate is very conservative, since most studies have shown a higher ratio of unsuccessful calls in reality.

You have determined that if a network with electronic mail is installed in this case, 8 of the 10 phone calls each day can be handled through electronic mail and 2 must still be made over the phone. Since electronic mail eliminates the need for call backs, only four messages need to be generated in place of 8 phone calls, for a total of 1000 electronic messages per year. Electronic mail is usually less expensive than a phone call—an estimate of $1.00 per message is used in the table. This one use of the network alone saves $3000 a year. When the payback period is computed, the balance of

Table 2-3.   Payback analysis of a LAN

Type of information transfer	Without a LAN			With a LAN		
	Number per year	Cost each	Cost per year	Number per year	Cost each	Cost per year
Phone call	2500	$ 2.00	$ 5000	500	$ 2.00	$ 1000
Electronic message				1000	1.00	1000
Cost without a LAN			$ 5000			
Cost with a LAN						$ 2000
Savings from LAN						$ 3000

$$\text{Payback period} = \frac{\text{Installation cost} - \text{Other savings}}{\text{Annual savings}} = \frac{\$15,000 - \$14,500}{\$3000}$$

$$= \frac{\$500}{\$3000} = 1/6 \text{ year}$$

the network cost not justified by the savings from hardware sharing is covered in only six months by savings in phone expenses. Among the hidden savings not even mentioned here is the reduction of unproductive time spent on the phone discussing matters unrelated to the message that needs to be communicated.

Network Applications
Software

Whether a network can do useful work for you depends on whether you can run the right software applications. There are two broad categories to investigate:

- Single-user software written for stand-alone PCs but able to take advantage of a network.

- Software written especially for a network and requiring some feature of a network to function.

If you are considering a network to enhance the environment of a group of stand-alone PCs, you will probably consider the first category most seriously; if you want to set up a new installation and networking seems important to achieving your aims, you are probably interested in the second category. Of course, you may have mixed requirements and need to consider software in both categories.

Network vendors have taken steps to ensure that most single-user software can be used in some fashion with their products. (The reason is that most software on the market is written for the single-user PC—by a considerable margin the most prevalent type of machine.) A PC network typically lets single-user software access the network printers and hard disks, and perhaps other shared peripherals as well. The ability to do this well is of key importance if you are considering adding networking to a group of existing PCs with applications that you have a financial investment in and that your users have spent time learning.

New software written specifically for a network often takes advantage of the network's ability to send data between PCs. In this class of software you will find electronic mail systems that let network users send messages to one another. Another use of this capability is to send files from one PC to another, a more direct and quicker form of sharing information than the nonnetwork alternative of copying data to floppy disks and mailing or carrying it to another PC user.

Most network system software has controls that let programmers store data on a network server where it can be accessed by two or more network PCs at a time. A number of multiuser-shared database systems are appearing for networks that provide not only all the features of single-user database systems but also extra controls for use in the network environment. If you use a database management system on a stand-alone PC and would like to be able to share databases with other PC users, this is the type of software you need. If you write your own programs for your database manager, you will need to learn some multiuser database update rules, which should be provided by the vendor of your network database management system.

Although its use seldom justifies the cost of a network, another popular application of networks is a multiuser personal calendar manager. This type of software lets you maintain your own daily appointment calendar, which can be read and updated by others on the network; and you or any of several network users may even schedule meetings for all who use the calendar manager to keep their appointments.

Connections to Other Networks

A *gateway* is a hardware device that connects two networks together and lets users on either network communicate with those on the other network. If the gateway happens to connect you to a public access network such as Telenet or Tymnet, you can communicate with other computer users who have access to the same public network. This capability is often used to send messages and files, or to log on to a remote computer using software that lets your PC act like a terminal.

Gateways are also used to connect with corporate mainframes, such as IBM systems networked with IBM's SNA. Many software packages let you access data on the mainframe (with proper authorization) and import selected information to your PC for local processing. The most common uses of mainframe data include putting it into a database or spreadsheet for manipulation, analysis, graphing, and reporting. If you have a number of users who need to do this occasionally, a single gateway on the network can give them all access to the mainframe, perhaps more economically than if everyone had individual connections to it.

Centralized Control and Distributed Computing

A network can also help you to establish centralized control over some important aspects of computer use in your organization, while still maintaining the benefits of distributed computing. A centralized, shared database is easier to manage than many small databases stored on individual PCs. And such a database is more appropriate for holding information that applies to or is used by more than one person. For example, if you store the names and addresses of customers in one centralized database that all your users can access over the network, a customer address need be updated only once, in the central database, and all users will see the latest version of the address the next time they access the database. If the address was stored in many different users' individual PC databases, they would all need to update it, requiring much extra effort and increasing the likelihood of error or omission of an update. The same principle applies to many other types of information stored by every organization.

Another advantage of centralized control of data is the ease of assembling information and analyzing and reporting it. If data that needs to be compared or merged is stored on many different PCs, gathering it can take much time and effort. Often, as a consequence, opportunities that require such an effort are simply bypassed.

Storing data in one place also allows security to be increased. Most network software lets you control who can access data and what they can do to it. If someone needs to view a file or a part of a file, the network manager can grant the person access to that data as necessary. Without a network, the entire file may have to be copied and given to the user, running the risk that it will travel further than intended, or that parts of it will be updated and then not merged in the original file, resulting in the creation of several versions of the file. It may be impossible later to reconstruct a consistent, accurate set of information. Networking does not by itself eliminate the problem: the network manager must set up the proper security controls for the benefit to be felt. If network users can freely copy files to their own PCs, the exact opposite scenario could take place, with many versions of the same file again in existence across the network.

While providing the benefits of centralized data storage, a network still keeps the attraction of distributed processing. Each user's having his or her own computer allows for consistent, predictable response time as long as all processing is being done on that local computer. If you add networking to a group of existing PCs, you should try to configure the system so that people can use their PCs just as before and get the same response times, or use new features provided by the network at its performance level. Since some parts of the network can be used by only one user at a time, access to the network is subject to delays—you may have to wait your turn to use the network disk or printer. Most waits for any single operation take only some thousandths of a second, but if many users stack up many requests, a delay can be several seconds or more.

SHOULD YOU WAIT TO BUY A LAN?

A local area network can represent a sizable investment, and many potential LAN purchasers have taken a "wait and see" attitude while they watch LAN hardware mature and LAN applications increase in number and capability. For a long time, LAN installations seemed best left to the pioneers, but many of the reasons behind people's decisions to wait have been addressed by today's PC networks.

Size of Investment

Large organizations have been especially hesitant to install networks for whole facilities or even the entire corporation. There is a very real concern that installation of the "wrong" network on such a large scale could be an enormous waste of money. Many customers in this category have been installing smaller trial networks as learning experiments, seeing how the network solution fits their needs. You may want to consider doing something similar, if you have enough time to make a decision.

On the other hand, managers of a small organization that needs a few PCs connected together to do a specific job may make their decisions under a different kind of pressure. Their goal may be to select a cost-effective network that gets the known jobs done, rather than making a choice that will be right for hundreds or even thousands of users, doing unanticipated things with the network for many years in the future.

Standards

The more you anticipate growth in the types of things you will do with connected PCs, the more important standards become. While a proprietary, nonstandard system may do the job perfectly well, a network that adheres to a published standard gives you the benefits of increased competition on its price, may give you a larger selection of vendors for hardware and software components, and is more likely to be the subject of long-term development attention from many vendors. You will find more information on specific networking standards elsewhere in this book.

Some of the benefits of having industry standards are being realized through a combination of de facto standards for networking software, such as Microsoft's MS-DOS 3.1 and IBM's NETBIOS, and published standards for networking hardware, mostly from the IEEE 802 committees. Selection of an IEEE 802 standard network does not guarantee that you can easily intermix software and hardware from different vendors and achieve a working result. The IEEE standards are an important part of the picture, but taken alone they do not address enough of the total network system to facilitate such a mix and match of components.

The IBM and Microsoft industry standards go a long way toward filling the software gap in the networking standards story. Many major PC network vendors are providing these standards for their networks, so software vendors can put their products on a large variety of networks by writing to the IBM and Microsoft interfaces. You should check to make sure the software you purchase will work on the hardware you have, but things are getting much closer to the state of single-user software on the IBM PC, where vendors know that by writing to MS-DOS and BIOS interfaces their software will run on many compatible systems. Another significant software standard has been set by Novell with their NetWare networking software, which runs on the hardware of a large number of vendors and provides a uniform user and programming interface.

Prices

The networking industry has recognized that price is an important part of any buying decision, and has worked hard at making LANs more affordable. The Ethernet system is a good example. The original Ethernet standard dictates an expensive hookup scheme that requires a heavy bus cable and an electronic transceiver box for every workstation and server. When combined with the network interface circuitry itself in each network node, the result was a high cost for every connection (well over $1000), plus an expensive cable strung throughout the installation.

It was recognized that this cost was keeping many people from installing networks, so an alternative system was developed. Called Cheapernet, it offers connection costs under $700; uses thinner, less-expensive coaxial cable; and requires no transceiver. The new system runs software written for the original Ethernet, transmits data at the same rate (although over shorter distances), and can be connected to a LAN based on the original Ethernet cable. The latest chapter in this story is the introduction of Star-LAN by AT&T, which supports the Ethernet standard and can use even less expensive twisted-pair cable (which is already installed in many buildings) to connect telephones to a local switchboard.

In addition to cheaper cabling schemes, LAN hardware is benefiting from custom VLSI (very large scale integration) circuit technology. This approach replaces dozens of discrete parts with a single large custom integrated circuit, increasing reliability and decreasing manufacturing costs because there are fewer parts per network connection circuit.

The entire networking industry is also enjoying the usual advantages that come with increased sales volumes, and the entry of major firms such as AT&T and IBM can only help this trend. The resulting economies of scale tend to lower LAN prices further; lower prices lead to more sales, and for a while at least the benefits should be felt all around. If you wait, you may pay less, but one disadvantage of waiting is that you postpone the benefits of networking. If you decide that a network is right for your organization but you don't want to pay more than is necessary, try to choose a network system that can expand sufficiently to meet your needs several years down the road, and buy only what you need today.

Software

The limited availability of network software has also been given as a reason to postpone installing a LAN. Good software has been available for networks for some time, but much of it has come from smaller firms with lower advertising budgets, so it does not have as obvious a market presence as the major single-user PC software. The large software vendors have delayed making their software available on networks not because of technical problems, but rather because of struggles over how to license software for a LAN. The problems are twofold: how to deal with a system on which the number of users may be constantly changing, and how to administer a scheme that charges fairly but doesn't put undue restrictions on end users.

Most vendors are settling on one of two schemes: either a flat-fee site license covering all users in one installation, or a charge per active user coupled with a software lock that lets only the licensed number of users run the product at a time.

Two other factors have helped increase the variety of software available for networks: standards and the increasing number of LAN installations. Software standards such as NETBIOS and MS-DOS 3.1 give software vendors a single interface that enables them to write their software for a large fraction of the installed network base. A bigger market usually attracts more vendors, and software developers are no exception. Even the major vendors that had deferred offering network versions of their software are starting to recognize the importance of the market and are offering network software.

The pioneering phase of networking PCs is over. Standards have emerged, networks have become affordable for many, and software for accomplishing many useful tasks is available. Although you still should make sure that the benefits of a network justify its cost, most of the earlier reasons to wait before purchasing a LAN have been largely overcome.

LANS AND MULTIUSER SYSTEMS

Many of the problems that are addressed by a local area network can also be solved by a multiuser time-shared computer system. A typical multiuser system has one central computer connected to several terminals, as shown in Figure 2-1. The system is called *time-shared* because the processing time of the central computer is shared among all the terminals. All the applications software on a multiuser system runs on the central processor, and the terminals are used for keyboard input and screen output only. By contrast, in a PC network each user's workstation is a full-fledged computer capable of running software on its own.

Each approach has its own advantages, and there are cases where a combination of the two approaches works best. In a combination approach, multiuser systems may be networked together, allowing easy transfer of information between them while retaining the benefits of multiuser systems where needed.

It is typically less expensive to add a user to a multiuser system than to a network—a terminal costs substantially less than a personal computer and a network connection (although that price gap is narrowing). The problem with this generalization comes when the performance limits of a multiuser system are reached. For example, it costs much more than the price of 4 terminals to add 4 more users to a 16-user installation based on a multiuser system that only handles 4 to 16 terminals. Replacement of the

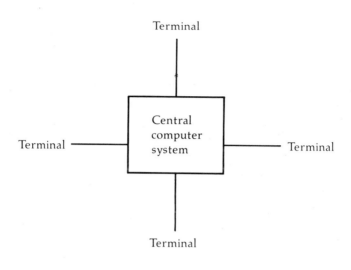

Figure 2-1.   A multiuser system

central computer itself may be required if the performance or the physical connection capability of the original central processor has been exceeded.

Adding workstations to a network tends to degrade performance more gradually than does adding terminals to a time-sharing system — as long as each workstation does a lot of local processing and does not drain the network servers as much as terminals do a central processor. However, networks also can have discontinuities in their cost-per-user curves. A discontinuity occurs at the point at which the network server is saturated and needs to be replaced or augmented by another server. Things can get very expensive if it is difficult to add a new network server and coordinate its use with an existing server. A multiuser system is more likely to be expandable with less impact on software, as long as there is some way to replace or upgrade the central computer with a more powerful system that can run the same software as the old system.

For some purposes, there is more software available for multiuser systems than for networks, especially software customized for specific vertical market segments such as law offices, wholesalers, construction businesses, and the like. On the other hand, PCs have fostered the development of excellent personal productivity software such as word processors, spreadsheets, and personal data managers, and many of these packages have built a strong following among end users, who may not want to give them up for the benefits of a pure multiuser system.

While use of the popular single-user software on a network is still the subject of investigation by many software vendors, multiuser systems have forced software vendors to deal with the multiuser licensing issue. In most cases the approach taken is to license for a single computer, but one that is a multiuser computer so that all the users connected to that machine can use the software.

Consistent response time is one of the personal computer's greatest attractions, and a network maintains this feature for software that runs on the workstation. In a multiuser system, since all the applications software runs on the central computer, response time varies according to the number of users active at its terminals. A network puts processing power in each workstation, buffering the end user from network data transfer times under many conditions.

Networks also may give each user more control over the placement of files than do multiuser systems. Files that must be kept secure can be kept on floppy disk and loaded only at the workstation, while a multiuser system requires everything to be loaded on the central computer. This reliance on a central computer can affect downtime, too. If the central computer needs repair, no user can use any of the terminals. A network can usually function in a degraded fashion, letting each user run any applications that run totally on the workstation until the server or network is repaired.

A network is most needed when a group of existing PCs need to communicate, or when the ability to run PC software that can't be used on a multiuser system is required. A multiuser system is a better choice when low-cost expansion up to the limits of the system is mandated, or when a specific software package that is not available on a network provides the best solution. You should also keep the coexistence approach in mind, since it may let you benefit from the best features of each approach.

SUMMARY

The decision to use a networking approach is a major one and should be driven by your needs and analysis of the costs and benefits of installing a LAN. The conditions for purchasing a LAN are favorable and continually improving. For those who decide that a LAN is a good solution for their requirements, the next chapter focuses on the process of choosing a particular network from the many available.

3

CHOOSING A LOCAL AREA NETWORK

This chapter outlines the process of choosing a LAN and gives some general guidance. As you read later chapters about installing and using a network, and especially as you read the reviews of some of the popular networks, you will add to this outline and develop a sense of what is important to you so you can do your own network evaluation.

As you analyze the features of candidate LANs, you need to consider their ability to handle not only your present needs but your future needs as well. An accurate assessment of present needs requires a detailed understanding of the problems you are trying to solve. Assessing future needs requires that you put your networking requirements into the context of your business or organizational plan, especially with regard to the need to transfer and process information. A network represents a sizable investment and should be one that can grow with your computer applications. Think about growth in areas such as the number of network nodes, capacity of disk storage, number of print servers, and the size of the physical area covered by the network. Also, if you will be using off-the-shelf software, how much software is available for the network you choose? The network vendor or your dealer may be able to provide you with a catalog of currently supported software applications.

GENERAL

Cost is always an important consideration. PC networking is a competitive business, and advances in electronic technology are currently driving costs down. (Highly integrated designs, for example, are reducing the number of parts required on a network interface card.) Follow two rules of thumb: choose a vendor who is actively working with new technology so that expansion of your LAN in the future will benefit from reduced costs, and do not buy more hardware than you need as long as prices continue to fall over time.

Ease of installing and using the network should be a major factor in your selection. The software used to initialize and manage your network is the biggest factor in this respect. Don't be fooled by the simple appearance of the floppy disk your network software comes on, compared to the pages of impressive-sounding specifications describing the hardware. The hardware must be right for you, but the software is even more important. This book will help you learn what to look for in network software—and you should plan to spend more time evaluating the software than the hardware in your network purchase.

You should evaluate your network vendor and its local representative to assess the support you will get during the planning, installation, and use of your network. Truly useful service requires expertise and time, so be wary of assurances that all the help you need is free. A certain amount of consulting and assistance may be covered in the cost of the sale, but free long-term assistance is probably either nonexistent or of low quality, or the assurance of such assistance a signal that the provider is new in business or won't be around very long. Reliable references from previous sales should be requested and checked. You should also request references before hiring a consultant to help with any phase of your network installation.

Once the network is installed, you and your end users will need training. You should evaluate your own situation and decide if you need classes for you, your staff, and your users. If so, see if your dealer offers them, how much they cost, and when they are given. Unless you have considerable in-house expertise or a lot of patience, you should not plan to depend entirely on reading the manuals, figuring it out for yourself, and training your end users. If your programmers are going to be modifying software for the network, consider the availability of technical documentation and training for them. Your network dealer or vendor should be able to assist you in locating these.

Maintenance of your system may be a critical factor. The more productivity depends on your network being up and running, the more vital it is that you have fast, dependable service for it. (The same consideration, of course, applies to any other computer equipment.) If you are used to a single-user PC environment, you may not be prepared for the way a network increases the dependency of many users on a single piece of hardware. For example, if several point-of-sale computers or a classroom full of student PCs all depend on a network disk server, the failure of that disk server may require that service be quicker than would the failure of a single PC. Many service options exist, ranging from on-site service within a couple of hours of the failure, through mailing the suspected component away for a couple of weeks. You must consider the options and make sure the appropriate ones are available for the system you select.

APPLICATIONS

The most important consideration in selecting a network is its ability to solve a problem, increase productivity, or enhance the operation of your organization. The first step in choosing a network has little to do with the network system itself. You must carefully determine what you want the network to achieve, and what applications software can be used to meet these goals. It may be off-the-shelf software from a third-party vendor, or it may be custom written by your programmers or a consultant. Your PC network should be chosen for its ability to run this software.

Existing Software

If you are networking a group of PCs that are already in use, you need to analyze how existing software will function in the network environment. Even if you decide that existing software will be used in the same way as before and will not take special advantage of the network environment, you must still be sure it does not conflict with the network in any way. In some cases a software package or hardware card may be unable to run at all on a workstation that is equipped with a network connection. Your dealer, network vendor, or application software vendor should be able to tell you what will and will not work together.

If you want to take advantage of the network with existing software, you should check the same sources to see if the version you own supports the network you want to install. You may have to purchase an upgraded version of the software that incorporates network support. Make sure the software works with the network in the way that you need it to. There is considerable leeway of interpretation in the statement "It works with networks," as is pointed out in Chapter 5.

If your applications are written by your own programmers, you need to understand how this software will function on a network. The same considerations apply as for outside-developed software, but you can't turn to an outside vendor for answers. It may be necessary to consult with the vendor of the programming language your applications are written in. Some implementations of programming languages work with networks, while others have problems. In any case, if you decide that achieving the desired results requires that your applications be modified, you or your programmers must first review the network to make sure that it supplies the functions you need. This phase of network selection is very technical and must be done by someone familiar with your applications and with multiuser programming environments, which present a new set of problems compared to single-user environments. You must perform a similar analysis if you need new, custom-written applications for your network. You may have more freedom of choice for a programming language for a new application.

New Software

If one reason for buying a network is to run new applications — such as shared database applications or electronic mail — that require a network, you may find a suitable off-the-shelf package from an outside software vendor. The vendor can tell you what networks the package supports, and you can evaluate the features of the package rather than its ability to run on a network. In this book you will find criteria for evaluating common network applications, as well as examples of some of these applications.

BASIC COMPONENTS

Any network you evaluate has three main components: workstations, servers, and connections. Most networks support only a limited number of choices in these three areas, so although you must evaluate your network selection in all three dimensions, you will probably have to make trade-offs in deciding which network system most closely meets your requirements.

Workstations

If you need to use non-IBM PC workstations on your network, you must select a network vendor that supports different types of computers on a single network. Make sure you understand how the different kinds of computers need to share such network resources as disk storage and printers, and be sure that the network you choose permits the right degree of sharing. For example, some networks may let you connect two different kinds of personal computer workstations to the same cable, but may require that each have its own separate disk server, and there may be no way to exchange data between the two computers.

The workstation hardware requirements that you need to evaluate include:

- Amount of random access memory (RAM) required
- Amount of local disk storage required
- Compatibility with other workstation hardware.

You should also consider whether the number of workstations supported by the network meets your current and projected needs. Your greatest evaluative effort should be spent on the workstation software, concentrating on such things as:

- Ease of installation and use
- Number of needed functions supported
- Ability to run application software
- Performance
- Flexibility and ease of modification
- Security.

As you read this book you should compile a list of the things that are the most important to you in each of these areas. There is a great deal of variety in workstation software, and you need to build your own model of essential applications.

Servers

Most vendors of IBM PC networks let you use IBM PCs as servers as well as workstations — at least to provide disk and print service to the network. Many vendors also provide proprietary hardware-based servers, usually claiming higher performance than can be had from PCs. Your choice of server can therefore extend beyond the issues mentioned under workstations to include the choice of the hardware itself.

Some networks offer you a choice between dedicated and nondedicated servers. A dedicated server is useful only as a server, while a nondedicated server can also be used simultaneously as a workstation. This is a cost/performance trade-off, for such use of a server as a workstation almost always diminishes its performance as a server (except possibly if it was being given very light use in either capacity). Another consideration is the vulnerability of a server used as a workstation: the workstation user should be running only well-tested software in a stable configuration, since any crashes or "hang ups" of this software can adversely affect a whole community of users with work in progress on the server.

Another choice must be made between multipurpose and single-purpose servers — between, say, use of a single PC XT as both a disk and print server and use of two PC XTs, one functioning as a disk server and the other as a print server. Again, this choice usually presents a cost/per-formance trade-off. Two XTs cost more than one, but if both functions are used heavily enough you will get better performance from two than if you try to implement both these functions on a single PC XT. If you decide to try a multipurpose server or a nondedicated server, you should set up an experimental configuration and see if the performance meets your needs before you order a full network configuration based on that choice.

Disk Servers   Some of the factors to consider when evaluating network disk storage servers are

- Number of mass storage servers supported
- Number, capacity, and speed of hard disks per server
- Method of splitting disks up between workstations
- Provisions for multiuser file sharing and locking.

You may have to choose between a file server and a disk server. The difference between the two is pretty technical, and you need not be too concerned about it as long as your applications work properly and you are satisfied with performance. The distinction has to do with the nature of the information that passes between a workstation and the server. Figure 3-1 shows a simplified view of a workstation application package accessing a disk drive through MS-DOS. The goal of any PC network is to allow the application to access the disk on a remote computer as if the disk drive were on the local computer. Thus, network software must first intercept the application's request to read or write a local disk file and send that request to the remote disk or file server for processing; it then must get the result that is returned from the remote server and pass it to the application, just as if it had come from the workstation's MS-DOS.

Workstation

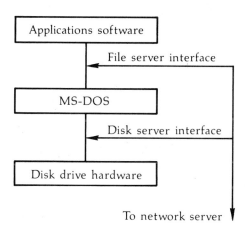

Figure 3-1.   Difference between file server and disk server

With a disk server, interception occurs between MS-DOS and the local disk drive. When an application requests a block from a file that is on a network disk server, the workstation MS-DOS does most of the work. MS-DOS computes the location of the disk block and requests it from what it treats as a local disk drive. The network system software intercepts this request and sends it to the disk server, which reads or writes the appropriate block on the server's disk.

With a file server, the workstation MS-DOS does not become involved with a network disk file access. The network system software intervenes before MS-DOS can receive a network disk file request. Instead, the entire request is sent over to the file server, which processes it and sends back the result.

Sometimes a single application request to read or write a file block can result in several disk input or output operations between MS-DOS and the disk drive. In such cases, using a disk server may generate more network traffic than using a file server: the file server sends the initial request from the workstation to the server and the server sends back only the final result; by contrast, the disk server sends the intermediate results back and forth, since the MS-DOS on the workstation must process the extra disk blocks.

You should try to find objective performance information comparing data access speeds for the networks you evaluate. The performance of the network disk or file server will have a strong effect on the performance of many applications and on the number of workstations you can connect.

Print Servers   Print servers, like disk servers, may be implemented on proprietary hardware or on IBM PC or PC-compatible computers. Some considerations when selecting a print server are

- Number of printers supported
- Interfaces supported, serial or parallel
- Printer models supported
- Print server software.

In addition to letting you share a printer among several workstations, a print server usually stores print output on a server disk drive and sends it to the printer as fast as the printer can accept it. This capability, called *print spooling*, means that the print server must have adequate disk storage to handle the volume of files your users will send to be printed. You will probably need a hard disk, then, and perhaps should consider using a disk server as a print server, too.

The software used to control the print server may vary from vendor to vendor, and you should be sure that it provides the functions you need. The reviews in later chapters give you some idea of the range of functions available on a print server.

Other Servers   Disk and print servers are the most widely used network service, but there are others that your applications may require. Some of the most common are

- Backup servers
- Gateway servers
- Remote communication (modem) servers.

You must plan for the backup of your network mass storage. Tape cartridges are a popular medium for storage, since you can often back up an entire hard disk on a single cartridge. You may prefer cartridge disk servers, or even a duplicate hard disk server that can hold as much as your primary network disk.

Gateways, used to connect dissimilar networks, are discussed in more detail later. Remote communication servers are useful if the network needs to be accessed from a remote site over a phone line using a *modem,* a device that converts data into tones that can be transmitted over the phone. Two computers connected to the phone with modems can send files and other information back and forth. A good remote communication server lets you use the network from a remote site just as if you were connected with a local workstation. Performance is usually slowed down by the limits of the phone lines. (Another seeming use of a modem on a network—sharing information among workstations—usually doesn't work out well because little of the PC communications software is adapted for this environment.)

Connections

It's ironic that the components most readily identified with a network— cables and network interface hardware—are in many respects the least important components. The applications supported by the network and the network-management software are what you use the most. The performance limits of the server software or hardware are usually reached before the limits of cable bandwidth (which is the data transfer speed) or network-interface hardware design can be approached. Still, there are many important choices to make with respect to connections, especially relative to costs.

There are three main areas to consider in choosing a network connection scheme: the cable type, the topology (or physical layout), and the low-level network protocol used to transmit data. Each LAN vendor usually bundles together a solution that addresses each of these three areas, so you don't have to decide on them individually.

Cable Types   The choice of a LAN limits your cabling options. Many LANs are designed to work with only one type of cable, although some can accommodate two or more types. In many cases the wiring is the most expensive part of installing a LAN, and the importance of this aspect of the cabling choice is clear. You must be sure you know the details of each

LAN's requirements before you estimate cabling costs. The most common cables are twisted-pair and coaxial cable (commonly called "coax"). Each of these is available in different grades at different costs per foot.

Twisted-pair, the least expensive medium, is simply two wires twisted together and covered with an insulating sheath. Twisted-pair has another cost advantage over coax — most buildings are already wired with twisted-pair for their phone systems. Networks that can use this existing cable can often be installed at significantly less cost than systems that require new wiring. The disadvantages of twisted-pair include greater sensitivity to noise, possibly resulting in the repeated transmission of network messages to correct transmission errors; shorter distance coverage than coax for some networks; and lower data rate than coax on some networks.

Coaxial cable is very commonly used in LANs, and it comes in several varieties, offering a range of

- Cost per foot
- Thickness and flexibility
- Ease of installation
- Usable lengths
- Bandwidths.

Network connections can be categorized as *baseband* or *broadband*. Baseband supports fewer channels of information than broadband; the connection is usually less expensive and the installation less critical. Ethernet and the IBM token-ring are examples of baseband networks. A broadband network cable is physically capable of carrying other signals such as video, voice, and security information as well as network data traffic. However, appropriate hardware and software is needed to take advantage of this low-level physical capability. The IBM PC Network is an example of a broadband network.

Fiber optic cables are by far the most expensive medium, but they are also the most resistant to noise and interference and thus have a very low error rate. There are fewer vendors of fiber optic LANs than there are of electrical wire-based systems, but commercial products do exist and are in use. If very high noise immunity is important to you, it may be worthwhile to investigate this choice further.

Repeaters   Cabling distances vary with cable and network card choices. If you expect to expand your network you should determine whether the maximum cable length supported is enough for your needs. Some networks can employ repeaters: hardware devices that considerably extend the maximum usable length of the cable. A repeater works at the physical level; that is, to the network software it is not distinguishable from the cable.

Bridges   Another way to extend networks is with a bridge. A bridge connects two identical networks and passes messages between them. However, it is a bit smarter than a repeater; it only sends messages to the other network that are destined for it, while a repeater transfers everything back and forth, just like a cable. Bridges can cut down on total network traffic by splitting up your network into clusters of those workstations and servers that most often talk to one another. Since the messages local to the cluster stay within that part of the network and don't go past the bridge, the amount of irrelevant network traffic on the other side of the bridge is reduced. However, a bridge can become a bottleneck if it is slower than a simple piece of cable or a repeater and if you put it in the wrong place, such as in between two or more network nodes that communicate heavily.

Topologies   Your choice of a network also involves selecting a layout of physical connections, or topology. The most common PC LAN layout is the *bus* structure, shown in Figure 3-2: a single cable is routed everywhere a connection is needed, and workstations and servers are connected to it. (Some networks, such as Ethernet, let you make the connection with a tap that does not cut the wire in two. You can connect a new workstation to

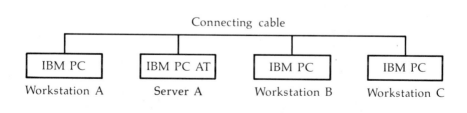

Figure 3-2.   Bus network topology

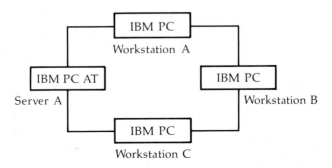

Figure 3-3. Ring network topology

the LAN or remove an existing one without disturbing the workstations on either side or shutting the LAN down during the operation.) A bus usually results in a shorter total cable length than the other topologies. It has the disadvantage that a single break in the cable may bring the entire network operation to a halt.

The second major cable layout, the *ring*, is like a bus structure with its ends tied together, as shown in Figure 3-3. One of the technical disadvantages of a ring is that at some level each node in the ring has to handle all the data being transferred in the network. For example, in Figure 3-3, for A to pass a file to C, B must handle the file as an intermediary. Failure of a single node can disrupt the entire network's operation. The main advantage of this topology is that it is more deterministic than a bus (explained below under the discussion of protocols.)

The *star* topology, shown in Figure 3-4, resembles many traditional multiuser or time-sharing systems: a central computer with separate lines to each workstation. This layout usually requires more total cable length than the bus or ring. Star networks often terminate each line with a cluster controller, a specialized computer capable of handling several workstations, thus improving the economy of the wiring. Furthermore, star configurations often use twisted-pair—the least expensive cable. Since each line is dedicated to carrying information between only two nodes, it can be of a lower bandwidth than a bus, which must handle traffic for all the nodes.

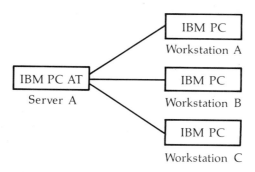

Figure 3-4.   Star network topology

Some star networks have been designed to take advantage of electronic telephone switchboards, or Private Branch Exchange (PBX) systems, sharing this wire with the phone system and providing a great savings in the time and cost of installing a LAN system.

There are many variations on these three topologies. IBM's Token-Ring Network improves on the basic ring topology with redundant connections to reduce the likelihood that a single failure will knock out the whole system. The IBM PC network has a hierarchical layout, explained in greater detail in Chapter 7.

Protocols   You can select a network with very little consideration of the protocols used to manage the network connection. Nevertheless, this topic still seems to come up often enough that it is useful for you to know what some of the common terms mean. The fundamental problem that network protocols solve is the sharing of a single wire — the network cable — among many workstations and servers, all of which may need to use it at any unpredictable time. The most popular network protocols are *token passing* and something called *carrier sense multiple access/collision detection (CSMA/CD)*. In brief, token passing is an orderly method of sharing a cable, while CSMA/CD lets every node use the cable when it needs to and handles collisions on the cable when they occur.

In a token-passing system, information is passed around the network from node to node. Messages are linked together, and the last message is followed by a special message called the *token*, which signifies the end of the group of messages. As each node is passed, it removes from the group any old messages that it sent, since if it is seeing them again, they must have gone all the way around the network. The node reads any messages addressed to it and marks them as having been read, then passes them on to the next node. When the token is seen, any new messages to be sent are added to the end of the group, then the token is passed.

The CSMA/CD protocol is an entirely different means of regulating message traffic on the cable. Each node monitors the network and waits to transmit until the level of network traffic has subsided. If two nodes try to talk on the network at the same time, a collision occurs — it is sensed by the transmitting nodes, and they wait a randomly selected interval before trying again. To avoid continuous collisions, each node waits a different amount of time before retransmitting.

CSMA/CD is used widely in PC LANs, the best-known example being Ethernet-based systems such as 3COMs. It is also used in the IBM PC Network product. Its main advantage is ease of reconfiguration — you can add a new workstation or server to a bus-based system at any time without shutting the network down. It is efficient under light use, but starts getting bogged down under heavy use because of the time spent recovering from collisions.

Token passing's main advantage is that it is "deterministic": each node gets a chance to transmit a message within a fixed amount of time. This feature is especially important in many manufacturing applications where a guaranteed response time is critical.

Token passing is also efficient under heavy use. Since there are no collisions, the bus cannot be overloaded. However, you cannot remove a workstation or server from the system without shutting down and reconfiguring, since removal of a node breaks the ring and the token stops in its tracks. It also takes some clever network software to recover from the loss or garbling of the token; in this respect token passing is more vulnerable than CSMA/CD.

In most cases, topology and protocol are not nearly as important factors as systems and applications software.

STANDARDS

Depending on your needs, standards can be of the greatest importance or only a minor consideration in your choice of a network. Standards are likely to be of more importance if you

- Plan to expand your network
- Need to connect to other networks
- Plan to run applications from several vendors.

Standards are of least importance if you are buying a small configuration that will remain fairly static and will not need to be connected to other networks, use devices from other vendors, or run many different applications programs.

There is more standardization among network hardware components than among software applications. You can probably find many more hardware products from different vendors that can physically coexist than software products that can share information. For example, you could buy a workstation and a print server from two vendors that claim Ethernet compatibility, find that they can be connected to the same cable without physical interference, but discover that you can't use the print server from the workstation because the two are incompatible in ways the Ethernet standard simply does not address. You must check very carefully for compatibility before you select network components from more than one vendor.

Software

The ISO Open Systems Interconnect (OSI) model described in Chapter 1 is a framework for describing network standards, rather than a standard itself. If you want to mix network components from different vendors, they must be compatible at some common OSI layer. Most of the current standards address only the lower levels of the OSI model. Applications software generally interfaces to the network at the highest levels, where there are very few widely accepted standard interfaces. This is one reason why applications software often needs to be modified for a specific network before it can run on it.

MS-DOS 3.1 and MS-NET   Although formal standards for network applications software may still be in the future, there are some promising de facto standards. Support for these standards may be important in your choice of a network, especially if you require wide availability of applications software.

Microsoft set a major standard in the personal computer world by releasing the MS-DOS operating system, called PC-DOS on the IBM PC.

MS-NET, Microsoft's network software, appears to be having a similar impact in the networking world. IBM's PC Network provides an implementation of MS-NET, and many computer and LAN vendors are adding MS-NET or MS-NET-compatible interfaces to their products. MS-NET is accessed via a set of system calls provided in MS-DOS Version 3.1, and these calls provide several important network programming functions. More and more software is being adapted to run under MS-NET and MS-DOS 3.1, so the increasing support for these interfaces may influence your choice of a network.

NETBIOS   Another important PC networking software industry standard is the OSI session level NETBIOS interface, first presented by the IBM PC Network system. Many other LAN vendors have since provided a compatible interface with their systems, and IBM itself has provided this interface to its Token-Ring Network.

Applications packages are more likely to use the simpler, higher-level MS-NET and MS-DOS 3.1 interfaces than NETBIOS. The NETBIOS interface is especially important for systems-level network software, such as programs for network servers. Unless you need to run a specific application that requires NETBIOS, it may be of slightly less importance to you than MS-NET compatibility. However, because it is supported in several IBM products, it appears likely to be used more as time passes.

Hardware

Hardware standards are most important in the fundamental parts of your network such as cable type and the low-level network protocols. If you choose a nonstandard, proprietary cable and protocol offered by only one vendor, you may be locking yourself into that vendor for all your future networking needs. A network conforming to one of the IEEE 802 standards opens the door to a broader choice of vendors.

IBM   IBM offers three networking hardware choices. The industrial token bus is designed for factory automation and process control. The PC Network uses broadband technology, and is discussed in greater detail in Chapter 7. The Token-Ring Network is an evolving system intended for use in large corporate networks, and is the basis for the IEEE 802.5 standards committee work.

IBM has suggested that, in an office environment, the broadband PC Network should be used to connect a small number of PCs together. The token-ring is seen as the building-wide network used to tie a large number of machines or clusters of machines together. A gateway product provides the connection between the broadband LAN and the token-ring. You can also use the token-ring as a local PC network, omitting the broadband network entirely. The Token-Ring Network runs the same software as the broadband PC Network (as described in Chapter 7). It supports the MS-DOS 3.1 and NETBIOS interfaces mentioned earlier. It can run over IBM's coax or less-expensive twisted-pair that meets telephone installation standards. Both wiring choices provide a bandwidth of 4 million bits per second, although you can connect more nodes and go a greater distance using coax.

The Token-Ring Network may be appropriate if you are planning to connect a large number of systems, including other IBM computers. IBM has expressed its intention to provide a complete corporate computer-network hookup, although the details for connecting more than just PCs together are being released very slowly.

Ethernet   The Ethernet standard is supported by many computer vendors, and several variations in cabling have evolved to reduce the relatively high cost of the original specification. Electronic devices called *transceivers* can be used to connect the different cabling schemes. The choice of cable generally has no impact on applications software, and is a trade-off between cost and performance, with respect to speed and maximum cable length.

Standard Ethernet requires a heavy trunk cable and a transceiver for every workstation. The transceiver connects to the trunk cable, and a wire runs from the transceiver to the workstation or server. *Cheapernet* uses lighter, less-expensive cable and has the same 10-million-bits-per-second capacity as Ethernet, but does not use an outboard transceiver and cannot support as long a cable as Ethernet. The review of 3COM's EtherSeries products in a later chapter contains more details on Ethernet.

StarLAN   AT&T's StarLAN is a competitor to IBM's token-ring in the corporate network arena. It uses a standard Ethernet trunk cable connected by a device called a *hub* to clusters of workstations. The workstations connect to the hub with standard telephone company twisted-pair.

You can connect hubs to hubs, increasing the number of workstations supported in a cluster and giving you more flexibility in wiring them together. StarLAN operates at a bandwidth of 1 megabit per second.

MAINFRAME CONNECTIONS

If you are selecting a PC network for use in an installation where there are other computers (especially minicomputers or mainframes), you should think about how you could connect your network to them even if you see no immediate need to do so. There are several classes of connection that may be important for you:

- Message and file transfer
- Terminal emulation
- Program-to-program communication
- Remote job entry.

Making a good selection requires technical expertise. You need to understand the host computer application, data-file structure, and communication connections, as well as the gateway connection between the host and the PC network, the PC network hardware, and the software that runs on the PC workstations to access the host.

Gateways

Figure 3-5 shows one means of connecting a mainframe to a LAN. The interconnection is via a gateway, which is a server designed to pass information back and forth between two dissimilar networks. In this case, an Ethernet PC LAN is connected to a 4300 series IBM mainframe with a gateway processor. The gateway translates low-level protocols and handles the speed differences between the two networks. Since all traffic between the two networks must pass through the gateway, you must carefully evaluate the performance capability of the gateway in light of the amount of data you expect to transfer through it. If it does not have enough capacity it will become a bottleneck.

Most major PC network vendors offer gateways to IBM SNA networks, and some offer gateways to other popular PC networks. You may have a

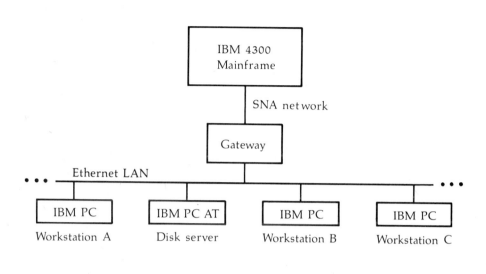

Figure 3-5.   A gateway connecting a LAN to a mainframe

choice between a dedicated gateway server computer and an add-on board for a PC. The trade-offs are similar to those between a proprietary disk or file server and the use of a PC to do the job. You should examine price and performance as you make your evaluation, as well as the software provided to make the connection between the two networks.

Direct Connection

An alternative means of connecting to a minicomputer or mainframe host is to run a direct connection from each PC on the LAN to the host computer. Many add-on cards are available to connect to host computers via most of the communications protocols available. However, this approach usually costs much more than the gateway approach and it makes little or no use of the PC LAN. For the extra cost, you may get more performance, or more consistent performance when you access the host, since there is a dedicated connection rather than a shared connection through a gateway.

Message and File Transfer

Message transfer and file transfer refer to electronic mail and document transfer, respectively. Many different kinds of electronic mail systems are in use today, and there is not yet a standard. Some systems cover only workstations connected to a common network and others connect also to public electronic mail services to cover a very wide area. The usefulness of electronic mail increases with the increase in the number of people you can communicate with, so be sure to consider ways to connect your PC work-stations to electronic mail systems if appropriate.

There is not yet an official standard for document transfer either, although IBM's DISOSS standard is widely supported. If you need to share documents with a DISOSS system, examine whether your network of choice can do so.

Terminal Emulation

Terminal emulation is a very common approach to connecting a PC to a host computer. To the host your PC appears to be a terminal, and the host lets you do whatever a terminal can do on it, such as accessing existing applications on the host (which is often very important). But with straight terminal emulation you can't do anything that takes advantage of the fact that you are using a PC. If you want to do terminal emulation, you should examine the available options with respect to:

- Faithful emulation of desired terminal
- Ease of use (how keys are mapped onto PC keyboard)
- Performance (how fast emulator can receive data from host).

Data Extraction

Another way of accessing the host from a PC on a LAN is to extract data from host databases and move it to the PC for processing. This is another highly technical area, and to do a proper evaluation you need an excellent understanding of the software that runs on both ends of the connection. The software that extracts data from the mainframe database must have a detailed understanding of the host data-file layout, and it is possible that a revision in host software will change something in the layout and cause the extraction software to stop working. If the data extraction software is not updated for a period of time, you may be unable to run your application until it is updated. If you can find data extraction software from the same vendor as for the host database-management software, it may be more likely that the extraction software will be updated concurrently with the database software — although there is no guarantee.

Remote Job Entry

Submitting jobs for processing on the host computer is another common need of PC users. A gateway or direct connection can provide the necessary data link for this remote job entry to take place, but PC software is also needed to do the actual job submission and control. Ease of use and matchup of functions against your needs list are the most important criteria.

Program-to-Program Communication

A relatively new area is program-to-program communication. IBM has introduced a standard called LU 6.2, and the full implications are still unfolding. Not much PC software is available that takes advantage of program-to-program communication, but as more software gets written for networks, this capability will grow in importance. The goal is to let a programmer set up two or more programs so they can execute on two different computers and pass information back and forth as they are running.

Security

You should closely examine the security provided by software used to connect networked PCs to a mainframe. In most cases the mainframe data files were created before the PCs had access to them, and security may not have been a big consideration when the files were first stored. It is very easy to miss a security problem when security is an afterthought rather than something designed into an application. In addition to straightforward security issues, such as who can access which files, there are more complicated ones to consider, such as the ability of any authorized user to access host data and store it on the local network hard disk. Without the appropriate additional security, other network users may be able to access your data. If any PC on the network has a modem and is used to receive incoming calls, then anyone who can call that PC may be able to "break into" your mainframe.

Hardware Compatibility

Before choosing your mainframe connection equipment, be sure any hardware cards that must be added to network PCs are compatible with other cards that you plan to have in the PCs. Communications cards are among those more likely to have incompatibilities with network interface cards than other types of cards. A complete list of the cards going into the workstations and servers should be checked out with your dealer and the board manufacturers.

4

PLANNING AND INSTALLING A LOCAL AREA NETWORK

Once you have selected a network vendor and system, you need to make a detailed plan of your specific configuration and then install the system according to the plan. This chapter deals with planning and installing a local area network. After it is installed and running, you can use it and must manage it. The next chapter discusses using a local area network. Most of the work involved in managing a network is similar to the installation process; some additional management responsibilities are discussed at the end of the chapter.

Although the installation process of each local area network is unique, there are many similarities among networks from different vendors. Hardware installation varies the least from one network to another; methods of cabling are generally the area of greatest difference. Software installation varies in its specifics, but several general concepts hold across most networks, and understanding these concepts helps smooth the planning and installation.

This chapter provides an overview of the installation process so you can decide whether you want to attempt it yourself, and if so, to give you hints to make things go more smoothly.

If you plan to install a moderate-to-large network using hardware or software that is new to you, it is highly recommended that you build a very small experimental network first. Many network vendors sell "starter kits" containing everything you need to connect two PCs together. A few days of experience with a couple of workstations and a server can teach you a lot about your particular situation. This small-scale experiment can also help you during the planning phase to make a better detailed plan and to purchase the right equipment when you order the bulk of your network hardware and software.

If your potential network users, who will share peripherals and information, are sophisticated with the PC, try setting a couple of them up with a server and your intended software configuration. If your network will be used to manage the operation of a business, it may be harder to set up a trial network. Use recent or dummy data for your network applications and have some of the eventual network users spend a few hours working with this data as they would with the real thing.

Figure 4-1 shows a sample checklist of things to evaluate after finishing the network trial. Note that it is only a sample — you should tailor it to your own environment and needs. When considering the items, also discuss them with the network users.

You will probably modify several aspects of your network configuration after the trial run. If this experiment seems to use more time than you would like to spend, consider the likely results of implementing a full network without the benefit of a trial. Unless you are exceptionally skillful or lucky, you will lose time in many ways:

- Users' time wasted running in a suboptimal configuration
- Your time spent reconfiguring all the servers and workstations
- Users' time wasted while you reconfigure the network.

Even worse problems are possible from an improperly installed network, especially if it is used to run a business — you could lose money, irritate customers, and upset employees. (Of course, none of these potential problems is unique to local area networks; they can arise from any change in data processing equipment or procedures.)

PLANNING THE INSTALLATION

There's an old saying that if you plan to go nowhere in particular, you're bound to get there. Although your needs — the components and how you should arrange them — may seem obvious to you, writing them down into a plan will probably reveal additional things you will need.

The complexity of your plan and the time you should devote to it will vary with the size of your network. A few hours to a day of planning may suffice for a network composed of four or five PCs run by knowledgeable computer users sharing a network disk and printer, while it may take

Disk storage

Performance
Responsiveness (delay from request to action)
Transfer speed (time to load and save files)
Consistency (variation in performance)

File placement
Convenience (ease of locating and accessing)
Usability (able to access disk from all applications)
Volumes (correct things on public and private volumes)

Print service

Performance
Usability (print from all applications)
Spooling (time workstation is tied up while printing)

Job management
Sharing (distribution of printers to users)
Separating (distinguishing different users' printouts)
Forms (need to change print forms often)

Systems software

Operating environment
Understanding (quality of training)
Ease of use (ease of doing necessary tasks)
Functionality (can do all necessary tasks)
Reliability (as compared to single-user PC)

Security
Functionality (keeps unwanted users out)
Convenience (not cumbersome to authorized users)

Applications software

Personal programs
Usability (can use programs on network as desired)
Licensing (do users understand license issues)

Multiuser network applications
Sharing (any problems with concurrent data access)
Functionality (does intended job)

Figure 4-1.   Checklist for trial network evaluation

months to plan for a hundred or more workstations running several different multiuser applications sharing a dozen network servers and linked to a corporate mainframe. If you are faced with such a complex task, don't hesitate to engage an experienced consultant to help with your planning.

Modern programming practices generally stress the importance of planning "top-down" and implementing "bottom-up." Planning and installing a network should be approached the same way. Briefly, top-down planning means starting with a high-level description of the overall task you are trying to perform. This description should help you see the separate components of a large, complicated problem. It is easier to deal with these components separately than trying to solve the whole problem at once. If the interfaces and connections between the components are well-defined and understood, you should be able to work out the details of each separate component by itself without concern for the details of the other components until you get to them.

Each individual component can be treated the same way: broken down into smaller pieces that can be separately considered. This process is called "successive refinement." You eventually reach a level of detail that cannot be further refined, and you have solved the problem. You are then ready to implement the solution — in this case, purchase and install the network.

Bottom-up implementation means you install the simplest, lowest-level pieces of your design, test them to see if they work as planned, then add the next level and test it, repeating the process until the entire network has been installed. Each successive level of implementation adds more function to the network, and is built on a previously tested foundation. This approach is very important, since problems are more easily found than if you wire an entire network together, load all the software, then try to determine why something doesn't work.

This chapter uses the above approach to planning and installing a network. The highest-level description of the network is at the applications software level: What are your end users going to do with the system? This question generates a list of needs, from which a description of the required application and system software configuration follows. The software configuration in turn suggests your server and workstation requirements, from which it is fairly simple to see how to cable them together.

This whole process requires that you have a good understanding of your application needs and use that understanding to select the right network software and hardware. Two critical skills may require a consultant's help: one is studying a system and turning that analysis into the right applications software setup — the job of a systems analyst; the other is determining a good network hardware and software configuration to support the applications software — best done by a local area network specialist (who could very well be the same person as the systems analyst). Make sure your in-house person or consultant has the right mix of experience and skills to make your installation a successful one.

Software Planning

Although the analysis of your application needs from a systems viewpoint cannot be covered here in its full scope, some of the special needs from a network perspective will be discussed. Before you start planning your network installation, you should have selected the applications software for your network on the basis of the considerations listed in Figure 4-2.

Business

> Problems to solve
> Improvements sought
> Conversion from existing system
> Financial resources to purchase system

People

> End-user computer sophistication
> End-user need and ability to modify applications
> In-house or outside custom programming availability
> Network management responsibility

Software

> Applicability to problems at hand
> User interface suitability
> Integration with other applications
> Shared database access across network
> Custom programming requirement
> Ability and need to modify source code

Figure 4-2.   Applications software selection considerations

Without a good understanding of the applications you will run, you cannot possibly plan the requirements or configuration of your network.

Your hardware and software plans are interdependent. As you work through your software plan, you will gather information that will shape the hardware plan. You may need to make a couple of passes through both plans, modifying earlier decisions as you gain a greater understanding of the interdependencies. For example, the number of servers you need in order to support your workstations depends on the applications software that will run on your network, and also on how that software is installed and used in conjunction with the network. Some software can be set up to make very little demand on the network, while other packages use the network constantly and heavily.

Figure 4-3 diagrams a piece of a network from a user's perspective. This viewpoint is helpful to guide you in top-down planning of your LAN. You must determine:

- Who your network users are
- Which applications each user runs on each workstation
- Which servers each application uses from each workstation.

As you can see in the diagram, the relationships may be complicated. A workstation may be used by more than one user, and a user may use more than one workstation. A workstation can run more than one application, and an application may be run on more than one workstation. The applications may use one or more servers.

To simplify this picture, identify the major components of your network and study each individually:

- Users
- Applications software
- Systems software
- Workstations
- Servers
- Connections.

Figure 4-3 also shows peripherals, such as disk drives, printers, and modems. They should be considered part of the workstation and server plans.

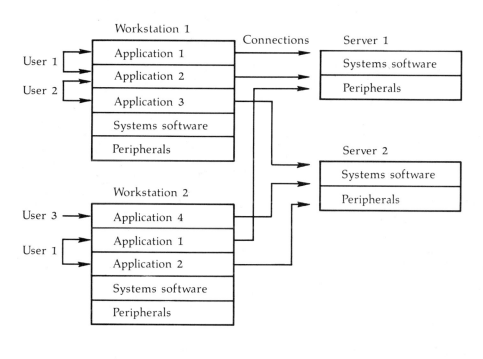

Figure 4-3.   Network usage diagram

Refining your understanding of each of these areas will yield insights that will help improve your understanding of the others. To best use this information, you should keep notes as you go; a worksheet helps to keep things organized. Figure 4-4 is an example of a worksheet that you can use for each user of your network. In addition to name, network log-on ID, and password, you need to know which applications this person uses, and from which workstations they are run. This use pattern, together with knowledge about the applications themselves, determines the workstation configuration you will need.

Applications Software   You need to understand the demands that each of your applications places on the workstation, on the servers, and on the

---

User Information Worksheet

Name: _____ System Manager Privilege (Y/N): _____

Network log-on ID: _____ Password: _____

(Repeat log-on ID and password for each account used if more than one)

Network Usage

List each application used by this individual along with the workstation number it is used on:

Application Name   Workstation Number

_____   _____

_____   _____

_____   _____

_____   _____

_____   _____

_____   _____

_____   _____

_____   _____

Figure 4-4.   User information worksheet

connections between workstations and servers. Figure 4-5 shows a basic applications software information worksheet that you can use to analyze your applications. It does not address connection requirements, since the larger context of applications, workstations, and servers determines these. This worksheet concentrates on the individual application characteristics, independent of context.

You should fill out one of these worksheets for every application you will run on your network. Some applications may be thought of as a single large unit that may be run as a collection of separate smaller components. For example, your accounting system may have been purchased as a single software package, but it may contain separate modules for accounts payable, accounts receivable, general ledger, and payroll; different users may run different subsets of this accounting package, perhaps not even all

Applications Software Information Worksheet

General Information

Applications program: _____   Version #: _____
Vendor: _____

Workstation Requirements

Microcomputer vendor and model: _____
DOS version #:
    Lowest: _____
    Highest: _____
Display adapter:
    (monochrome, graphics, special): _____
Monitor type:
    (monochrome, B&W composite, color composite, color RGB): _____
Random access memory:
    Shared memory in kilobytes: _____
    Unshared memory in kilobytes: _____
Disk storage:
    Floppy drive A: storage needed in kilobytes: _____
    Floppy drive B: storage needed in kilobytes: _____
    Hard drive C: storage needed in kilobytes: _____
    Number of files used: _____
Printers:
    Type of printer 1: _____   Forms for printer 1: _____
    Type of printer 2: _____   Forms for printer 2: _____
Plotter:
    Type of plotter: _____
Modem:
    Type of modem: _____
Pointing device:
    (mouse, digitizer): _____
Other peripherals:
_____

Figure 4-5.   Applications software information worksheet

Server Requirements

Server vendor and model: _____

DOS version #: _____

Random access memory:
   Shared memory in kilobytes: _____
   Unshared memory in kilobytes: _____

Disk storage:
   Shared read-only in kilobytes: _____
   Shared read/write in kilobytes: _____
   Unshared read-only in kilobytes: _____
   Unshared read/write in kilobytes: _____
   Number of files used:

Printer:
   Type of printer 1: _____   Forms for printer 1: _____
   Demand on printer 1 (% of capacity): _____
   Type of printer 2: _____   Forms for printer 2: _____
   Demand on printer 2 (% of capacity): _____

Plotter:
   Type of plotter: _____

Modem:
   Type of modem: _____

Other peripherals:
   _____

(Repeat server information for each server accessed by application)

Figure 4-5.   Applications software information worksheet (*continued*)

on one workstation. If the modules put different demands on the system, each should be considered separately.

Often, the same workstation can satisfy many requirements of both single-user PC and multiuser versions of an application. The DOS version number you use should be within the range you have marked on the worksheet to indicate the lowest and highest revision of DOS that the application can run under. The need to display graphics or text and the subsequent choices between display adapters and monitors are familiar problems faced by all PC buyers. Some applications can run on any monitor; if this is the case, indicate so by writing "any" in the blank. Application memory requirements are mostly independent of use in a network, although some applications may require additional space to manage multiuser access to data. Indicate the minimum memory required by your application, or if you know from experience that you need more than the minimum to obtain satisfactory performance or functionality, use that amount.

Disk storage questions must be reviewed in light of the network environment. Many applications can be run completely from the network's disk storage and need no local storage. Some of the most common reasons for requiring local workstation storage include:

- Copy protection requires local disk drive to start program.
- Program is incompatible with the network software and can only be run locally.
- Program is hard-coded to use local drive letters A: or B:.
- Security considerations prohibit putting data on network disk drives.
- Performance is improved by local storage of data or programs.

Performance considerations are hard to generalize, but how long it takes to access data depends on where it is stored. The storage options considered here are RAM disks, hard disks, and floppy disks. A *RAM disk* uses random access memory to emulate a very fast disk drive. Some networks support all three options in both the workstation and the server; others support a subset of them in one place or the other.

The graph in Figure 4-6 shows the relationship between network load and the data access speed of these storage options. No one graph can accurately depict the performance relationships under all conditions. (For example, on a particular network it may always be faster to get data from a local hard disk than from a server's RAM disk.) Nevertheless, the following rules usually apply:

- Workstation storage access speed is independent of network load.
- Given equally fast floppy disk drives and hard disk drives, data can be accessed more quickly from a local device than from across the network, even when the network is lightly loaded.
- Network data access slows as network loads increase.

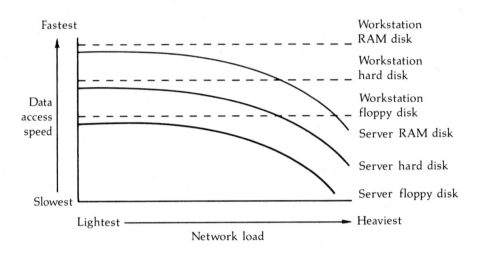

Figure 4-6.   Access speed versus network load

The last point is critical, as Figure 4-6 demonstates. (Network load refers to the drain on the server from all the competing workstations.) If you stored frequently accessed data on a network hard disk and the network load was light (on the left side of the graph), performance would be somewhere between that of a local hard disk and a local floppy disk — probably quite adequate. But if the network load turns out to be heavy (on the right side of the graph), the data access speed may be considerably slower than a local floppy disk — possibly inadequate. (In most cases, the limits of the server will be reached long before you use all the bandwidth of the connecting cable.)

Performance considerations encourage storing not only some data on the local hard disk, but other software elements as well, including program overlay files. The WordStar word processor, for example, includes two such files, WSOVLY1.OVR and WSMSGS.OVR. Overlay files contain program subroutines that various applications commands require. The application (in this case WordStar) loads part of the file to get the appropriate subroutines. If these must be loaded over the network each time they are used, there will be a delay of several seconds each time while the overlays are read into memory from across the network. If this delay is not acceptable, consider storing the overlays locally, or copying them from the server to a local RAM disk at the beginning of each session with the application. An MS-DOS batch file should be used to automate the process. Remember, however, that some software licenses prohibit this practice.

You also need to know the maximum number of disk files your applications have open at any one time. The workstation must be set up to allow for the right number of files, which also affects the amount of workstation random access memory you will need. There is more information about this topic later in this chapter. You should carefully evaluate the application's use of printers with respect to how your network is used. The trade-offs between attaching a printer to the workstation and using the network printer are mostly between cost and convenience. A local printer may be needed if your application requires:

- Immediate printing
- A specialized printer not suitable for other users
- Preprinted or multipart forms that must stay loaded in the printer.

For example, if your workstation is used as a cash register and prints multipart invoices while the customer waits, it may be best to dedicate a printer to that workstation. On the other hand, use of a shared printer on a network server may be in order if your application specifies:

- Infrequent use of a printer
- That delays in printing are acceptable
- An expensive printer (which must be shared to justify cost).

Plotters and other output devices can generally be analyzed by the same methods as printers. Some applications require modems—devices that connect your computer to a telephone line for transferring data between the workstation and a remote computer not on the network. If your application requires a mouse, digitizer, or other workstation peripheral, note that that on the applications worksheet, too.

Next you need to determine the requirements each application places on network servers. If a specific type of server is required, that fact should be noted. Many applications can be used with any network server, but some require specific server features—such as an application that is split into two parts, one running on the workstation and the other on the server. Such an application may also make a demand on the server's random access memory, and that requirement should be noted.

Server disk requirements depend on the decisions made earlier regarding how the programs and data will be partitioned between the server and workstation. Network server disks may be the storage option of choice when:

- Many users use a program or data file
- Only one user needs the file, but from different workstations
- Network disk capacity is greater than local capacity
- Network disk speed is greater than that of local disks.

Once you have decided what to place on the server, you also must decide whether to place it in shared or unshared, read-only or read/write storage. Most network systems require you to categorize the server's storage according to these or similar terms. If the data is accessed by more than one user at a time, it must be stored as shared data. If it is not only read but also modified, it must be read/write. Shared files may include applications programs, DOS utilities, network utilities, and multiuser databases.

It is usually only necessary to keep one copy of a shared file on the server. For example, the network software may include utility programs to display and modify the print queue for network printers. Rather than storing copies of this utility on every workstation, you can place one copy of it in shared storage on a network disk. Unshared storage is typically used to hold files pertaining to a single user, such as:

- Private data files
- Single-user licensed applications
- User profile information
- System management files
- Software under development.

On the worksheet estimate the shared and unshared, read-only and read/write server disk space required under each of these categories. If your applications require a certain number of files to be open on the server, note this fact also. Refer to your network documentation for more details, since some network servers handle network file opening independently of the MS-DOS file system, and the MS-DOS CONFIG.SYS FILES parameter (explained soon) is not the way to control this operation.

Next you must determine print server requirements for the application.

In the previous discussion you saw that your application's needs guide your choice between a local printer and a shared printer. If this application will use a network printer, you should estimate the percentage of the printer's capacity that the application will use from each workstation. For example, if a printer can print 100 plane tickets an hour and a ticketing agent's workstation can handle 20 customers per hour, each workstation may use up to 20% of the printer's capacity. You would expect that the printer could handle a maximum of five workstations. It may be appropriate to perform a more detailed analysis taking into account such things as the time it takes to turn the printer off-line while removing a ticket, reloading forms, and so on.

You should fill out an applications software information worksheet for every application that will run on the network. Be sure to include network utilities and special applications such as electronic mail. From your information about all the applications that will run on the network, and about which users will run which applications, you can derive the system software, workstation, and server configuration of your network.

Systems Software   Systems software integrates the applications software with the network hardware. Your systems software plan is determined by the applications you will run, the needs of the users who run the applications, and the exact configuration of servers and workstations you choose. Since you have planned only the first two items so far, you can't complete the systems software plan until you have determined the workstation server configuration. Since doing so is easier if you understand the basic principles of your network's systems software, it is important to review the documentation and make sure you understand the areas discussed in the following sections as they are implemented in your network.

One piece of important systems software probably doesn't come from your network vendor. Most PC networks use the MS-DOS operating system on the workstations and on the servers. In most respects MS-DOS is used in a LAN environment exactly as on a stand-alone PC, but some issues should be considered, especially performance and ease of use.

The exact details of how to configure MS-DOS for your LAN PCs vary from network to network, and you must follow the directions supplied by your vendor. Two important MS-DOS system files usually come into play: CONFIG.SYS and AUTOEXEC.BAT. These files contain plain ASCII text and can be created and modified by most text editors, such as the EDLIN program that comes with MS-DOS.

CONFIG.SYS contains system configuration information that can affect network performance. One important entry is the BUFFERS parameter. A line in the CONFIG.SYS file like:

```
BUFFERS=20
```

tells MS-DOS to allocate 20 buffers in RAM for storage of disk blocks. These buffers fill up with blocks read from disk. If a program accesses a block that is already in memory, that data is available at memory speeds, which are much greater than disk speeds. However, allocating too many blocks can have a detrimental effect, since the blocks must periodically be written back to disk for permanent storage, and there can be quite a pause while this happens if you allocate a large number of buffers. Additionally, each block takes 512 bytes of workstation memory, which is subtracted from memory that would otherwise be available for applications and systems software.

Another important CONFIG.SYS file entry is the FILES parameter. Structured like the BUFFERS entry, it tells MS-DOS how many files can be open at a time. For example,

```
FILES=15
```

tells MS-DOS to allocate enough local memory and DOS file control information to allow 15 files to be open at once. To set this parameter correctly, you must understand the needs of your applications and systems software.

The AUTOEXEC.BAT file is used to automate the setup of a workstation or server running under MS-DOS. All the commands it contains are automatically executed every time you start the PC. Each LAN vendor's software puts different requirements on the contents of this file, and some vendors even custom build the file for you automatically. Using this file enables all the network software to be loaded and an application to start running before the end user touches the keyboard.

During planning you must also determine what version of MS-DOS you will run on your workstations and servers. Many networks let you mix different revisions on the same network, but the safest course is to use only one version everywhere. Using the applications software information worksheets, you will determine the lowest and highest acceptable revision levels for MS-DOS on your system; it is advisable to use the highest revision level uniformly across the network.

Most of the new systems software you have to deal with controls the network itself. It is easiest to plan to install this software as two components: the workstation component and the server component. In each case there are two further major subdivisions to consider: resident operating software and utilities. The operating software is the part that must be configured and installed. It controls the network hardware for you while you are using the network, just as MS-DOS controls your PC's disk drives and other devices. The utilities are used to configure, extend, and maintain the network. They are programs that you run briefly to do a specific operation, like the MS-DOS FORMAT command.

Which systems software to install on the workstation varies from vendor to vendor; several examples are presented in the later chapters of this book. Generally, you need to know which network resources — especially disks and printers — you will be using from each workstation. In some cases, you just install an all-purpose software driver, and the resources you can use from that workstation depend on the user account established for you on the server. Occasionally you need to know whether the users of this workstation will be using such network applications as electronic mail, and adjust the workstation software accordingly.

In any event, you need to consider this software in the light of overall workstation requirements. The applications software information worksheet (Figure 4-5) contains most of the relevant questions that you need to answer. Your network documentation probably describes how much overall software support, with respect to memory, disk, and printer, is required by the network software that runs on the workstations. Using this summary information, fill out an applications software worksheet so the needs of the network software can be factored into the workstation configuration. This single sheet can probably be used for most of your workstations. If workstations differ in the applications they run (for example, some have electronic mail privileges and some don't), you may consider those applications separately, creating a worksheet for each.

Most LANs come with a variety of utilities used to configure and operate the network. Referring to the network documentation, determine what is offered and what your network users need. This software is a prime candidate to load into network disk storage, since it will probably be used at most workstations. In most cases it includes, at a minimum, software to:

- Connect and disconnect to network disk storage
- Connect and disconnect to network printers
- Monitor and modify network print queue status.

You must decide whether it is appropriate for your users to have access to these utilities. In some cases, you may want to provide a batch file that executes the utility in a predetermined way. Consider the sophistication of your users and the possible damage that can be done by accidental or malicious misuse of these utilities. Software that you probably shouldn't make widely available includes network utilities to:

- Create and modify user accounts or user profiles
- Create and modify network disk volumes
- Alter network security.

These utilities should be used only by you or the designated system manager, and they should be stored securely so they can't be misused.

Network software for the server can also be treated during planning as two parts: operating software and utilities for managing the server. The operating software handles workstation requests for server devices such as disks and printers; utilities set up the server so that its resources can be shared with the network. Again, consult your network documentation to see what options are available for configuring the server operating software. In some cases, you simply load it and answer a couple of questions. For other systems you have to make many configuration decisions to suit the type of hardware attached to the server.

If your server is also used as a workstation, make note of any special restrictions in the way it can be used or the software it can run. When configuring the hardware, consider the demands of both workstation and server software. For example, there must be sufficient random access memory to support the memory-resident software of both the workstation and server.

Most LAN software controls network disk allocation by means of *volumes*, or *directories*. Among the many reasons for grouping files in volumes are the following:

- Security
- Write protection
- Ease of finding and accessing files
- Applications software requirements
- Providing personal disk storage.

You must understand your applications with respect to each of these categories. Also relevant is the previous discussion about grouping files according to their being shared or unshared, or read-only or read/write. In many systems these paired categories are mutually exclusive: an entire volume or directory must be declared, say, shared and read-only, or unshared and read/write. Some systems allow a finer level of differentiation, letting you assign these attributes to individual files instead of to the volume or directory. Read your system manuals to see what your network software supports. You should thoroughly understand your applications software needs and systems software capabilities in this area, since making a change usually involves redoing major portions of your installation. The applications worksheets should be reexamined to see if the server disk requirement sections are adequately filled out.

Next examine the network provisions for print service to assess flexibility. In some systems you identify your printer by name and the basic setup is done automatically. Others require you to use printer control codes to make your printer do things like go to the top of the next page or reset to standard character pitch. You must understand your application's printing requirements, your network software's printing options, and the relationship between the two. (Several options for server print management appear in the review chapters later in the book.) Consider the amount of memory that the software on the server needs to drive the printer. Sometimes you can specify a print buffer size; a large buffer may speed network printing but also takes memory away from other server software.

Your network security requirements depend on your user community, the sensitivity of your data, your applications software, and your network software. In some cases you may plan to install the network with security turned off. For example, an elaborate security system may be more trouble than it's worth in a software development environment where the users are computer knowledgeable, code under development must be shared among all users, and network-licensed compilers are uniformly used. By the time you give everyone the appropriate privileges, everyone may have access to everything anyway.

Even in such an open environment, you may help prevent accidental damage if you use read-only volumes or directories to store compilers and archived copies of the code you are developing. In a different setting, such as a retail store where the network holds the business's accounting system, point-of-sale workstations, and electronic mail between branch stores and the home store, elaborate security may be necessary.

Since the security provided by each network varies, it is difficult to create a planning worksheet that is generally useful. Base yours on the

Workstation Configuration Worksheet

Workstation Requirements by Application

Application	Memory Usage		Disk Drive Usage			Files Used	Display Type	Printer Type	DOS Version		Other Devices
	Unshared	Shared	A:	B:	C:				Low	High	
MS-DOS											
Network											

Workstation Hardware Summary
Memory:
Floppy disk drive(s):
FILES= in CONFIG.SYS:
Display(s):
Printer(s):
DOS version:
Other devices:
Serial ports:
Parallel ports:
Expansion slots:

Figure 4-7. Workstation configuration worksheet

type of security your network offers and fill it out during the planning process. Your network security arrangements could address the particular user on a specific application; or you could save time and effort by assigning the same security arrangement to all users who fit in a similar class — for example, all secretaries may have the same security level, check-out clerks another level, and bookkeepers a third.

Hardware Planning

Once you have a good understanding of your users, applications, and systems software, you can derive your needs for workstations, servers, and connections. You need to determine the workstation and server hardware configurations and the connection scheme you will use to tie the workstations and servers together.

Your user information worksheets identify all the applications each workstation uses. Collect this information on a workstation configuration worksheet so that you can determine what hardware the workstation needs. By analyzing all workstations, you determine the number of servers needed to support your workstations and the hardware configuration of each server. Finally, on the basis of your network's data dependencies — that is, which workstations communicate with which servers — you must build a connection plan for your cables and network transceiver cards. This plan is usually the most straightforward and is dictated by the architecture of the network system you choose.

Workstation Planning   The configuration of your workstations is determined by the applications and systems software that run on them. Your user information worksheets tell you who uses what applications software on each workstation. Your analysis of systems software reveals the hardware dependencies it imposes. You now combine this data to determine the workstation hardware configuration.

One approach to collating this information is to use a workstation configuration worksheet, shown in Figure 4-7; it identifies the major hardware requirements of each piece of software that will be run on each workstation. You need such a worksheet for every workstation — although, of course, you can duplicate the same information for workstations with identical requirements. The first two worksheet entries are for the MS-DOS and network software requirements; fill them in now or as soon as you have enough information.

The user information worksheets you completed earlier contain entries for applications and workstations. For each workstation, extract the name of each application run on it and put an entry in the left-hand column of the worksheet. From the applications worksheets transfer the relevant information to the proper line of the workstation configuration worksheet. (If you are proficient with a PC database management package, you can automate this process, especially if your package can handle relationships among multiple databases.)

Once you have all the information about all the applications that must run on this workstation, you can see what your workstation hardware configuration must be. Analyze the data in each column and enter the results in the summary table at the bottom of the worksheet.

1. RAM must be at least as much as the sum of all the unshared memory plus the largest shared memory requirement that must be in use concurrently. Typically this is the sum of the memory requirements of your network driver software, any memory-resident utility programs, MS-DOS itself, and the largest application program you run.

2. Some applications may require one or more floppy disk drives. (If this is a hardware expense you would rather avoid, substitute a network shared disk if possible.) Your total floppy disk space requirements gives you an idea of how to load software on each diskette and how often your users will have to swap them.

3. Some applications may require a hard disk. The minimum disk size needed equals the sum of all the applications disk space requirements. Again, add this expense to each workstation only after you are sure the network drive is not an option.

4. The total number of files opened by all the software that must run concurrently gives you the value for the MS-DOS FILES= entry in the CONFIG.SYS file. Consult the MS-DOS manual to determine how much RAM is thus consumed and make sure that figure is included in the MS-DOS memory requirement on this worksheet.

5. For each workstation you assign a video display of the type required by most applications. Determining this demands some nonnetwork PC hardware expertise. If any of your applications require graphics, you will probably need a graphics display adapter and monitor. Most such display devices can also handle your text requirements, although often the quality of text is not as good as on a text-only monitor.

6. If any of your applications require a printer, it must be allocated here. If several of your applications require different kinds of printers, you may want to limit the number of printers you must purchase for each workstation by reallocating applications and users among workstations.

7. The DOS version needed is one between the maximum of the low entries and the minimum of the high entries listed in the workstation configuration worksheet. If the first number is higher than the second number, you have a conflict in DOS requirements and must separate the conflicting applications. Check with the vendor of the software that requires an older DOS revision and see if an upgrade is available for the newer version.

8. Any other special peripherals (such as modems, mice, digitizers, or plotters) should be entered in the last column. You will probably need only one each of these, but make sure your choice is compatible with any two or more applications that require them. For example, if you have two different graphics applications, choose a plotter they both support.

9. Depending on the types of devices you attach to your workstation, you may need one or more serial or parallel I/O ports. This information can be derived from the documentation for the peripherals and your workstation itself. There are many ways to add these ports, and some PCs include them as standard equipment.

10. You must also make sure your workstation has enough expansion slots to hold all the peripherals you want to attach to it. Consult your owner's manuals for the workstation and the peripherals. Most network attachments take up one expansion slot. Make sure you account for slots needed to supply serial and parallel ports and to connect special devices such as mice.

At the completion of this exercise, you should have a good idea of the hardware configuration you need for each workstation. Review the systems software configuration needed to support that hardware, and factor any additional demands on the workstation back into the worksheet. If you can do so without being wasteful, be liberal enough in your figures to make sure your configuration will not fail if some piece of software needs a bit more memory than its documentation states. In performing this analysis for all your workstations, you may also decide that a different grouping

Server Configuration Worksheet

Server Requirements by Application

Application	Number in Workstation	Memory Usage		Disk Usage		Files Used	Printer Type	% Capacity Used	Other Devices
		Unshared	Shared	Unshared R-O R/W	Shared R-O R/W				
MS-DOS									
Network									

Workstation Hardware Summary
Memory:
Floppy disk drive(s):
FILES= in CONFIG.SYS:
Display(s):
Printer(s):
DOS version:
Other devices:
Serial ports:
Parallel ports:
Expansion slots:

Figure 4-8.   Server configuration worksheet

of applications on the workstations can reduce cost with no loss of function. But be careful not to sacrifice the problem-solving goals that motivated your installing a network.

Server Planning   The next stage in your plan is the determination of network server configurations. Figure 4-8 shows a server configuration worksheet. If your network is small enough to function with a single server, planning is fairly simple. If you have dozens of workstations, determining your server requirements not only requires careful analysis but may benefit from some creativity as well.

To minimize cost, you will probably want to use as few servers as possible. Naturally, you need to know how many workstations a server can support. The right number depends heavily on the type of applications you are running, your pattern of using them, and the ability of your network software and hardware to support that pattern. You derive your estimate from experience with your applications and from the network vendor's information. Figure 4-9 gives some very rough estimates of the number of PC workstations that can be typically supported by some of the more common types of servers under varying network loads. Actual rates of use are subject to wide variation according to individual circumstances, so these figures should not be used as the only basis of your estimate.

A light load might consist of word processing or spreadsheet processing during which only the data file resides on the server, or execution of an electronic mail program. A moderate load could consist of interactive database queries and interactive transaction processing. A heavy load would be software development or batch database work such as report generation.

	Light Use	Moderate Use	Heavy Use
PC XT server	8-12	4-8	3-4
PC AT server	12-18	8-12	4-8
High-performance server	18-36	12-18	6-12

Figure 4-9.   Typical number of workstations supported by different types of servers under different network loads

These examples are intended to give you a feeling for the problem. The true criterion is really the amount of server access required per minute. If the server is accessed only occasionally and most of the processing is local to the workstation, there is only a light load on the server and it can handle more workstations. If almost every command given on the workstation sends a request to the server, this represents a heavy network load, and the server can handle fewer workstations.

You need to know how many workstations a server can handle for each application you will run. If you need more than one server, you must decide what files and print service to place on each server. There are several reasons for grouping program and data files on a single server:

- The applications software requires it
- Network loads suggest the configuration
- Redundant storage of the files on other servers is reduced
- All the server resources for a group of workstations are provided, and cabling costs are minimized for that group.

From these and other factors that are important in your environment, you must come up with a trial server configuration, deciding the workstation/application pairs that will use that server for network resources.

After you fill in all the information about your applications and the network software, you can analyze the worksheet in Figure 4-8 and at the bottom write your estimate of the server hardware required. Note that this worksheet tells you only what is necessary, not what is sufficient. Performance considerations determine the latter. Here are some things to consider during your analysis:

1. Server memory should be at least equal to the sum of unshared memory times the number of workstations requiring it plus the largest program that can use shared memory at any one time. If more than two or more shared-memory programs can run at once, you must sum their memory requirements together. Your network software documentation should help you determine this requirement.

2. Network disk capacity must be large enough to hold all the unshared files times the number of workstations requiring them plus the total amount of shared disk storage used.

3. The maximum number of files in use at any one time determines the FILES= parameter in the MS-DOS CONFIG.SYS file. Some network

software opens multiple-user files as a single MS-DOS file, so you should consult your network documentation when computing this value.

4. Your server needs one printer of each type required by the workstations. The printer's use rate is the sum of the percent of capacity used by each application times the number of workstations running that application at once. If your use rate exceeds 100%, either your server needs more than one of that type of printer or you need another print server.

5. Other devices such as modems, tape drives, and communication gateways should be noted in the server configuration. Make sure you have a way to back up the disk storage for the server.

6. Using your projected configuration, you can ascertain the number of serial and parallel I/O ports your server needs, and you can determine the number of expansion slots required to hold all the peripheral adapter cards.

If the summary turns out to be a realistic configuration, go on to the next server. If you find you require more of some resource than can be configured on a single server, you need to rethink your allocation of servers to workstations.

Connection Planning   The final major step in your plan is usually the most straightforward. You need to determine how you will connect the workstations and servers of your network. Connections are needed whenever data must flow between two network nodes. For example, a connection is needed if an application needs to get a data file from a disk server, or send output to the printer on a print server, or send a message to another workstation by electronic mail.

A connection can be physical or virtual: a physical connection is a direct one by connecting cable; a virtual connection is one achieved by routing the data through one or more intermediate nodes. Be sure you understand the possibilities implicit in this distinction, since virtual connections add no cabling costs, although they may extract more of a performance penalty than a direct connection.

Different networks have different connection rules. Some of the most common ones are described in the second part of this book. The exact details of your network must guide your choices. In any case, you should start with a logic diagram showing the data dependency paths of your network, such as in Figure 4-3. From this diagram, your network cabling rules, and your physical site map, you can construct a connection blueprint for your LAN.

Site planning for the workstations and servers themselves is usually no more complex than planning for stand-alone PCs. Adequate power typically requires no more than a convenient wall outlet with stable power, and adequate cooling usually requires only comfortable temperatures. Cable stringing is another matter, and can quickly get you involved with local safety and building regulations. Your best bet is a good electrical contractor with some previous experience in installing LANs. In addition to following electrical codes for safety, LAN cabling needs to conform to the vendor's rules regarding:

- Minimum separation between connections to the cable
- Maximum lengths of cable runs
- Proper termination at the ends of the cable
- Use of drop cables from the trunk to a workstation or server
- Repeaters to boost the signal over long distances
- Routing away from sources of electrical interference such as AC wiring, motors, and fluorescent light fixtures.

Finding the problem with an improperly laid cable can be frustrating and time-consuming, so you are well advised to learn the rules of the LAN in advance and make sure you follow them. A carefully worked out map of your site drawn to scale and showing all workstations, servers, and connecting cables is a must. Study the map and make sure all the length constraints are met. Leave some room for expansion in your cable runs. For example, allow a workstation to be moved from desk to desk within a room if possible. Run bus cables near enough to potential future network node sites so you can easily add the node later.

You must also be sure to follow the cable length rules that pertain to the exact type of cable you are using. Different cable grades with compatible basic electrical characteristics may have different signal-loss rates, meaning that you may be able to use 5000 feet of one type of cable but only 2000 feet of another. Different network topologies can result in radically different cabling diagrams for the same siting of workstations and servers. For example:

- A bus may require one cable strung past all the nodes.

- A bus with drop cables sends a single cable into each office; one not using drop cables may appear to send two cables into each office (it's actually the same cable entering and leaving the node).

- A star may require much more wire than a bus, especially if the workstations are closer together than to the server at the hub.

Once your cable diagram is drawn, you can decide whether to use precut cables or custom-made ones. You must balance the cost of the unused lengths of the precut cables against the labor costs of making exact-length custom cables. In many areas this difference may be slight, since the labor costs of running a single cable far exceed the material costs. If you decide to use precut lengths, be sure they also meet your cabling rules — as far as the network rules go — 20 feet of excess precut cable in a 1-foot diameter coil still counts as 20 feet.

DOING THE INSTALLATION

If you have built a trial network to learn about your system and carefully analyzed your network as described in this chapter, the actual installation is a matter of executing your plan. You should build your network in testable sections, making sure each one functions according to your expectations before continuing with the installation. For example, you may install one server and its workstations and make sure they work together before adding another server.

The order of installation may be dictated by your network vendor, but it typically follows a sequence such as:

1. Set up the server and workstation hardware
2. Make sure the combination works stand-alone
3. Install the network cards and cables and connect them
4. Install the system software on the server and test it
5. Install the system software on the workstation and test it
6. Bring up your applications and test them.

You can see that the order of implementation is practically the reverse of the order of planning and design. You start implementation with the lowest-level components of your network, make sure they work, and then build on that foundation, testing each successive layer to make sure it works, too.

Hardware and Software Installation

If you are reasonably sure about your network layout you can run cables at the same time you set up workstations and servers. Make sure that the cables you need first for system testing are installed early enough. If you are unsure about your network in any way—for example, whether it will have adequate performance—run only enough cables to perform a test. String more cables when you are satisfied with your design.

Set up the servers following the instructions provided by the server and network software vendor. Connect all the peripherals identified in your server worksheet and make sure the minimum requirements for memory and disk storage are met. Workstations should be set up the same way. In most cases you can test the workstations to see if they function as stand-alone PCs. You can frequently also test the server this way, especially if it is a PC XT or PC AT.

Next, the system software should be installed on the servers and workstations configured as the documentation and your worksheets suggest. The worksheets should greatly assist you in the areas that might otherwise require a lot of guesswork, such as allocating server storage to volumes or directories, making different network resources such as printers available to your end users, and setting up system security.

Cable your server and workstations together and start testing the system. Your LAN documentation probably suggests some simple tests you can perform to make sure the basics are functioning before you start trying your applications. When you are satisfied that all is well you can start loading and testing the applications.

Diagnosing Problems

If all does not go well, consult your network documentation and look for an explanation of common problems or interpretation of error messages. Building and testing your network in small pieces should help you to locate the point at which things stopped working. Like most system problem solving, half the battle is isolating the problem to a small part of the system, then fixing the faulty part or repacing it with a good part. A network has many parts, possibly strung out across a large area, and can be formidable to debug. Some techniques for isolating problems follow.

1. Make sure every workstation and server works alone, outside of the network environment.

2. Test network connection cards with loopback plugs, if they are available, or hardware diagnostic software.

3. Test cables for short circuits with an ohmmeter. There should be no direct connection between the network cable conductors. Short circuits may be induced by a kink or pinch in the wire.

4. Test applications software on local disk drives and printers if possible.

Try to narrow down the number of system components whose working status is unknown. Do this by swapping in components known to work. Consider using this technique with server and workstation PCs, network connection cards, cables, and even applications packages that use the same or similar server resources as the suspect applications. It may be difficult to swap a cable strung through the wall or ceiling, so if you suspect it is bad, try moving the workstation or server to another location with a known good connection on the network and see if it works there. If it does, your suspicions about the cable should be heightened.

Training Network Users

Once you are satisfied that your applications are installed and working, you need to train the users of your network, tuning the training to their needs. Technical users may just want copies of the network documentation and they will learn what they need to know when they need to know it. End users who don't care at all about system implementation or utilities may only need to be trained on the applications. In any case, you should plan for some time to be spent on training and if your system is installed by or with a lot of help from a consultant, plan for that consultant to spend several days at your site to answer questions and make adjustments in the initial configuration.

Managing the Network

Every network needs a manager who is responsible after the installation. If your network is fairly static in the applications it runs and its configuration of workstations and servers, it may be enough to assign a nontechnical user who can handle daily backups of the servers, answer questions about the applications, and assign new user accounts as needed. A consultant can be called in when network management needs go beyond these simple ones.

If your network environment is dynamic (new applications are frequently brought up, new workstations and servers added, security requirements undergo change, and the like), you may need an experienced person in-house or a consultant on call. Many management tasks can be handled by someone who is not a computer expert but who has received the proper training on the network.

5

USING A LOCAL AREA
NETWORK

There are a variety of ways in which a local area network can be used. A LAN can reduce hardware costs if an expensive peripheral (such as a laser printer) is needed by more than one PC user. It can provide a means for passing information between users, eliminating the need to send diskettes, or replacing a hard copy interoffice mail system. These applications are for convenience and efficiency, and are among the most common uses of LANs today.

There are also many applications that simply cannot be implemented through the use of several isolated PCs. Any time more than one user needs instant access to the latest version of a particular piece of data, such as an inventory count or the status of a reservation list, a multiuser application package is required. As discussed earlier, a network is not the only way to satisfy the need for instant access, since a shared central computer may also be used. But as far as networks are concerned, this type of application is the most sophisticated and the least likely to be available off the shelf.

OVERVIEW

Figure 5-1 illustrates the broad spectrum of network uses, ranging from sharing hardware to sharing and modifying information. As you move to the right, along this axis, the sophistication of network systems and applications software increases, as does the amount of interaction among network users. The simplest use of a network is sharing hardware. In this environment, no one network user is very aware of the others. Each user can view the network pretty much as consisting of his or her own machine with its own collection of programs and data files. Users become aware of other network users primarily through their impact on shared devices, such as printers and tape drives, that can be used by only one user at a time. If someone else is using a device that you want to access, you must wait your turn. You may also notice a slowdown in response from shared

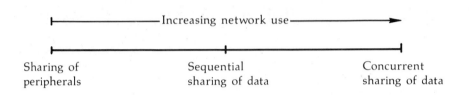

Figure 5-1.   Spectrum of network use

hardware that can be accessed by more than one user at a time, such as disk drives, communications gateways, or the network bus itself. In this case, the network software makes the shared peripherals appear to be attached to the workstation as if they were a local device. In a sense, the network is nothing more than an intelligent extension cord, in that it provides some measure of conflict avoidance. Usage requests for devices that can only be accessed by one workstation at a time may be queued up, or an error message returned indicating that the device is in use and you must try again later.

Concurrently accessible devices like disk drives are partitioned by the network software into separate logical devices, each of which is a self-contained system that can be accessed without interference from other workstations. The next stage of network software sophistication permits users to share information electronically but not concurrently. This use is analogous to passing diskettes around in a nonnetworked, multiple-PC environment. Network users are aware of other network users, but they still operate mainly in a private environment, passing information to each other by the network instead of manually. Using the network to transfer information is more convenient than passing diskettes around, but it introduces two new problems. Consider that when someone hands you a diskette and says "here's the latest copy of the budget, add your department's data to it" you automatically know two things:

1. You have the latest information
2. Nobody else is going to modify the data on that diskette until you are finished with it.

The first problem of network information transfer is version control; when you are handed a diskette, unless the person has made a mistake, you are assured you are being given current information. The second problem is concurrent update control; when you are the only one who can physically modify the data file, you can be sure that it does not contain partial information from several different users that results in an inconsistent picture. When you replace this manual system with an electronic system, such as a LAN, you need some new means of providing these controls. You need some way of informing other users which files to access and when. If several versions of the data are in a shared volume that everyone can access, you must prevent different workstation users from accessing different files and making their modifications in an uncontrolled order. You can still use single-user MS-DOS software for this type of application, but some extra care must be taken in setting up the network and in establishing use procedures. Some networks are better than others at providing automatic safeguards against accidental damage to data files.

The most complex network application is one in which many network users must have simultaneous access to the same information, both to read it and modify it. Many real-life business applications fall into this category; reservation systems, sales from inventory, banking systems, and manufacturing control operations are just a few examples. The users' view of this system is more unified than in the previous two scenarios. Many workstation users are simultaneously using the network to manage and control a single application or process.

Each user may interact with one, two, or even all the other users from moment to moment. Two reservation agents may try, only seconds apart, to reserve the last room in a hotel; the first one should get the reservation, and the second one should see instantly that the room is no longer available. The systems and applications software needed for this kind of application must be carefully designed. Most PC networks provide some support for this type of environment, but the level of support varies, and it requires a knowledgeable and experienced systems analyst to evaluate a particular network's suitability for a specific application. The applications are likely to require custom programming, as perhaps are the systems. This need is especially likely if the end users of the network are not computer-knowledgeable, and the application must be easy to use and reliable and its data must be relatively safe from accidental damage. For example, in this type of environment it is probably not sufficient to require users to type in manual commands to lock data files before updating them.

SOFTWARE CAUTIONS

Since network hardware for personal computers was developed before network applications software, the network operating software was designed to allow most existing MS-DOS software to run without modification, even though that software was developed for the single-user PC. Programming functions were provided so that new multiuser software could be written, or single-user programs could be adapted for the multiuser LAN environment.

There are degrees to which you can successfully run single-user software on a LAN; the range of adaptability runs along that same axis shown in Figure 5-1. At the left end is software most similar to that for a single, dedicated PC. The network provides some additional peripherals and the software to manage them and make your application see them as local peripherals. This configuration presents the least risk and extra work on the part of the system manager and users. Most single-user MS-DOS programs can run in this environment.

The middle range of the scale in Figure 5-1 represents the use of single-user programs with carefully controlled resource sharing. The sharing mechanisms are outside of the application software. Procedural mechanisms include a previously agreed-upon method for creating or updating shared information and coordinating access among users. Network commands to lock files for access or update can also be manually typed by the user.

This sharing is not "transparent" to the end user; that is, it is not managed automatically by the application. A single-user application is being used in a multiuser environment. If the established procedures are not followed, there is a risk of data loss or damage.

The right side of the scale requires the use of software written specifically for the network environment. When properly designed, this is the safest environment, since the applications and systems software together prevent accidental data damage by system users. Such network software is discussed later in this chapter.

Many existing MS-DOS applications run without modification on a network. The following sections examine their use and suggest ways to best configure them for a LAN environment. First, it's important to look at some of the problem areas that restrict function or even prevent some packages from working at all.

Copy Protection

Many of the best-selling personal computer software packages are copy-protected to prevent purchasers from making copies of the disk and sharing the software with unlicensed users. You cannot load such copy-protected software to a network disk and have all your workstation users access and run that software. (Even if you could, it would probably be in violation of the license under which you are using the software.) However, there are still ways you can make use of many such packages in conjunction with a LAN: you can run the software on your workstation and use the network for disk and print service, or you can load the software to the network disk and run it from a single workstation just as if you had loaded it to that workstation's hard disk.

Most current software lets you access network disks and printers. You can use the network's disk or file server to hold the program and data files. Only one workstation is licensed to use the program, however, and that workstation may need the original program disk in order to start the software, depending on the type of copy protection used. (Before hard disks increased in popularity, almost all copy-protection schemes required the use of the original distribution diskette, called a *key disk*, to start the software. The program checks to see if the key disk is in drive A:, and if it isn't, the program does not start. The normal MS-DOS disk-copying utilities cannot copy the key disk, so only one user can run the package at a time.)

As the number of PCs with hard disks increased, users complained about key disk copy-protection schemes, since they wanted to load their software to the hard disk and take advantage of its speed and convenience. Software vendors responded with new copy-protection schemes that allow users to load the software onto a hard disk and run it.

Using this type of copy-protected software on a network disk is much riskier than the key disk scheme. The copy-protection apparatus uses low-level details about a PC's hard disk organization that may not be duplicated by the network environment. It may directly access the hard disk controller, bypassing MS-DOS and the network software, guaranteeing that it will not work on the network disk drive. This type of copy-protection scheme may also depend on the exact placement of the protected programs on the hard disk. If the system manager makes a backup of the network disk, then reloads it later, it may come back in a different place on the disk. The package's copy-protection scheme will sense that the software has moved and make it fail to run.

Even if you find that a package does install successfully on your network hard disk, the burden is on the system manager to enforce the single-user, single-machine license restriction. The key disk enforces this restriction for you, but software installed on the network hard disk may be accessed from more than one workstation. If you want to use such a configuration, a password or other security mechanism should be used to restrict access to the software. If you have any questions about the licensing issues involved, consult the software vendor.

Disk Access

Unintentional multiuser update of a file can occur during shared use of programs that write system information to the disk during the program's execution; such information can be about program configuration, user profiles, or internal data structures.

If a software package is loaded to a network disk and run by several users, not only data files can be unintentionally updated. For example, you may store your desired default word processing settings in a program configuration file. If this file is stored in the directory that the word processor resides in, your settings can be overwritten by another user's the next time they are changed.

There are two ways around this problem of accidental change to data and program files. First, if the application package lets you specify the name or directory of the system file, you can set up separate files for each user. (This approach is the most conservative of disk space.) If this cannot be done, your second recourse is to provide each user with his or her own copy of the software in a private network directory.

The single-user program's documentation may not state whether the program can be written to disk (since this may not be an important concern in the single-user environment). You will have to find out for yourself. If the program saves any information between executions, such as user profile or program configuration data, it is writing something to the disk. If you are not sure, consult the software vendor. If you can't obtain this information, you can experiment by putting the program in a write-protected or read-only directory or volume on the network disk. Don't try to create or modify any critical data while you do this experiment, since the application's handling of a write-protect error, should one occur, may cause you to lose the data file. Most packages will not lose your data, since they may be run on write-protected floppy disks, but you should not count on this. If you can execute the program's functions without problems, it does not need to write to the disk, and you can share it over the network among multiple users.

More and more network software requires MS-DOS Version 2.0 or higher. If your software requires that you run MS-DOS 1.0 or 1.10, check with the network vendor to make sure that the system supports that version. In any case, it is a good idea to use only one revision of MS-DOS throughout your network, both for servers and workstations. You may be able to successfully mix revisions, but it is not recommended.

Some programs also depend on certain disk-access features that survive from the CP/M operating system. These are technical and have to do with direct manipulation of operating system data structures or dependence on undocumented operating system behavior related to opening, accessing, and closing files. Most network systems software has been modified to handle the common violations of operating system protocol, but if an application bypasses the operating system completely, there is no way the network software can prevent problems.

Printing

Most applications can be made to work successfully with a network printer, but you may run across one or more of the following problem areas:

- Direct hardware access by the application
- Network software filtering of control codes
- Network software interjection of control codes
- Conflict between the network and application print buffering
- Nonrelease of shared printers by the application
- Setting of printer parameters by different applications.

Don't let this list alarm you, since you may not hit any of these problems. However, printing problems can be especially frustrating, so it is worthwhile to go over some of the more frequent causes and solutions for them.

Nearly all network systems software that provides sharing of printers can redirect print output that the application sends by an MS-DOS call to the MS-DOS PRN: or LPTx: device. Many networks can also intercept print output sent to the PC's BIOS, a lower-level programming interface.

If, however, the application software directly accesses printer port hardware on the local PC, there is little that can be done to get that application to use a network printer.

Fortunately, this most common problem area is also often remediable by a user configuration option. Many applications packages use the hardware interface directly when configured to print to a serial printer, but use an MS-DOS or BIOS interface when printing to parallel printers. If your application does not seem to work on the network, check to see whether you have chosen COM1: or COM2: as the printer port. Even if this designation identifies the physical port that the printer is connected to on the server, you may be able to make your printing instructions work by telling your application that the printer is connected to LPT1:, or PRN:, or that it is a parallel printer and following the network instructions for redirecting that device to the network printer.

Less frequently, you may have a problem even when you have selected a parallel printer from your application. Some programs check the hardware directly for printer status information that is not available from MS-DOS or BIOS. This is especially likely if your program has a built-in print spooler. If you can disable the spooler, try to do so; you may then be able to start printing on the network printer.

Many applications let you print to a disk file instead of to a printer. In other words, the print output is stored as text in a file. (The command to do this varies from application to application.) You can then print this text file either by using the network print command, or by using the MS-DOS COPY command to copy the file to the network printer:

```
COPY file LPT1:
```

(This example assumes that the network printer is redirected from the local printer named LPT1:.)

The second common printing problem occurs when your application needs to send special control codes to the printer and your network software either filters them out or interprets them as having special meaning for some network function. For example, say your network software supports a command to immediately stop whatever is printing on the network printer; when you issue that command from your workstation, the network software sends a certain character sequence to the print server, and, upon seeing that character sequence, the print server software stops the printing process. The problem arises if, by coincidence, your application program sends that same character sequence to the network printer, intending a different result but stopping the printer instead. For example, an application printing high-resolution graphics to a graphics printer may send practically any character sequence to create a complicated graphics image. In addition to graphics images, control character sequences are generated to control special printer functions such as microspacing, super-scripts, and subscripts, or to print simple character graphics or foreign-language characters.

If the network you choose does not implement print commands as described, you may have nothing to be concerned about. On the other hand, if your application prints perfectly when connected to the local printer but has problems on the network printer, character sequences are an area to investigate. You should note the exact function in process when the problem occurs and check with your network vendor for a possible solution.

A companion problem occurs when the network print software tries to be helpful and adds formatting control to your print output at the same time that your applications program is supposed to be in control of the printer. The result is a poorly formatted printout, the most common symptoms being extra linefeeds, formfeeds, or slowly creeping output that starts lower and lower on each successive page. The simplest solution to this type of problem is to turn off the network print driver's control of output format. If there is no single command or configuration choice for doing this, look for settings in the network print control software like:

- Page length
- Line length
- Skip over perforations?
- Margins
- Borders
- Page offset.

Make these settings equivalent to the physical limits of the paper you are using. For example, for 8 1/2- by 11-inch paper, you would want the following settings: page length of 66 lines, do not skip over perforations, top or bottom margin of 0, left and right borders of 0, and page offset of 0.

Another possible source of problems is conflict between print buffers. It is common for print buffering to take place in:

- Your applications program
- The workstation (if an installable print spooler is used)

- The network print server
- The printer itself.

Sometimes these buffers work together, but at other times one buffer gets hung up waiting for input from another. You may also have a problem such that the last line or few lines of a file never get printed. In any event, it is seldom efficient to have more than one print buffer working on the same print output. All that extra handling of the print output may use extra system resources with no net reduction in waiting time. The solution is to reduce your print buffering software to the minimum and see if the problem goes away. Even if you are not experiencing a problem, try disabling your application's print spooler if you can, or don't load the workstation print spooler, and see if there is any noticeable difference in printing performance or in the delay between the start of printing and the time you regain control of your workstation. If there is no degradation, leave the print spooler disabled or unloaded.

There is also the general problem of having a shared printer instead of a dedicated printer. When you are the only user of a printer, there is no need to know when you are through with it, since nobody else is waiting to use it. Your software can send it data continuously or at a leisurely pace, and the next character sent to the printer will follow the previous one exactly, with no intervening data from other users. Programmers have written their applications with this in mind, and very few programs use MS-DOS system calls to release or "close" the printer when they are done printing.

In a network environment it is necessary to know whether you are truly finished with a particular print job or are just pausing to compute the next thing to be printed. Every network provides one or more ways to release the printer, such as:

- An explicit user command
- A software sequence
- A printer inactivity timeout.

Your network system documentation should provide adequate information on how to use this printer-release feature, and you should be aware of the need to use it on your network. If you do not, you could have seemingly random problems with network printing. For example, if your system provided a timeout value of, say, 30 seconds, and 95% of your printing never paused for more than 30 seconds but 5% of your printing did, 5% of the time the network printer would appear to mysteriously stop in the middle of one print job and start one on behalf of another workstation.

Similarly, if a software character sequence is used to release the printer, you could have problems similar to those with network software filtering of control codes. Your application could coincidentally send the control code sequence that releases the printer, when in fact it was attempting to control the printer in some other way.

Finally, in a shared environment, you must manage the use of different printer settings by different applications software packages. Modern printers are capable of many fancy printing operations, and an applications package can set the printer up to use different fonts, character widths, lines per inch, and so on. You should establish a default condition for the printer, and if an applications program changes the printer configuration, it should set it back when it is finished. Some network print server software allows you to establish a character code sequence that is sent to the printer before starting every new print job. If your print server software supports resetting the printer, you should enter the character sequence that resets the printer to the condition expected by your network users. No matter what each user's individual print job does to the printer configuration, the printer is then restored to a known state before each new print job, independently of what the application program does.

If your print server software does not have such a feature, then you must be sure that your users send the equivalent sequence from their applications whenever they have changed the printer configuration in the course of a print job.

Another common cause of user complaints is related not to network software but to operating procedure. Whenever you remove output from the printer, be sure to turn the printer back online so that it can be used by other workstations. If the printer is out of earshot, a long time may go by before the user realizes that his or her print job is not ready because the printer is off-line, not because some other user's output is printing.

Shared Servers

When a network server is also used as a workstation, it is especially vulnerable to system crashes caused by application software bugs or user errors. When a server is also a workstation, the safest user software to run is an applications program that is also running on the other workstations.

For example, a cash register program that has been in use for a period of time and appears to be fairly stable is not likely to cause the server to crash. When the server also acts as a workstation, the riskiest thing to do is to allow the user to run many different programs, including some that have not been tried on that workstation before. The IBM PC environment offers no hard protection against an applications program crashing the system, and one that behaves well on a single-user PC may have a conflict with the server software that shows up only at the most inopportune moment.

Some programs that work well on a stand-alone PC may have a problem on a shared network server, so be sure to try them in a noncritical environment first. You should be especially careful about memory-resident programs that are activated from within another program by an unusual key sequence. Even if they don't crash the server PC, these programs may shut off the server's interrupt system and result in temporary suspension of network service. If network response time seems to suddenly slow down by a very large factor, make sure no one is running such a program on a shared server.

It almost goes without saying that trying to develop software on a PC that is also acting as a network server is a sure recipe for disaster. New software invariably has bugs that can hang up or crash the system and bring the network server down at the same time. Likewise, software that is self-booting or runs under an operating system other than MS-DOS certainly cannot be used while the PC is acting as a server.

If the application running on a shared network server appears to be hung up — that is, there is no response from the keyboard — you should try to salvage the most you can out of the situation. In some cases, the server software may still be running and only the applications package is hung up. Have all the workstation users of the network server finish what they are doing and log off the server before you shut it down and restart it.

USING APPLICATIONS

Now that you've seen how things can go wrong, it's time to look at the brighter side of the picture — taking advantage of the network environment. The most popular PC application categories include word processing, spreadsheets, database managers, accounting systems, and graphics packages. For each of these applications there is a different common-use scenario, with different requirements for sharing and modifying data.

Word Processors

One of the most common uses of personal computers is word processing. Seldom does more than one person using a word processor need to update the same file at the same time, so single-user word processors generally work well in a network environment. The network's disk or file server should be used as you would use a local hard disk: for storing the program and document files.

Another advantage of a network for word processing is that you may be able to afford a faster, more-expensive printer if it can be shared by many users. Some of the new laser printers are especially well suited for such uses, and they combine text output of near typeset quality with graphics output capability. Not only can they improve the professional appearance of your firm's correspondence, presentations, or documentation, they may further justify their cost by allowing you to make less use of some outside services such as for typesetting of advertising copy.

Many installations share several common document formats, often referred to as boilerplates. You should take advantage of this commonality wherever possible and establish a shared public volume or directory containing the frequently used boilerplates. This saves disk space and painlessly enforces consistency among many users.

Finally, the network provides an easy means for users to share finished documents. Simply place a document in a shared directory and inform the intended recipient of its location. Users can read or print the document right from its storage location without creating another space-consuming copy. An electronic mail system makes it even easier to inform network users of the documents and their location.

Spreadsheets

In their patterns of use spreadsheets present many analogues to the word processors. A spreadsheet is created and modified by a single user, then perhaps shared with others. The network is a fast and convenient way to share a spreadsheet among several users — far superior to making many diskette copies and carrying them to the other users.

Consider using shared volumes or directories to store commonly used spreadsheet templates or macros. Most spreadsheet users spend a fair amount of time developing special routines to handle dates or some locally unique data such as supporting tables for sales forecasts. Share these with other network users by saving them on the disk server.

A major trend in patterns of PC use is to extract data from corporate mainframes and load it into spreadsheets to generate "what-if" scenarios. A network with a gateway or bridge to the mainframe should work with this strategy; if your users need such a capability, make sure the network software and hardware provide it.

Database Management Systems

There is more likely to be a natural need for several users to simultaneously read and modify the same database than to access a document or a spreadsheet. Database applications fit into the LAN, being natural candidates for using shared network storage, printers, and other services. The caveats and procedures already discussed apply to them as well, with emphasis on the need to control access to data files, especially if you use a single-user database system with manual controls over file access. Make sure that any manual protocol to be followed is well understood by your users, and consider using safeguards such as storing data files in private directories where the network automatically restricts access to one workstation at a time.

Accounting Systems

Many applications are used for accounting, including point-of-sale, inventory control, general ledger, accounts receivable and payable, and payroll. If more than one user needs to access the same accounting file at the same time, you need to invest in a good multiuser accounting system for your business. It is especially crucial to guarantee data security, integrity, and recovery. You should not rely on error-prone manual controls over any of these critical areas.

Data security requires that your network software provide adequate protection against unauthorized reading or modification of accounting information. The larger the number of users and types of applications running on the network storing your accounting data, the more critical protection becomes—and the less able a simple security scheme is to provide enough flexibility to allow authorized users to do their work without allowing unauthorized users to tamper with vital data. In many cases, you may want to provide several levels of access to the same file; for instance, the assistant bookkeeper may be able to read the values of salaries, but only the head bookkeeper can change them.

Data integrity refers to the freedom of data from corruption. The damage done by the failure of two users to synchronize their access to a word processing document pales by comparison to the possible damage done by a corrupted accounting data file.

Even if you have done your best to prevent data loss or corruption, you should plan for its occurrence. You must be sure you can recover from it when, not if, it happens. Don't be among the majority of users who start worrying about recovery after the disaster strikes. In most cases, planning simply means that you back up the network disk files as often as necessary so that if you lost everything but the backups you should have to reenter no more than one business day's worth of transactions. (You should, of course, have hard copy or some other suitable backup of the day's transactions so you can reenter them.)

Graphics Software

Like word processors and spreadsheets, there is not much call for multi-user concurrent update of a graph or the data used to generate a graph. A LAN can contribute to the usefulness of a graphics package in several ways, though. You have already seen how a LAN makes it easy to share information between PC users. Graphics packages generally only need to read a data file to produce a graph, and thus they can unobtrusively retrieve data from common network databases for graphing. Graphics output devices such as plotters and 35 millimeter slide makers may be difficult to justify for a single PC, but easy to justify when an entire department can share one on a LAN.

NEW SOFTWARE FOR LANS

As more PC LANs are installed, more software is being written specifically for the network environment. The majority of software running on LANs today is single-user software, but several of the applications areas described earlier are seeing a steady growth in network versions. Other applications are, by their nature, unique to the network environment. Foremost among these is electronic mail, a system for sending messages and files to other users on the network. There is a wide range in the functions provided by PC electronic mail systems, and the following section details some of the features you may want to look for.

Electronic Mail

A good electronic mail system is both useful and addictive. The term "electronic mail" is somewhat misleading, since the system not only transmits information that would otherwise be sent through interoffice or U.S. mail, but also replaces short telephone calls with electronic messages sent back and forth. Every user on the network has a network name or address, and the mail system lets you compose a message and send it to another user or users. The message is stored on the network server, and the user is notified that it is waiting for retrieval. If a user is not logged on when a message arrives, the system stores the fact that a message is waiting and notifies the user the next time he or she logs on. Some systems are less automated and require users to start the mail software on the workstation to check the status of waiting mail.

There are many desirable features of an electronic mail system; for example, you can:

- Send and receive messages and files
- Forward incoming messages
- Save, print, and reply to messages
- Retrieve, edit, and resend saved messages
- Send messages and files to lists of users
- Temporarily forward mail to another user
- Access external networks
- Access public electronic mail systems.

Sending and receiving messages and files should be quick and easy, requiring a minimum of keystrokes. You can send more than one file at a time by specifying an MS-DOS filename template. You should be able to forward a message to another network user, adding comments to the message to explain the reason for forwarding it. Replying to a message should also be very easy to do; the system should automatically supply the name and address of the sender as the recipient of the reply, rather than forcing you to remember it and type it in.

You should be able to save messages and files on any convenient disk as well as being able to print them locally or on a network printer. You should be able to edit messages by pulling up an old message from the disk, modifying it, and sending it off to a new destination. The electronic mail system should make it easy to maintain distribution or mailing lists and to share such lists among network users. In other words, you should be able to mail a message or a file to a group of users all at once by simply giving the name of the list you created.

Temporary mail forwarding is useful if you are going to be away from your desk for an extended period of time while someone else, such as a secretary, watches your mail for urgent messages. Finally, access to users outside of the local area network obviously extends the benefits of the system to whatever size group you can access. A uniform electronic mail system across an entire division or corporation can be a great productivity boon. An even wider circle may be accessed if you can use your electronic mail system to interact with a public electronic mail system.

The benefits of electronic mail include:

- Reduced "telephone tag"

- Increased speed of disseminating information

- Lower direct and indirect mailing costs

- Improved corporate communications.

In a typical business environment, an inordinate number of phone calls result in "telephone tag"—the leaving of messages to call back rather than completion of the communication. Often the message is brief, (it could be written in a page or less) but is too long to dictate to the secretary or whoever answers the phone. Although not all business use of the telephone falls into this category, a great deal frequently does. If the party you need to converse with can be reached over the network, and has access to the electronic mail system, the exchange of "please call back" messages can be drastically reduced or even eliminated.

Electronic mail is very fast, operating practically at the speed of data transfer over your network. Combined with the reduction of telephone tag this is a double benefit. Not only is your message more likely to get to its destination, it does so more quickly than it could through the normal mail or even an express courier service.

The sources of savings from electronic mail are several. There are direct savings in paper, envelopes, postage and telephone costs. There are indirect savings in the reduced labor of handling paper mail, and productivity is increased because less time is wasted on unsuccessful telephone calls.

Improved corporate communication is a major intangible benefit, for which the electronic mail system must be extended beyond the local area network to cover a large number of people, such as a division or corporation. The most common business problems can be traced to poor communications. Most of the people that each employee needs to communicate with daily should be reachable over the network. You may quickly discover that the benefits of electronic mail outweigh those of any other single use of the network.

Electronic Calendar

Electronic calendar applications are slowly gaining in popularity among local area network users. An electronic calendar is a specialized database application that lets you enter and retrieve your daily appointment calendar. Among other things, a good electronic calendar system allows you to:

- Enter appointments quickly and easily
- Schedule meetings based on someone else's calendar
- Search for appointments by time, day, and description
- Reschedule appointments without reentering data
- View and modify another user's calendar
- Print or view calendar for entire day, week, or month
- Store appointments that recur daily, weekly, monthly, or annually
- Determine scheduling conflicts among all participants in a meeting
- Schedule reservations of meeting rooms.

It is important that entry of appointments be fast and easy. It's hard to beat a calendar on the desk for quick view and entry of appointments, so the software that provides this function must be usable with a minimum of keystrokes and delay. Recall of appointments must be equally quick, although here the system can have some advantages over a paper system, especially for someone with a very full schedule. Appointments are frequently changed, and the system must handle this quickly and with a minimum of typing. The system should automatically reschedule appointments that recur on some regular basis.

It should be no surprise that the benefit of a LAN in conjunction with an electronic calendar is the ability to use other people's calendars when you schedule a meeting.

Intelligent calendar systems can handle requests like "schedule a one-hour meeting Thursday afternoon between Tom, Lee, Sally, and Bob." If all these users keep their calendars updated, the system can check the calendars for a common one-hour slot and, having found one, add that meeting time to all their calendars. Of course, if no common time is available, the system must report this and allow you to try another time.

Some calendar systems can schedule other resources such as meeting rooms — another example of how a network provides a big improvement over a system of isolated PCs. If all users can access the schedule of your meeting rooms from the PC in their office, there is no need for anyone to wander around the building looking for an available room.

Remote access via a telephone connection and modem is also very desirable if you are often on the road. You can check your calendar to see what new appointments have been made for you, and you can let people back at the office know where you will be and when you will be there.

Multiuser Shared Databases

Another major use of PC networks is multiuser shared database management. A multiuser system should provide all the features of a single-user system, and allow convenient but controlled access by more than one user to the same database. A LAN database system may be used alone or as the basis for a multiuser application such as an accounting system.

Different network database systems control shared access to different degrees. All such systems provide basic locking mechanisms, but they differ mostly in how much responsibility they place on the user to lock in the correct sequence in order to prevent erroneous database updates or deadlocks between database users. The least control is offered by a system that simply provides the lock and unlock commands but does not integrate them into the database access operations. In such cases, any user can execute all the database access commands even if another user has issued one or more lock commands. Clearly, the integrity of such a database depends totally upon everyone's proper use of the lock and unlock operations.

A more sophisticated system may detect the fact that one user has locked a certain file and will not allow other users to access that file until the first lock is released. The same protection applies to individual data records. Deadlocks occur when each of two or more users holds something locked that another needs. Each user ends up waiting for a resource held locked by the other, and nobody gets any further. Automatic detection of such a situation is possible but is complicated and unusual in microcomputer database systems. Security is often more of an issue for a multiuser database than for many other network applications. Its importance depends on the contents of the database, but you should carefully evaluate the security provided by the combination of your underlying network software and the database system's own security features. A database system can assign security safeguards much more precisely than the network software. For example, the network may provide security at the directory or file level, but you may want to limit some users' update privileges to certain fields in a database record while letting them read a larger set of fields or perhaps the entire record. The network software can't help you assign security measures selectively, but a good multiuser database package can.

BACKUP STRATEGIES

The need to back up a network's disk storage has been stressed already. Part of the benefit of a network is that it is usually one person's responsibility to make sure the backup gets done, and that data stored on the network server by everyone and anyone is backed up when the network is backed up. If the network server is lost and the backup has not been done, everyone loses data, potentially causing a major disaster. The system manager should set up a backup procedure and make sure it gets implemented.

As a general rule, you should consider the effects of losing the network disk server at any given time. If you wouldn't want to have to manually recover the information stored or modified since the last backup was done, it means that another backup should be scheduled. As a practical matter, you should back the system up at least once a day.

It is not imperative to save the entire contents of the network disk drives, since many if not most files don't change daily. The MS-DOS BACKUP utility, and most other network backup programs, allow you to specify that only files modified since the last full backup need to be saved. This utility should make your daily backups go much faster. If they don't go faster, examine the files being backed up. It may be that some extremely large files are being backed up in their entirety although only a portion of each file is modified each day. Consider whether such a file can be split up into smaller portions and whether such a change might speed up the daily backups.

Restoring a disk server from a loss of data requires one of two possibilities:

- The last full backup and all the partial backups must be restored
- The last full backup and the last partial backup must be restored.

The first case holds if your backup program saves all files that have been modified since the last backup, be it a complete backup of the disk or a partial one. In this case, you should do a full backup once a week or so, since the number of backups you must restore gets larger every day. In the second case, your backup program can keep track of files that have been modified since the last full backup and save all of them. This may be done by specifying the date of the last full backup and saving all files modified after that date. Here you need only restore two backups, the full one and the last partial one. The trade-off is that this partial backup is cumulative and thus gets larger every day, while in the first case the sizes of the partial backups are proportional to the amount of data modified since the last partial backup. In the second case, you will want to do a new full backup when the partial backup starts taking too long or approaches the size of the last full backup.

SOFTWARE LICENSING

Using applications in a network environment raises the important issue of licensing. Most software vendors have well-established policies regarding the use of their products on single-user systems but are vague about how their software fits into a multiuser network. Of course, a vendor who sells software specifically written for a network environment usually has a well-defined policy. But personal computer networks have caught many vendors by surprise, and you will discover policies ranging from progressive approaches with liberal discounts for multiple users and one-time site licenses, to "head-in-the-sand" policies that don't address local area networks at all.

Single-User Licenses

Most MS-DOS software is sold with a single-user, single-machine license, meaning that it is intended to be run by one user on one PC. If you purchase software like this to run on a network, you cannot use it from more than one PC at a time without violating the license agreement. Some licenses prohibit the use of the software on more than one PC at any time, even if it is never used on two PCs at once.

Multiuser Licenses

As more multiuser PC software appears, vendors are establishing licensing procedures to cover its use. One common approach allows you to pay by the number of users. Some policies consist of an honor system whereby you agree that your installation does not have more than the specified number of users of that particular application. Other vendors have installed "counting locks" in their software, allowing the specified number of users to run the package at one time. When a user over the limit tries to run the package, an error message is returned explaining that the limitation has been reached. If you find the limit too restricting, you can usually purchase the right for additional users to run the package concurrently.

Site Licensing

A new approach among PC software vendors to the multiuser licensing problem is *site licensing*. You usually pay a fixed fee for the right for an unlimited number of users to use the software at a particular installation. This approach is gaining in popularity as major corporations, faced with spiraling software expenses, are making strong demands for it. A site license for a package can save money in the long run, and it appeals to a central data processing department in that it provides some measure of control over the software in use on the company's personal computers. If a corporation purchases a site license for a particular software package, it is more likely that all the users in that company will standardize on that package. There is a side benefit to the company that purchases a site license: there need be no more worrying about lawsuits arising from employees' making unauthorized copies of single-user packages.

The demand for this type of license is so strong that many smaller software vendors are making inroads in the corporate market by offering such a license while some of the major vendors are dragging their heels. This can only increase the pressure on the major vendors, making it likely that site licenses will be more and more widespread in the future.

II

EVALUATIONS OF POPULAR
LOCAL AREA NETWORKS

6

INTRODUCTION TO THE
EVALUATIONS

The following chapters contain overviews of five popular PC LANs:

- IBM PC Network

- 3COM EtherSeries

- Corvus OMNINET

- Novell Advanced NetWare

- Orchid PCnet.

These LANs were selected from a large number of networking products because of their popularity; in addition, each network illustrates one or more major aspects of personal computer network architecture. Many other fine products are available. This list is not to limit your choice to these products, but to give you a sense of the range of networks available for your PCs and to identify some of the ways in which they differ.

As you read the reviews you will get a clear picture of the features and user interface offered by each system. Screen displays are included to show the actual dialogue that takes place during setup and use of the network. You will see that there is a considerable range in user interface, from teletype-style question-and-answer displays to full-screen displays with pop-up windows and menus. This presentation is the next best thing to having hands-on experience with each system.

By studying these chapters, you will hone your skills in evaluating PC network systems, and you can apply this knowledge to choosing the right system for your needs from the many that are available, including, but not limited to, the five described here.

METHODOLOGY

Each network system described in this book was loaned by the manufacturer or a retailer. The latest version of hardware and software was used. The networks were set up with a server and two workstations, following the manufacturers' documentation. Several of the networks support a variety of servers, including an IBM PC XT or AT and a dedicated server of proprietary design. In order to show you the range of network product designs available, the proprietary servers were used whenever possible.

The emphasis of the reviews is not in comparing the networks to establish which one is "best," but rather to solidify the ideas presented in earlier chapters. This guideline allows a wide range of products to be described, covering a lot of ground in both performance and price. Each LAN has its strengths and weaknesses, and by reading these discussions you should understand better which features really matter to you. This increased understanding will help you evaluate other networks besides the ones discussed in this book.

There is a natural tendency to dwell on hardware features when contemplating computer equipment purchases, perhaps because hardware is tangible and easier to understand than software. If you get nothing else from the review chapters, you should see how the differences between the various vendors' hardware are not nearly so large as the differences in network and utility software. Once the hardware is installed, if it functions well, it becomes less important. The software is something you interact with every day, and you should choose carefully to get the right combination of features you need.

Each review chapter takes you from an architectural overview through installation and use of the network. Separate sections describe hardware, software, and documentation. The outline of this chapter is similar to the review chapters' and explains the contents of each section, pointing out things you should especially note and helping you to interpret discussions and results.

Network Architecture

The technical details of the network architecture are described early in each chapter. Physical layout varies considerably among systems, and you will see examples of the major topologies described earlier in the book. Bus and star topologies currently seem to be dominant, with IBM's Token-Ring Network building support among large corporations.

This section describes general cabling features, including the maximum length of cable segments. This last detail must be studied carefully, since the maximum length often depends on the type of cable used. Lower signal loss cable is more expensive, but sometimes allows you to use longer cables to build a larger network. Some networks require minimum distances between network nodes as well.

The limit on the number of workstations and servers allowed is described for each network. In most cases, as long as you stay within that maximum number of nodes, you can use any combination of workstations and servers you like.

Low-level network protocols are becoming a less controversial subject as commercially successful products are introduced using the various protocols. Each product's low-level protocol is discussed, but most readers can ignore this information; also provided is the network communications bandwidth, but it, too, is less of a concern in many installations than was once thought. Experience has shown that the limit of the network bandwidth is seldom reached before some other limit has been reached, such as the server's ability to handle multiple disk I/O requests.

Workstations and Servers

Each network was set up with a server and two workstations. Two different models of the IBM PC were used as workstations:

- An IBM PC with 640 kilobytes of memory, two 360-kilobyte floppy disk drives, and a monochrome display and adapter.

- An IBM PC Portable with 256 kilobytes of memory, two 360-kilobyte floppy disk drives, and a black and white display driven by an IBM Color Graphics card (the standard PC Portable setup).

The PC was used for the single-workstation benchmarks, and both were used for the two-workstation benchmarks. All of the networks tested can use any member of the IBM PC family as a workstation (except for the IBM PCjr, which is frequently not supported). Most of the systems can use true PC-compatibles, too, and some can even mix non-PC-compatibles with IBM PC-compatibles in a single network.

Every network tested provides some kind of mass storage and printer service to the network. Disk servers are the most prevalent, although file servers are increasing in popularity (especially since IBM announced the IBM PC Network, which is a file-server-oriented system). Proprietary microcomputers dedicated to providing network disk or file service are becoming increasingly popular, and an interesting cross-section of these is discussed in the reviews. All of the vendors offer a network that uses an IBM PC XT or PC AT as a disk or file server.

It is important for a disk or file server to have a hard disk drive, and IBM PCs that have been upgraded with IBM or third-party hard disks can frequently be used as servers. Most vendors caution against the use of a PC XT or AT server for more than a small network with moderate traffic, and those that offer their own proprietary server usually claim it is designed to handle larger configurations than can be served by a PC XT or AT.

Several of the networks allow almost any device to be connected to a network server for sharing, including floppy disk drives. You certainly wouldn't want a floppy disk to be more than occasionally accessed by the network workstations; nevertheless, such a feature may be useful—for example, to copy the contents of a floppy disk over the network to another workstation.

There is quite a range of workstation and server memory require-ments, and although the cost of memory has dropped considerably, it can still have an impact on your network cost—especially if it makes the dif-ference between requiring a memory expansion card or not. When you read the memory requirements, remember that you must add your appli-cations software requirements to the network and MS-DOS requirements.

Another way to save money is to use diskless workstations, if they are practical for your application. Support for diskless workstations is common—although in one case, the IBM PC Network, the hardware supports it but the software supplied by IBM doesn't.

You will see several different approaches to providing print service to your network, offering a wide variety of cost and performance trade-offs. You will see how an item that may seem minor at first can have a big impact on the cost and function of your network. Another detail to keep in mind is whether support is provided for parallel printers, serial printers, or both. All of the networks reviewed allow multiple print servers.

Another issue for consideration is the concurrent use of a server as a workstation. Several of the reviewed networks provide this capability. Its practicality depends on the performance characteristics of your network environment.

Every network has some provision for mass storage backup. All allow backup to a floppy disk, but in practice this is a cumbersome method to use. Several of the vendors provide their own tape backup system or sup-port a third-party hardware vendor's tape backup. Networks that allow use of multiple servers let you use a separate hard disk for backup.

INSTALLATION

The networks reviewed differ more in the details of installation and setup than in day-to-day use. There is a wide variety in the amount of planning and work that must be done. The reviews deal with each of these areas separately, further subdividing planning and doing into hardware and software components. Most of the work done during setup applies to later expansion of the network as well, so installation should not be thought of as a one-time task.

As you read the installation section of the reviews, you should think about how your present levels of experience and skill match those required by the product. But don't eliminate a product from consideration solely on the basis of its complexity of installation if you think its operational features match your needs. You may, however, have to add the cost of a consultant to your network cost estimate, or locate an experienced and helpful dealer.

Hardware Installation

To perform the reviews in the chapters following, a few computers were networked together in a single room. In a permanent installation, stringing cables is a much greater task than it was in the test lab. The cabling guidelines supplied by each vendor are discussed in this part of the reviews. This aspect of any network should always be evaluated carefully. A mistake can mean that your network will cost far more than you anticipate, or it may even mean that the setup you had planned is not feasible because it exceeds cable length restrictions.

Besides cabling, hardware installation is largely a matter of positioning the workstations and servers, installing printed circuit boards, and plugging in cables. Although time-consuming, this part of hardware installation is fairly uniform from network to network. The greatest differences are in the amount of configuration required on the network interface cards. Most cards come preconfigured to run with a typical PC. If your configuration is not "typical," you may have to modify jumpers or switches on the board. The degree to which doing this is necessary or possible is discussed for each network.

Software Installation

You will see a great variety in how the different software products are installed. The process ranges from one involving interlocking programs that must all be configured properly, to a simple, brief question-and-answer session with a single program. As you read the reviews, consider how complexity of installation reflects the availability of features. A good middle ground is a system that has a lot of flexibility but also assumes reasonable default values and lets you easily make changes later.

Another factor to consider is the need to perform the installation process for every one of your workstations. Some networks let you create a prototype of the workstation software and then use that on all the workstations. Others require you to repeat the entire installation process on every workstation.

Some networks work entirely within an MS-DOS framework, so you deal with that familiar environment throughout. In other networks, the server runs under another operating system, and you may be required to install that operating system and learn its commands in addition to those of MS-DOS.

USING THE NETWORK

This section in subsequent chapters describes what it is like to use each network. It presents a typical sequence, from turning on the computers and running your applications, through backing up network mass storage.

All the networks tested extend the single-user MS-DOS operating environment. Network files and printers are accessed as a natural extension of the local workstation's resources, using the MS-DOS conventions such as drive letters C:, D:, and so on, and printer designations such as LPT1: and LPT2:. The networks differ in the way they are used beyond this MS-DOS extension. There are two other important areas to evaluate: managing the network and using the network. Network management includes creating and maintaining disk volumes, print queues, user accounts, and so on. Network use includes establishing a connection to a server (logging in), accessing files stored on the server, using network printers, and sending messages and files to other network users. You will see a range of approaches to providing these features, such as relying heavily on MS-DOS commands, running special utility programs, or using new commands. These approaches differ in their ease of use, and features like built-in help systems are important if many end users need to run this software.

SECURITY

Security is an area of major importance to most networks. The systems reviewed offer a range from simple password protection to complex systems of privileges dispensed according to user account name and user group membership. It is important to understand how your users and your applications will function in a multiuser environment, and how security can prevent both accidental and malicious loss of data or damage. If security is of little concern, some systems allow you to run with security turned off. If you are uncertain as to the degree of security you will need, it is better to start with too much rather than too little.

MULTIUSER SUPPORT

Every network supports many users at some level. The differences in support are often technical and subtle, but can have profound impact on the usefulness of your network in your particular situation. All the networks provide ways for programmers to control access to network resources in order to avoid data corruption, but not all network systems allow the same operations. Make sure you understand how the network software controls two users who need to append to more than one file in the same directory at the same time, or to update different records in the same file at the same time.

A related area to investigate is protection against data corruption through unintentional violation of one of the multiuser restrictions, such as simultaneous attempts to write to the same file. Several systems prevent two users from opening the same file when the file is accessed in the old single-user MS-DOS way. They allow the extended, multiuser access only through new system calls that are not available under single-user MS-DOS, and thus should not be present in single-user MS-DOS applications programs.

UTILITIES

Several of the networks reviewed provide an electronic mail system. Those reviewed vary in sophistication, and if you plan for electronic mail to be a major feature of your network, you should look carefully at the functions provided. Some of the systems are primitive and not likely to satisfy your needs.

Features to consider include storing messages to disk, forwarding mail to other users, and sending mail automatically to a list of users. Some systems let you mail not only messages but files as well.

Another task performed by utility programs is mass storage backup. Several networks provide special programs intended to speed up or ease the backup process. Nothing was seen that is significantly faster or more functional than the MS-DOS BACKUP and RESTORE programs, although in some cases you must use the network software, since the MS-DOS programs can't handle certain features of that network's file structure.

Other utility programs include extended diagnostic programs, useful for setting up or testing hardware; configurable menu systems that let the system manager build a set of menus to guide inexperienced users through the use of the system; and many programs for checking network status and modifying parameters to improve performance. Not all vendors provide all these utilities, and some are available only at extra cost.

DOCUMENTATION

There are two general types of documentation to consider: system managers' manuals and end users' manuals. Most networks use this division in their documentation set. The manuals generally contain all the information needed to set up and use the networks, but they vary both in the ease with which they guide you through the installation process and in the ease of accessing needed information later.

Things to look for in documentation include logical organization that takes you through planning your network, setting it up, installing the software, and using the system. Concise, easy-to-read manuals that concentrate on explaining how to use the system and omit system management details are a nice plus for your end users. Also consider the system manager's need to answer users' questions on any topic and to expand the network. A good index and table of contents, as well as sections describing error messages and their probable causes, can be invaluable through the life of your network.

If you plan to do multiuser programming, make sure adequate technical reference documentation is available. Programmers need to know how the network's file-locking system is controlled, and how to direct information to a particular node in the network.

PERFORMANCE

Benchmark tests were run to see how the networks handled popular third-party software packages and to show how the various networks compare in performance. In-depth performance evaluation of any one network could easily fill a book this size, and the performance characteristics often depend just as much on your applications software as on the network itself. Also having considerable impact on performance are the number of users on your network and the nature and frequency of the network traffic they generate.

Given the difficulty in generalizing about performance, the emphasis is on showing you how performance compares in a few standard benchmark tests that represent a spectrum of network use from light to heavy. The configurations tested are not necessarily the lowest- or highest-cost system available from the given vendor, but rather a system demonstrating a particular approach to LAN service, emphasizing proprietary servers when they were available. You should not try to reach a conclusion about a particular vendor's typical system cost from these configurations; instead you should note how, in several instances, spending additional money on the server can result in increased network performance.

The software used in the benchmark tests is single-user MS-DOS software. Lotus 1-2-3 and dBASE III are copy-protected, and the copy-protection key disk has to be in the workstation's disk drive when the software is started. The tests use network mass storage to store all program and data files, and they are network printers. The multiuser tests are set up so that two users share the same program files but write to different data files on the same server. This simulates a typical pattern of network use—a public directory stores common programs and each user stores his or her data files in a private directory.

The workstations and server were set up according to the vendor's documentation. The MS-DOS BUFFERS parameter was set to 20 in the CONFIG.SYS file on the workstations and on the server, when applicable. The following sections describe the specific benchmarks.

Lotus 1-2-3

The benchmarks use Lotus 1-2-3 Version 1A. The time to load 1-2-3 is measured from the moment the ENTER key is pressed after **LOTUS** was typed at the MS-DOS command line, to the appearance of the 1-2-3 spreadsheet on the screen, waiting for a user command. Between these two events, the ENTER key must be pressed twice, and it is hit as soon as requested.

A 14,000 byte worksheet file containing a home mortgage calculation spreadsheet is loaded next. The time to load this spreadsheet is measured from the pressing of the ENTER key to the appearance of the spreadsheet and movement of the cursor to the upper-left corner cell.

A 5-column by 35-row portion of the spreadsheet is printed to LPT1:, which was redirected to a network printer before Lotus 1-2-3 was entered.

The time from pressing G to getting back control of the keyboard was measured. Also noted was whether printing works across the network or not.

The file manager is a Lotus utility that lets you display and maintain lists of filenames, and perform operations such as copy, delete, and the like on them. The file manager was tested on a network server directory to see if it could perform all these functions there.

WordStar

The benchmark tests use Version 3.30 of MicroPro's WordStar word processor. The time to load WordStar was measured from the pressing of ENTER after the typing of **WS** at the MS-DOS command line, to the display of the WordStar Opening Menu. A 40,000 byte document is loaded, and the time to do this is measured from the pressing of ENTER after the filename was typed, to the instant when the file can be edited.

Next measured is the time required to position to the end of the file when CTRL-QC is pressed. The next time measured is that needed to append this document to itself when CTRL-KR is used to read the file in and append it at the current cursor position. Finally, the time needed to save the file and exit is measured, from the pressing of CTRL-KX to the appearance of the MS-DOS command line prompt.

dBASE III

Tested next in the benchmark sequence is Ashton-Tate's dBASE III database manager, Version 1.00. Its load time is measured by criteria similar to those used for the previous programs. Two benchmark tests are each run twice, once from a single workstation and then simultaneously from two workstations operating on separate but identical data files. The data file contains 160 229-byte records, each consisting of 15 fields; 3 of the fields are keys—a 7-byte numeric key, a 20-byte character key, and a 4-byte character key. The first benchmark test is to sort the file based on the 7-byte numeric key field; the second benchmark test is to reindex the entire file on all three keys.

BASICA

The final programs are four small file-access benchmark tests run under the IBM PC BASICA interpreter Revision 3.1. They are from *BYTE* maga-

Sequential write

```
105 PRINT TIME$,"Start"
110 A$="12345678123456781234567812345678"
120 B$=A$+A$+A$+A$
140 NR=500
160 OPEN "D:TEST" FOR OUTPUT AS #1
180 FOR I=1 TO NR
200 PRINT #1,B$
220 NEXT I
240 CLOSE
260 PRINT "Done"
270 BEEP
275 PRINT TIME$,"Stop"
```

Sequential read

```
100 PRINT TIME$,"Start"
300 NR=500
320 OPEN "D:TEST" FOR INPUT AS #1
340 FOR I=1 TO NR
360 INPUT#1,B$
380 NEXT I
400 CLOSE
420 PRINT "Done"
440 BEEP
460 PRINT TIME$,"Stop"
```

Random write

```
100 CLEAR 1000
105 PRINT TIME$,"Start"
110 A$="12345678123456781234567812345678"
120 B$=A$+A$+A$+A$
140 NR=500
160 OPEN "R", #1, "D:TEST"
170 FIELD #1, 128 AS Z$
180 FOR I=1 TO NR
200 LSET Z$=B$
210 PUT #1,I
220 NEXT I
240 CLOSE #1
260 PRINT "Done"
270 BEEP
275 PRINT TIME$,"Stop"
```

Figure 6-1.   BASICA benchmark programs

Random read

```
100   CLEAR 1000
105   PRINT TIME$,"Start"
140   NR=500
160   OPEN "R", #1, "D:TEST"
170   FIELD #1, 128 AS Z$
180   FOR I=NR TO 1 STEP -1
210   GET #1,I
220   NEXT I
240   CLOSE #1
260   PRINT "Done"
270   BEEP
275   PRINT TIME$, "Stop"
```

Figure 6-1.   BASICA benchmark programs (*continued*)

zine's standard benchmark repertoire. Figure 6-1 shows the programs, which write and read 500 records to two files, a sequential file and a random file. The random-file-access benchmark tests seem to access the network disk the most heavily, causing the disk activity light to stay lit almost continuously. This heavy use of the disk is reflected in the fact that, for several networks, the time required to run the program from two workstations is double that for one workstation.

IBM PC Network

Hardware: IBM PC Network Adapter card
IBM Translator Unit

Software: IBM PC Network Program Version 1.00

Manufacturer: IBM Corporation
P.O. Box 1328
Boca Raton, FL 33432
305/241-7614

Cable type: RG-11 cable TV coax

Max length: 1000-foot radius, 2000-foot maximum separation
(larger installations possible with custom design)

Topology: Tree

Data rate: 2 megabits per second broadband

Protocol: CSMA/CD

Max nodes: 72 with IBM cable, 1000 with custom design

7

IBM PC NETWORK

IBM's Personal Computer Network product was announced in August 1984 and delivered in early 1985. The product is an interesting blend of third-party and IBM proprietary technology. A small company called Sytek designs and manufactures the network interface cards and Microsoft's MS-NET is the basis for the network software. However, several critical software components were developed or extensively modified by IBM, including the file server and a menu-driven user interface program.

The IBM PC Network hardware is broadband, in contrast to most personal computer local area networks, which are baseband. Broadband networks can carry many channels of information (such as video) as well as digital data. The broadband network hardware is more expensive to produce, but IBM's offering is priced competitively with most PC LANs. Standard cable TV coax is used to wire the network.

OVERVIEW

IBM uses its own PC family machines as both workstations and servers. IBM does not sell a dedicated network server, but the PC AT is advertised as the machine of choice for providing network service. The PC AT can have one or two fixed disk drives per network server. You can have more than one server on a network. In fact, every PC on the network can simultaneously be a server and a workstation.

The network cabling is more complex than that of most of the other systems discussed in this book. Figure 7-1 shows the layout of a small IBM PC Network setup. Every network requires a *frequency translator* and various coaxial cable junction blocks in addition to the usual cables running to the

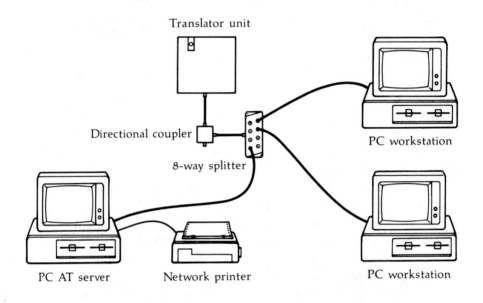

Figure 7-1.   Small IBM PC Network configuration

network nodes. Achieving a balanced network also imposes strict limits on cable lengths.

Using the IBM PC Network software is much easier than cabling the network. The software is among the easiest to use and install of all the networks reviewed in this book. The software can operate in a command mode or a menu-driven mode. If you are familiar with networking concepts you can probably get the software installed and running without even consulting the manual, although doing so is not recommended.

Each workstation PC must contain at least 128 kilobytes of RAM and one floppy disk drive. This minimal configuration can use network disks and printers and send messages to other nodes. If your workstation has a hard disk and at least 320 kilobytes of memory you can perform all the network operations.

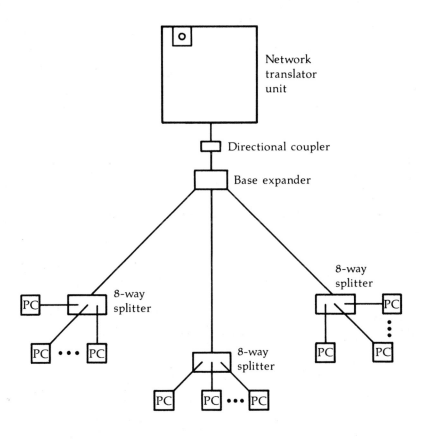

Figure 7-2.   IBM PC Network is tree-structured

Network Architecture

IBM's cabling layout is a tree, as seen in Figure 7-2, with a special frequency translator unit at the root of the tree. This frequency translator acts as a master node of the network. Every network node transmits on one frequency and receives on another. The translator receives all network transmissions, converts them to the frequency that network nodes can receive, and sends them to all the nodes.

As far as the network software is concerned, this tree structure is an unimportant detail of the network hardware. Network users and software programmers are unaware of the tree structure, since every node can talk to every other node. Even though the frequency translator handles every message, it does not process the information in any way. You can cable a small network in a way that resembles a star configuration, as shown in Figure 7-3.

A network built from all IBM or IBM equivalent cables and connectors can have up to 72 nodes with a maximum radius of 1000 feet. Each node may be a workstation, a server, or both. The network is built up from standard cables of 25, 50, 100, or 200 feet in length. The cables can be combined to form a segment up to 1000 feet.

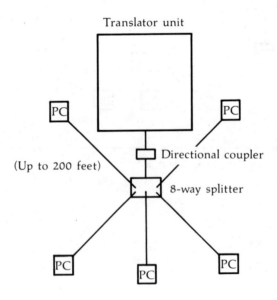

Figure 7-3.   A star-like configuration

The IBM PC Network must be electrically balanced to operate properly. This balance is achieved automatically by use of the IBM cables, which are precut and supplied with matching electrical attenuators. If you need to use non-IBM-standard lengths, you should consult with a professional broadband or cable TV engineer. Such an expert may be able to design an IBM PC Network of up to 1000 nodes with a varied physical topology, including a true bus layout.

As discussed earlier, broadband networks generally allow a single cable to carry more than just digital data. However, the IBM frequency translator can translate only PC Network data, and if you want to share the cable with video or other signals you need a special frequency translator, which IBM does not support.

IBM provides an interconnect between the PC Network and their Token-Ring Network. The PC Network is sold as the network to cable a small to medium number of PCs; the Token-Ring Network is intended to cable a large corporation.

The IBM PC Network uses a Carrier Sense Multiple Access/Collision Detection (CSMA/CD) protocol and transmits data at a bandwidth of 2 megabits per second.

Workstations and Servers

Any member of the IBM PC family (except the PCjr) can be connected to the IBM PC Network. A network server requires a hard disk but a workstation needs only a floppy disk. A hard-disk-based PC, PC XT, or PC AT can be simultaneously a workstation and a server, because of IBM's extensive modification of portions of Microsoft's MS-NET server software. This modification is one of the major differences between the IBM PC Network and MS-NET (which Microsoft sells to many computer manufacturers, and on which IBM based its PC Network product).

Table 7-1 shows the amount of memory needed to perform the various network functions. Each configuration listed provides 64 kilobytes for applications software, so any additional memory needed by your applications above 64 kilobytes should be added to the workstation memory requirements shown. The smallest configuration, an IBM PC with 128 kilobytes of memory, has some odd restrictions, such as the ability to send but not receive messages. Fortunately most PCs have at least 256 kilobytes of memory, enough to perform all the workstation functions except sharing of local devices.

Table 7-1.   Relationship of memory size to capability

RAM	Functions that can be performed
128K	• Send messages • Use network disks, directories, printers
192K	All of above plus • Receive messages • Save messages
256K	All of above plus • Use network request keys (CTRL-ALT-BREAK) • Receive messages for other names • Transfer messages to other computers
320K	All of above plus • Share your disks, directories, printers with network (must have hard disk)

Every network node must contain an IBM PC Network Adapter card, which takes up a long expansion slot. These cards can be configured to boot or start a workstation from a remote server disk, but the IBM PC Network program does not provide this capability. Thus, diskless workstations are not supported unless you write custom system software. A single disk drive is needed for each workstation.

Network disk servers can be PC XTs, PC ATs, or PCs with add-on hard disks up to 32 megabytes. Although IBM does not explicitly support non-IBM hard disks, truly compatible ones normally work. You can have as many servers on a network as you want, up to the physical limit on network nodes.

To use the IBM PC Network program you must run MS-DOS Version 3.1 or higher. These versions of MS-DOS contain the software needed to transfer data requests to the network when necessary.

Network print service can come from any PC with a hard disk. This PC can simultaneously share its files and its printer or printers and be a workstation. You can share as many printers as you can connect to your PC, including all the standard MS-DOS parallel ports (LPT1, LPT2, LPT3) and serial ports (COM1, COM2). Additionally, if you use the MS-DOS installable device driver feature to connect any other custom devices, you can also share them on the network. The PC Network Adapter cards come preconfigured to work in most IBM PCs.

IBM does not sell any special servers for backing up the network hard disks, although you can use the MS-DOS BACKUP and RESTORE commands to do so. Many tape backup systems for the IBM PC family are also available from third parties.

INSTALLATION

The IBM PC Network is easy to install if you can use the preconfigured IBM cables. If you need a larger network or don't want to use precut cables, you need assistance from a professional broadband or cable TV engineer to help design the network cable layout. RG-11 coaxial cable is used throughout the network, except for some RG-6 cable that connects to the translator unit.

The software is exceptionally easy to install. A program called the Installation Aid not only takes you through the network software installation process, but also automatically installs MS-DOS and network applications software purchased from IBM. The Installation Aid is menu-driven and includes many help messages.

Planning the Hardware Installation

The IBM PC Network is a balanced network, meaning that the signal strength is the same at every network node. To achieve this balance, the electrical characteristics of each cable segment must be carefully controlled. IBM sells a set of cables and attenuators that guarantee electrical balance. Using these cables, you can design a network of from 2 to 72 nodes, covering a circle 1000 feet in radius. If you need a larger system, it must be custom-designed.

Every network must contain one frequency translator unit. This device is housed in a small white metal box about the size of a textbook. It has its own power supply and must be located near an AC electrical outlet. The translator unit receives signals from the network adapter cards at a frequency of 50.75 megahertz and retransmits them to the network at a frequency of 219 megahertz. The IBM PC Network Adapters require a channel approximately 6 megahertz wide at each frequency. You don't need to worry about this unless you are designing a broadband network that combines IBM PCs with noncomputer devices such as video cameras.

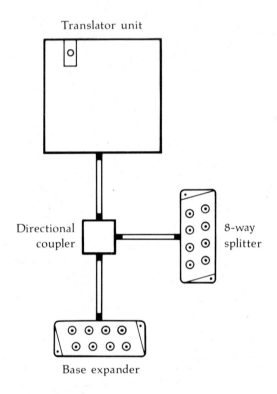

Figure 7-4. Root of the IBM PC Network tree

Figure 7-4 shows the root of an IBM PC Network tree. The translator unit is at the root, and is connected by a 5-foot cable to the directional coupler, a small junction block with three male cable-TV-type connectors. One output of the directional coupler goes to an eight-way splitter, which is another junction block with one input and eight outputs. You can connect up to eight PCs to the splitter, using a precut cable of from 25 to 200 feet in length. The other output goes to a junction block that looks like the eight-way splitter but is called the *base expander.* The base expander is the key to increasing the number of PCs on the network beyond the eight supported directly by the eight-way splitter block.

You cannot connect PCs directly to the base expander. You cable them to other eight-way splitters by using the IBM Short Distance Kit, the IBM Medium Distance Kit, or the IBM Long Distance Kit. These kits are balanced cables and attenuators of 1 foot, 400 feet, and 800 feet in length, respectively.

Each expansion-kit cable is terminated in eight-way splitter blocks. Each eight-way splitter can connect an additional 8 PCs, but no more base expanders. You can connect 8 PCs directly to the eight-way splitter on the translator, and 64 more PCs to splitters hooked up to the base expander, for a total of 72 PCs in a network built from IBM preconfigured cables.

There are several cabling guidelines you must follow when you plan an IBM PC Network. You can build a 400-foot segment from four 100-foot cables or two 200-foot cables, but you cannot use smaller pieces, such as eight 50-foot cables, because you cannot use more than three mid-run connectors in a row. Similarly, the 800-foot expansion must consist of four 200-foot cables. A 200-foot cable can be built from 50- or 100-foot pieces but not 25-foot pieces. (Of course, you can use a single 200-foot length as well.)

Any PC with a hard disk can be a server, and any server can also be a workstation. Each workstation can access more than one server at a time, up to a total of 26. Any PC that acts as a server can share its printers with the network. Each server can share as many printers with the network as can be physically connected to it. Files sent to the print server are stored temporarily on the server's hard disk, which therefore needs more space than is needed for network files.

Planning the Software Installation

It is possible to set up a small IBM PC Network with very little advance planning. It is a good idea to connect a two-PC network together and load the software in order to learn the system. This hands-on approach helps you to plan your full network better.

There is a great deal of flexibility in deciding whether a node should be a server or not (assuming it has the minimum 320 kilobytes of memory and a hard disk). In fact, every time you turn the PC on you can choose whether to make it available to the network as a server or not. In most cases, the users of your network expect to find the network environment stable, and designating one or more machines to always be servers is a good idea.

Every PC on the network is identified by a network name. This is an eight-character name, and you may want to derive it from the name of the person who most frequently uses that PC. If your PCs are shared, you can use names associated with their location or function, such as FRNTDESK for the front desk machine or ACCNTING for the PC in the accounting department. The network name is used by all network users to address messages to a particular PC, or to establish access to a PC's disk or printer.

Each server can offer one or more MS-DOS directories or disks to the network for shared access. This directory or disk is also given a network name, which does not need to correspond to the actual MS-DOS directory name. Your application software requirements may help determine the directory structure on your server's hard disk, as well as which directories need to be shared with the network. If not, the Installation Aid automatically creates directories on your server's hard disk to store systems and applications software.

A workstation user associates an MS-DOS disk drive letter, from A: to Z:, with the directory or disk the server shares with the network. From the workstation users' perspective, the shared directory or disk behaves exactly like a local disk with the specified drive letter. MS-DOS commands and application programs can access files on the network disk by referencing the disk's drive letter in the usual fashion.

Access controls may modify this familiar behavior somewhat. Just as a write-protect sticker applied to a diskette prevents your computer from modifying information on that diskette, a directory or disk may be restricted. Table 7-2 lists the ways file access can be restricted. The level of access permitted is established when the directory is offered to the network for sharing.

Table 7-2.   Options for sharing directories with the network

Option	Access
/R	Read-only
/RW	Read/Write
/W	Write-only
/WC	Write/Create/Delete
/RWC	Read/Write/Create/Delete

Full access (Read/Write/Create/Delete) lets workstation users treat the network directory just like a local disk. Restricted access, such as Read-only, prohibits workstation users from performing operations beyond what is specified. The access control applies to all files in the directory; there is no way to provide different levels of access to different files in the same directory. You can, however, offer one directory under different network directory names and associate a different level of access with each name. This lets you offer full access to one user and restricted access to another.

A public subdirectory is defined as one with Read-only access, meaning that all users can read its files concurrently. A private subdirectory has Read/Write/Create access, so only one workstation can access its files at a time, unless the application software has been modified to support simultaneous file updating by several users.

Printers are shared in much the same way as files. Network printers must be on network servers, which must also have a hard disk. You must also decide on names for network shared printers, following the same conventions as for network computer names.

Security is provided by passwords. Each device or directory that is shared on the network may have a password. Passwords are optional, but if they are used, each password must be provided when initial access is granted to the directory or device. This may be all the security you need, but it is not nearly as flexible as some of the other network systems discussed in this book.

Doing the Installation

Before starting the installation you should run the tutorial and demo contained on the diskette labeled "Exploring the IBM PC Network." This is a fast-moving explanation of network concepts and includes many animated graphics sequences. You may even want your network users to view it before using the network, especially if they will use network commands.

Physical Installation   Every IBM PC Network starts with a translator unit, directional coupler, and eight-way splitter, as shown in Figure 7-4. If you are going to have more than eight PCs, you need a base expander and an expansion kit for each additional eight PCs.

The translator unit connects to the directional coupler with a 5-foot RG-6 cable, terminated with cable TV coax connectors of screw-on style. The directional coupler is a small junction box, connecting the translator to an eight-way splitter via a 1-foot cable.

For every PC you need a network adapter board. It is easy to install. The network adapter takes a long slot, and requires configuration only if you have an unusual combination of expansion cards in your PC.

The possible cable configurations using precut IBM PC Network cable were explained in some detail already. If none of them are right for you, a custom design such as a bus layout may be appropriate. The *IBM PC Network Technical Reference* manual contains the specifications to be followed.

Software Installation   Every node on the PC Network has equal priority and capabilities. There is no "master" node or host that controls the network or through which all data must be processed.

This system architecture is reflected in the software installation process. The same program is run on all network nodes, and the main difference between workstations and servers is in your answer to the questions about sharing your directories and printers with the network.

The ease of installing the software is largely due to the cleverly designed IBM PC Network Program Installation Aid. It not only installs the PC Network program (building directories and batch files and modifying your CONFIG.SYS files), it can also be used to install MS-DOS itself on your hard disk, as well as the applications programs IBM sells.

The installation aid program can be used to install software only to a hard disk. However, an INSTALL.BAT batch file is provided for building network diskettes for use on diskette-based workstations.

If you need to create a custom configuration, you can completely bypass the installation aid program and do everything by hand. For the first installation, you should see how easy IBM has made a complex software installation process.

Since your network needs at least one server, you should start by using the installation aid program on it. This program does everything needed to complete an installation:

- Installs MS-DOS on your hard disk so network users can access the MS-DOS utilities.

- Installs the PC Network program on the hard disk.

- Installs IBM applications software packages on the hard disk so they can be shared by other network users.

- Builds subdirectories for each network user who needs to access your server's hard disk.

- Prints instructions for network users of your server.

```
                          IBM PC Network Program Installation Aid

                     MAIN MENU
      Choose one of the following:

      1.   Install your IBM applications

      2.   Name the network users who can use your applications

      3.   Display information about your installed applications

      4.   Display how network users can use your applications

      1 Choice




      Enter - Continue
      Esc - Exit                                          F1 - Help
```

Figure 7-5.   Main menu of installation aid program

Using the installation aid is a matter of loading the diskette in the PC's drive A and giving the G command. You are asked if you need help, then are given a main menu (Figure 7-5). Additional descriptions of each menu choice are available by pressing function key F1.

The first step is to install MS-DOS and the network program (select menu item 1). The up and down arrow keys move a highlight cursor through the list of applications that the installation aid can install. A graphics bar separates the DOS and PC Network program entries from the rest of the list to signify that DOS and the PC Network program are system programs that should be installed on every server, whereas the remaining programs are applications that you may or may not have purchased.

When you press ENTER, the program under the highlight cursor is installed. Directories are built on your hard disk, and the installation aid prompts you to load the applications software diskettes one by one into the diskette drive. When it is finished copying the files to the hard disk, you are returned to the installation menu.

After you are through installing software on your hard disk, you can name the users who can use your applications. This is not a security measure (since any user with access to your disk can use the programs it contains) but, rather, is used for organizing a disk. The installation aid creates directories in which each user can store his or her private data files. When you finish this step, options 3 and 4 from the main menu give instructions for you and other network users. The instructions tell you how to answer the prompts seen when the workstation starts up in order to use the applications set up for you on the server.

The installation aid automatically creates the MS-DOS directory tree shown in Figure 7-6 on your server's hard disk. When you install MS-DOS, the installation aid makes sure the root directory C:\ contains the usual MS-DOS startup files, COMMAND.COM, AUTOEXEC.BAT, and CONFIG.SYS. The next subdirectory level contains the NETWORK and BATCH subdirectories; these contain the PC Network program files used by the server. The installation aid automatically adds a command to your AUTOEXEC.BAT file that puts the \NETWORK and \BATCH directories on your MS-DOS PATH so that they are automatically found no matter what directory you are in. Thus, you can execute the network software regardless of your current directory on the server.

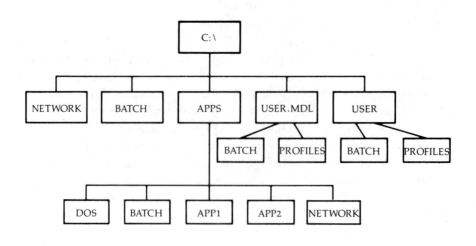

Figure 7-6.   Directory tree created by the installation aid

Next along the second level is the APPS subdirectory. This holds all the program files used by network workstations. The \APPS\DOS subdirectory, for example, gets all the MS-DOS utility programs when you install MS-DOS. The \APPS\BATCH subdirectory holds batch files created by the installation aid for network users. These batch files are used to run the various applications programs installed by the utility. The \APPS\NET-WORK subdirectory holds copies of the network programs used by workstation users. This spares workstation users from having to keep their own copies of the network program on diskette. The subdirectories labeled APP1 and APP2 represent particular application directories.

The USER.MDL subdirectory is a model for the creation of user subdirectories. Every user you named as a user of applications on your server has a personal directory created after this model. Any files that you place in USER.MDL are automatically copied into subsequently created user directories. The \USER.MDL\BATCH subdirectory contains batch files specifically created for a remote user who needs to run a particular application. The \USER.MDL\PROFILES directory is reserved for applications that need to create user profiles—files containing information about the way a user wants to run a program. The subdirectory labeled \USER represents a particular creation of a subdirectory tree for a user named USER. Such a subdirectory tree is created for every user.

Installing the network software on floppy disk workstations is even simpler, since no server functions can be performed. You need to start the workstation under MS-DOS 3.1, format a blank diskette, put the IBM PC Network program disk in drive A, and give the command

```
INSTALL B: DS
```

The **DS** stands for double-sided floppy. If you have only one floppy disk drive, the system prompts you to swap diskettes when it needs to access B. If you are installing to a high-capacity IBM PC AT 1.2-megabyte floppy disk, use **HC** instead of **DS** in the command.

The INSTALL program creates AUTOEXEC.BAT and CONFIG.SYS files on the floppy disk that automatically create the correct environment for the network software and start the network program when you boot the disk. The installation aid program does the same thing on your hard disk. If you already have an AUTOEXEC.BAT file in either case, it is renamed AUTOUSER.BAT and run at the end of the new AUTOEXEC.BAT file created by the installation process. If you already have a CONFIG.SYS file, the network installation software adds the lines needed to run the network to your existing file.

At this point you have installed all the network software and are ready to set up your workstation and server configurations. When you planned the network software installation, you decided which server directories, disks, and printers to share with the network. You also decided how these disks and printers would be accessed from each workstation; that is, the MS-DOS drive letters and printer device names such as C: and LPT2:, respectively. The configuration process lets you record your decisions about workstation and server configuration with the network. The configurations are easy to change later if necessary.

The configuration process, along with most network usage, is managed by the NET program. This program has two modes of operation, menu- and command-driven. NET normally starts in menu-driven mode. By answering simple questions, you provide all the information needed to set up the configuration of a workstation or server. Explanatory help screens are available at any point when function key F1 is pressed.

The NET program can also be accessed at any time by pressing the key sequence CTRL-ALT-BREAK. This combination is referred to as the *network request keys*. Even if you are running another applications package, you can press these keys to inquire about network status; see what network disks, directories, and printers you have access to; send messages to other workstations; and the like. If you don't want your users to be able to perform these functions, the network request keys can be disabled, although doing this also precludes you from receiving messages for other names or from forwarding messages.

Although the menu-driven mode of NET is the easiest to use for the first-time user, the command-driven mode is better suited to automation. A series of NET commands with various parameters can be put in a batch file and run without any user interaction to set up a workstation or server. The menu-driven NET command builds an AUTOEXEC.BAT batch file containing just such a sequence of commands when you tell it to save the network configuration you have created.

After you have installed the network software, the NET program is started automatically the first time you reboot your computer. After it displays a banner screen, and you press the ENTER key, it puts up an initial screen. You must type in the network name of your PC, which is the name used by other network users to identify it. If your PC has a hard disk and enough memory, you are asked if you want to share your printer, disks, and/or directories. If you answer yes, you are offered more options later in the configuration process.

```
                                             IBM PC NETWORK
                     Change Defaults for Starting the Network
      5   Number of devices to be used? (1 - 32)

   1600   Size of buffer for messages waiting? (256 - 60000 characters)

      1   Number of additional names that will be receiving messages? (0 -
          12)

     10   Number of devices to be shared? (1 - 150)

    512   Size of buffer for printing? (512 - 16384 characters)

     10   Number of network computers that will be using your devices? (1 -
          25)



      Enter - Continue                    F1 - Help
      Esc - Previous menu                 Tab - Cursor to next field
```

Figure 7-7.   Changing the network defaults

On the basis of your hardware configuration and the way you answered the startup questions, the next screen shows you the things you can do with the network. If you want to perform a different set of tasks, you can restart the setup process at this point and change the list within the constraints of your hardware.

Figure 7-7 shows the options available for changing the defaults used for starting the network. The number of devices to be used reflects the number of network disk drives, directories, and printers you can use. The message buffer area is space set aside to hold messages sent to you over the network until you read them (if you don't reserve enough space here, you can lose messages). You can receive messages for additional names — for example, if you want to receive messages sent to your first name, last name, or both. The next parameter establishes the number of different names for which you can receive messages. The number of devices to be shared is relevant only if your PC is a server. It must be greater than or equal to the total number of disks, directories, and printers you are sharing with the network.

The next question asks the size of your server's print buffer. You should allocate at least 16 kilobytes if you can spare it, since this memory allows the network printer to be driven more efficiently. The final default parameter is the number of network computers that will be using your server devices. No more than 29 can use a single server at once.

At this point, the main menu appears. The network is now in operation, and from this menu you can perform most of the network functions. Some of the functions have to do with changing your configuration, such as controlling the directories you make available to the network or the ones you use. Other functions make use of the network, such as sending and reading messages.

At any point you can save the current network setup. This option saves the commands needed to automatically recreate your current configuration the next time you start the PC. If your PC is acting as a server, it saves settings for the directories, disks, and printers you are sharing with the network. If your PC is a workstation, it saves settings for the network directories, disks, and printers you are using.

The main menu selections for disk or directory and printer tasks allow you to set up your environment with respect to sharing or using disks, directories, and printers on the network. You can set up disks and directories to be used or shared. As a file server, you must share your disk or a directory with the network.

Figure 7-8 shows the menu for sharing directories. The first item is the local MS-DOS pathname to the directory you want to share with the network. If you give C:\, the entire disk is shared. If you give a subdirectory name, like C:\APPS in this example, only the files and subdirectories beneath that subdirectory are shared. The second item you must supply on this screen is the network name for this directory. This name need not match the MS-DOS directory name—as in this case, where the network name is RDISK and the directory shared is \APPS. You can provide the directory password in the next blank (SECRET in this case). Next you tell the network software what access to give to the directory, from Read-only through full Read/Write/Create/Delete access. When you finish this menu, the directory is available to others on the network.

A similar process lets you use a directory on another PC on the network. You choose a local MS-DOS drive name, then specify the network name of the remote PC, the network name of the directory you want to use, and its password, if it has one. For example, a workstation user might choose to associate the MS-DOS drive name D: with the directory RDISK on a server PC. From that workstation, all access to drive D is automatically redirected to the \APPS directory on the server PC. MS-DOS com-

```
                                                          IBM PC NETWORK
                         Start Sharing Your Disk or Directory
     DOS name for disk or directory
          C:\APPS

     Network name for your disk or directory
          RDISK

     Password for disk or directory (Optional)
          SECRET

     Other users can
     1. Read only                4. Write/Create/Delete
     2. Read/Write               5. Read/Write/Create/Delete
     3. Write only

     5   Choice

          Tab - Cursor to next field
          Enter - Continue                F1 - Help
          Esc - Previous menu             Ctrl-Home - Return to Main Menu
```

Figure 7-8.   Telling the system how to share a directory

mands such as DIR and COPY, as well as applications programs accessing data or program files, can access files on drive D: just as if it were a local drive on the workstation.

Network printers need to be set up by selecting the print tasks option from the main menu. You can start or stop using or sharing a network printer, print a file, change the number of characters per inch or lines per page printed, and show status information about your network environment. If you choose to share a local printer with other network users, you must provide the local name of the printer, such as LPT1, LPT2, or LPT3. You then give the name your printer should have on the network. Other users refer to this name to access your printer. If you want, you can password-protect the printer, so that it can be used only by those users supplying the password.

If you want to use a printer on the network, you need to know the network printer name, the network name of the computer it is physically attached to, and its password if it has one. You also supply the MS-DOS printer name you want to use to refer to this printer. Once this has been set up, any program that prints to the MS-DOS printer name you chose will have its output directed to the network printer.

Output sent to network printers is kept in a file and printed when the file is closed. This printing of output happens automatically when you finish using the application and return to MS-DOS. It can also happen from within the application if the program uses the MS-DOS system call to close the print file. Most programs written for a single-user MS-DOS computer do not do this, however. Programs tailored for a multiuser network environment are more likely to close the printer when they are through with it.

You can force the network printer file to be closed by pressing the special key sequence CTRL-ALT-PRTSC. When you type this sequence, the output your workstation has sent to the printer goes into the print queue and is available for printing.

USING THE IBM PC NETWORK

After you have finished the installation and configuration process, you should save your configuration by selecting the option that does so from the main menu. As mentioned earlier, this operation builds a CONFIG. SYS file and an AUTOEXEC.BAT file that together serve to bring the network up automatically the next time you start your machine. Among other things, the AUTOEXEC.BAT file contains a series of NET commands that recreate the configuration you built up by following the menus. All the disks, directories, and printers that you specified are immediately available for use.

In addition to providing access to network printers and disk drives, the NET command lets you view the status of the network. By giving the NET command or using the network request keys, you can view the tasks and then view or modify the print queue on this or another computer. (The print queue is the list of files waiting to be printed on a network printer.) You can also display the network environment — the network devices you are using and the local devices you are sharing with the network.

The Pause and Continue Tasks menu lets you temporarily disable and reenable

- Using network disks and directories
- Using network printers
- Sharing local disks and printers with the network
- Receiving messages from other network users
- Printing files on local printers.

Table 7-3.   NET command options

Option	Function
CONTINUE	Restart after NET PAUSE
ERROR	Check network error status
FILE	See if a file is open or locked
FORWARD	Forward messages to another workstation
LOG	Store messages in a disk file
NAME	Receive messages for additional names
PAUSE	Temporarily stop network access
PRINT	Print to a network printer, display a network print queue
SEND	Send messages to another workstation
SEPARATOR	Start or stop printing separator pages between print files
SHARE	Offer a disk, directory, or printer for sharing
START	Start accessing the network
USE	Use network disks, directories, and printers

Table 7-3 summarizes the options available when NET is running in command mode. The NET START command has the most options for performance tuning, mostly trading off memory for speed.

PRINT MANAGEMENT

The IBM PC Network software lets you share with the network any printer that is attached to a server. This printer may be attached to a parallel port or serial port; it may also be accessible via an MS-DOS installable device driver. As long as the printer has an MS-DOS device name, it can be used over the network.

The NET program provides an extensive set of commands for creating customized print-separator pages. The print server prints the separator page before each file is printed. This page helps you to find the boundary between separately printed files. The customization language lets you insert the current time and date, use large block letters, insert the network name of the computer that sent the file to the server, and do many other

```
                                                              IBM PC NETWORK
                        Check or Change the Print Queue

    1. Update queue      ID  User Name       Size     Device   Status
                                           -- Start of Queue --
    2. Hold              001 ROWLAND             237 LPT1      PRINTING
                         002 ROWLAND             521 LPT1      WAITING
    3. Release                             --  End of Queue --

    4. Cancel

    5. Print next

    6. Print now


    3  Choice


        ↑  and  ↓ - Select file          PgUp and PgDn - Scroll List
        Enter - Change queue             F1 - Help
        Ctrl-Home - Return to Main Menu  Esc - Previous menu
```

Figure 7-9.   Displaying and modifying the print queue

things. If you don't want the server to print separator pages, this feature can be turned off with the NET SEPARATOR command.

The print queue can be displayed by remote computer users and modified by the user at the server's keyboard. The Print Queue Tasks menu is available from the main menu of the NET program. Figure 7-9 shows a representative print queue display. The queue is shown on the right side of the screen. This queue contains two files; one is PRINTING, the other is WAITING to be printed. Other status codes you might see in the print queue are shown in Table 7-4. Using the print queue management commands listed in Table 7-5, you can change the status of a file or change the order in which it is printed.

SECURITY

The IBM PC Network provides a very basic, simple security mechanism. Every directory, disk, and printer shared with the network may be protected with a password. But passwords are not required, and if no password is assigned when a device is offered to the network for sharing, no password is needed to access it.

Table 7-4. Print queue status

Status	Meaning
CANCELLED	File will not be printed
HELD	File will be printed when it is released
PAUSED	Printer has paused, no printing occurs until it is continued
PRINT FILE ERROR	File could not be found
PRINTER ERROR	Problem with printer
PRINTING	File is being printed
SPOOLING	File is being copied to the server's disk
WAITING	File is waiting to be printed

If some of the network devices you want to share are password-protected, you can choose whether or not to store the passwords in the AUTOEXEC.BAT file used to start the network. If you edit the file to include an asterisk instead of the password, you are prompted for the password when the command is executed. You must type the correct password from the keyboard before that network device can be accessed.

Table 7-5. Print queue commands

Command	Function
HOLD	Don't print file until released
RELEASE	Print a HELD file
CANCEL	Don't print this file
PRINT NOW	Current printing stops and this file is printed
PRINT NEXT	This file prints as soon as current file is printed

Unauthorized users are thus prevented from accessing sensitive data by simply turning on a network workstation.

You can exert some degree of discriminating control by offering disks and directories to the network for sharing under different names protected by different passwords. For example, on your server you may have a directory named C:\PAYROLL containing files that several bookkeepers can read but only your accountant can modify. You can use the following two NET SHARE commands:

```
NET SHARE BPAYROLL=C:\PAYROLL ELISE /R
NET SHARE APAYROLL=C:\PAYROLL LIBBY /RWC
```

The bookkeepers access the directory with the network name BPAYROLL and the password ELISE. The /R parameter limits their access to Read-only. The accountant uses the network name APAYROLL and the password LIBBY. The /RWC parameter allows the accountant to modify and create files in this directory as well as read them.

MULTIUSER SUPPORT

The IBM PC Network allows more than one user to read or write a file simultaneously. As with all PC networks, allowing more than one *reader* to have simultaneous access to a file is easier than allowing more than one *writer* to access a file. If a directory is offered for sharing as Read-only, several PCs can read the files in that directory at the same time.

Most MS-DOS applications programs use single-user MS-DOS system calls to access files. On the PC Network these calls are automatically translated into *exclusive file access* calls, meaning that only one remote computer can access a file. New system calls are provided in MS-DOS 3.1 and the PC Network program for shared file access. If your applications package uses these calls, then more than one user can write to the same file.

Most PC network software provides locking functions for programmers to use in order to control access to files. The IBM PC Network supplies a generalized lock function that can lock any region of a file specified as an arbitrary string of bytes within the file. Several additional calls are provided that are somewhat unusual, including one to create a temporary file with a name that is guaranteed unique. This call is useful when your applications programs need to create temporary files, and several copies of that applications program might be running at the same time using the same network directory to store data.

UTILITIES

The IBM PC Network allows you to send messages over the network. As with all the other network functions, you access the message functions with the NET program. You can:

- Send messages to other network users
- View messages sent to you by other network users
- Save messages to a disk file
- Receive messages for another network name
- Forward messages to another network name
- Review the names for which your computer can receive messages.

Sending messages is easy. By specifying an asterisk instead of a particular node name, you can send the message to all users. If you choose to use an asterisk, your message can be no longer than 128 characters. The message editor is very simple, and you can type as much as fits in the message window shown on the screen and perform limited editing functions such as inserting and deleting characters or reformatting a paragraph.

When a message from another user arrives at your computer, its speaker beeps and a small text block appears on your screen notifying you that a message is waiting. By pressing the network request keys, you can view the message on the screen. If several messages are waiting you can view them individually. You can also print a message or save it to a file. If you don't want to be interrupted at the moment a message arrives, you can instruct your PC to start saving messages to a disk file so you can review them when you are ready.

You can also receive messages for another user name; for example, that of a coworker who is on a business trip. If you forward your messages to another computer on the network, they are automatically routed to that machine.

DOCUMENTATION

The IBM PC Network manuals are very much in keeping with the IBM PC documentation standards you are probably used to by now. The hardware is documented in many small-format three-ring punched manuals, one for each major network hardware component. Included are manuals for the Network Adapter, the Network Transformer and Translator Unit, the

Network Base Expander, and the Network Short, Medium, and Long Distance Kits.

The Network Adapter manual provides the bulk of the installation instructions. It comes in two versions, one for the IBM Portable PC and one for the PC, PC XT, and PC AT. These manuals are clearly written and illustrated, and take you in great detail through the entire process, from taking the covers off your PCs, inserting the network cards in the expansion slots, putting the covers back, to hooking up the cables. In case your network does not work, a complete step-by-step diagnostic procedure you may follow is also explained.

The microscopic detail offered by these manuals may make the installation process look harder than it really is. Once you read through the manual and install one PC, you can probably install the adapter cards in each PC in 5 or 10 minutes.

The IBM PC Network software is described in the *IBM PC Network Program User's Guide*. This manual discusses installation, configuration, and use of the network. The *User's Guide* is easy to follow although vague in some places. The PC Network program itself is so easy to use that the manual is likely to be used more as a reference than as a how-to guide.

If you need information about the network, the optional *IBM PC Network Technical Reference* manual continues the tradition of fully disclosing the architecture of IBM PC products, including detailed programming interfaces and electrical specifications. This manual also describes the specifications that you must follow to design a custom network if you choose not to use the precut IBM cables or the IBM Translator Unit.

EXPANDING THE NETWORK

The peer-to-peer structure of the IBM PC Network makes expansion relatively easy, especially from a software standpoint. Depending on the specific details of your installation, extending a cable to a new node may be simple or moderately complex and expensive.

To add a new workstation or server, you need an adapter card and a cable connection to an eight-way splitter within 200 feet. If all the splitter's connectors are in use, or if it is too far away, you need a base expander and a short-, medium-, or long-distance kit. This expansion of the cable is seldom as easy as on a bus-structured network like Ethernet, where you are likely to need only a drop cable to the nearby network bus.

RELATIONSHIP TO MS-NET

It is common knowledge that the IBM PC Network product is based on Microsoft's MS-NET, or Microsoft Network program. Microsoft does not sell MS-NET directly to end users, but only to computer manufacturers, who make it run on their hardware, modify and extend it, and then resell it to their customers.

IBM has made many modifications to the Microsoft product. It is important that you understand that fact, especially if you are considering a non-IBM network that claims to be compatible with the IBM PC Network because it, too, is based on Microsoft's MS-NET. (Of course, this potential difference between the two vendors' MS-NETs is an issue only if compatibility is important to you.)

Unless the manufacturer has compatible network hardware (most likely licensed from Sytek) and is running compatible low-level network system software, you cannot connect the MS-NET system directly to an IBM PC Network. It may be that you can connect an IBM PC Network and another vendor's incompatible hardware by using a communications *gateway*, a special piece of hardware or a PC that contains network interfaces for both physical network types and software to pass messages back and forth across the gateway.

The major software enhancements made by IBM to MS-NET include:

- The ability of the server to also be a workstation
- The NET program with its menu-driven mode
- The installation aid for easy software setup
- The program that lets you send and receive messages.

The first item is important only if you want to be able to use a single PC as both a server and a workstation. Performance on such a PC is generally not as good, but this capability does increase the flexibility of your network.

The MS-NET product has everything you need to use the network, but the programs it provides are all command-driven. Many of the commands are closely related to the various NET subcommands. A particular manufacturer may provide a menu-driven equivalent to NET, but if such an equivalent is important to you don't assume it is available without checking.

The message utility provided by IBM is a nice extra, but again, the particular manufacturer you are interested in purchasing an MS-NET system from may provide a similar or even more sophisticated program. If not, you may be able to purchase one from the manufacturer or a third party.

IBM has also defined a very important programming interface to the network called the NETBIOS (*Network Basic Input/Output System*). You can write applications that use the network only by means of the standard Microsoft MS-DOS 3.1 system calls, and applications that do this have a chance of running on non-IBM Microsoft Network systems. However, the NETBIOS provides a number of useful functions that may also be used by your applications. A "compatible" network may or may not provide a programming interface that is functionally compatible to IBM's NETBIOS. Microsoft does not define a standard programming interface at the same system level as the NETBIOS, so unless the network vendor provides a compatible NETBIOS, important applications programs may not work on that network.

RELATIONSHIP TO
TOKEN-RING NETWORK

Before the IBM PC Network product was introduced, IBM announced the IBM Cabling System and encouraged its customers to use it in the construction of new buildings that might someday contain local area networks. In October 1985 IBM announced the Token-Ring Network, the LAN that makes use of the IBM Cabling System. If you are considering purchasing an IBM network, you should understand the relationship between the IBM Token-Ring Network and the IBM PC Network.

IBM positions the Token-Ring Network as the system to use for networking a medium- to large-scale facility. IBM has announced its intention to provide Token-Ring Network connections for most of its present and future computers, from PCs to mainframes. The PC Network is intended for use by smaller companies or departments in larger companies. Gateways between the Token-Ring Network and the PC Network are available, making use of a gateway server PC connected to both networks and running the IBM Token-Ring Network/PC Network Interconnect Program.

The Token-Ring Network conforms to the IEEE 802.5 committee

standard, giving it the advantage of having an open architecture with published specifications. Vendors other than IBM can build products that connect to the Token-Ring Network, and several have already announced compatible products.

Three types of cables are supported by the Token-Ring Network; two are "data grade" cables specified by IBM in its initial Cabling System product announcement and the third is standard twisted-pair telephone wire. All three cables use baseband signals and a token-passing protocol at a bandwidth of 4 million bits per second. You can connect up to 260 nodes with data grade cables and up to 72 nodes with telephone cables.

Every PC on the network contains a Token-Ring Network Adapter card that takes up a single expansion slot and provides the interface to the network. An 8-foot cable runs from each PC to the network cable. Individual network cables are run to a junction box called a *multistation access unit*. This cabling system makes the Token-Ring Network look like a star in topology, with the multistation access unit at the hub; electrically, however, it is a ring. Each network cable contains two twisted-pairs, and the multistation access unit connects twisted-pairs from each two adjacent cables to create a ring containing a single twisted-pair.

A multistation access unit can connect up to eight nodes, and larger networks are built by connecting multistation access units together. The cables from the nodes to the multistation access units can be up to 330 feet if telephone cable is used, and up to 1000 feet if data grade cable is used.

Although the Token-Ring Network hardware is very different from the PC Network hardware, the network operating software is compatible. The Token-Ring Network runs the PC Network control program described in this chapter, providing the same user interface to network facilities. PC workstations on the Token-Ring Network run PC-DOS Version 3.1, so network applications that use PC-DOS 3.1 system calls to lock and access network resources can run without change on the Token-Ring Network. Applications that use the more sophisticated PC NETBIOS system calls provided by the PC Network can also be run on the Token-Ring Network. But to do so you must purchase and install the IBM Token-Ring Network NETBIOS program on your workstations.

The basic Token-Ring Network adapter software requires 7 kilobytes of PC RAM. This is in addition to the memory requirements previously outlined for PC-DOS and the Network Control program. If you need to use the Token-Ring Network NETBIOS program, you must allocate an additional 46 kilobytes for it.

Table 7-6.   Standard benchmarks on IBM PC Network with PC XT server

Program	Task	Time	
Lotus 1-2-3	Load program	13.2 seconds	
	Load worksheet	6.7 seconds	
	Print portion of work-sheet to spool file	3.0 seconds	
	File manager	works OK	
	Copy protection	OK with key disk in workstation disk drive	
WordStar	Load program	6.6 seconds	
	Load document	5.8 seconds	
	Position to end of document	19.8 seconds	
	Append document	66.6 seconds	
	Save document and quit program	31.3 seconds	
	Printing	works OK on network printer	
		13.5 seconds	
dBASE III	Load program	OK with key disk in	
	Copy protection	workstation disk drive	
		ONE USER	TWO USERS (AVG.)
	Sort	62.8 seconds	104.8 seconds
	Reindex	71.1 seconds	87.3 seconds
BASICA	Sequential write	51.0 seconds	51.5 seconds
	Sequential read	44.7 seconds	45.3 seconds
	Random write	20.5 seconds	37.5 seconds
	Random read	65.5 seconds	119.3 seconds

PERFORMANCE

Although the IBM PC Network ran all the benchmarks successfully, it is not an especially strong performer. Table 7-6 shows the results of running the benchmarks using a PC XT for a server, and Table 7-7 is based on a PC AT server, the configuration IBM recommends.

Some of the results differ greatly from those obtained for the other networks in this book, perhaps indicating a software problem that may

Table 7-7.   Standard benchmarks on IBM PC Network with PC AT server

Program	Task	Time	
Lotus 1-2-3	Load program	8.6 seconds	
	Load worksheet	6.1 seconds	
	Print portion of work-sheet to spool file	2.4 seconds	
	File manager	works OK	
	Copy protection	OK with key disk in workstation disk drive	
WordStar	Load program	6.2 seconds	
	Load document	5.2 seconds	
	Position to end of document	17.0 seconds	
	Append document	56.1 seconds	
	Save document and quit program	25.4 seconds	
	Printing	works OK on network printer	
dBASE III	Load program	11.4 seconds	
	Copy protection	OK with key disk in workstation disk drive	
		ONE USER	TWO USERS (AVG.)
	Sort	50.3 seconds	66.9 seconds
	Reindex	63.7 seconds	74.3 seconds
BASICA	Sequential write	48.0 seconds	49.5 seconds
	Sequential read	42.3 seconds	41.5 seconds
	Random write	15.0 seconds	18.0 seconds
	Random read	55.0 seconds	70.5 seconds

eventually be corrected to improve network performance. For example, the BASICA random read test ran more quickly than the random write test for all the other networks, yet it ran more than three times more slowly on the PC Network.

Using an IBM PC AT as a server resulted in only a 10% to 30% speed increase over using the PC XT as a server. The difference shows up most in the two user benchmarks, where the AT runs two users no worse than 33% slower than one user, while the XT slows down by as much as 83%.

3Com EtherSeries

Hardware:	EtherLink Network Interface card 3Server dedicated network disk and print server
Software:	EtherSeries Revision 2.4
Manufacturer:	3Com Corporation 1365 Shorebird Way PO Box 7390 Mountain View, CA 94039 415/961-9602
Cable type:	RG-58 A/U or C/U, Belden 8259 for up to 1000 feet, or Standard Ethernet cable for up to 3280 feet
Max length:	3280 feet per segment, or 9840 feet with two repeaters. Up to 2.5 kilometers from end to end
Topology:	Bus
Data rate:	10-megabit-per-second baseband
Protocol:	CSMA/CD
Max nodes:	1024

8

3COM ETHERSERIES

3Com Corporation distinguished itself as the company that delivered the first standard Ethernet system for the IBM PC. The 3Com network products are called the EtherSeries; they support both standard DIX (Digital Equipment Corporation, Intel, Xerox) Ethernet 2.0 and "thin" Ethernet and conform to the IEEE 802.3 standard. 3Com has worked to reduce the cost of an Ethernet system, and pioneered the use of thin cable and onboard transceivers for the IBM PC. This technology lets you install an Ethernet connection using a single expansion slot in your PC, and connect to the network with a single BNC-style T-connector.

OVERVIEW

The EtherSeries product line includes a dedicated high-performance disk and print server called the 3Server, shown in Figure 8-1. The 3Server can handle six 70-megabyte hard disks (one is standard), two printers, and a 60-megabyte tape backup device. You can also use an IBM PC XT, PC AT, or compatible, as a disk, mail, and print server. The PC can be used as a workstation while it is performing its server functions. You can have multiple servers on a network, including a mix of PCs and 3Servers.

The 3Com EtherSeries software includes:

- EtherShare, which allows you to share hard disks on the network.
- EtherPrint, which allows you to share a printer on the network.
- EtherMail, which allows you to send files and messages across the network.
- EtherMenu, which allows you to customize menus for system control.
- EtherBackup, which allows you to back up a hard disk to tape.

Figure 8-1.   3Com 3Server (courtesy 3Com Corporation)

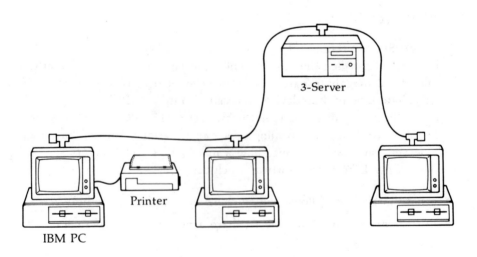

Figure 8-2.   EtherSeries network with 3Server (courtesy 3Com Corporation)

- EtherTerm, which allows you to do terminal emulation.

- Ether 3270, which allows you to do 3270 family emulation.

These packages are priced separately from the hardware, so you must check the total price carefully when you determine the cost of an EtherSeries network.

Figure 8-2 shows a sample EtherSeries network. The 3Server functions as the network disk server and print server. Table 8-1 lists its technical specifications.

Ethernet uses Carrier Sense Multiple Access/Collision Detection (CSMA/CD) protocol over a baseband cable with a bandwidth of 10 megabits per second.

Table 8-1.   3Com 3Server specifications

Feature	Specification
Dimensions	5.25 inches high by 15.5 inches wide by 17.5 inches deep
Weight	31 pounds
CPU	Intel 80186 microprocessor
Clock Speed	8 megahertz
Ethernet Interface	Intel 82586 multibuffer DMA Ethernet controller
Memory	512 kilobytes RAM, expandable to 896 kilobytes
Disk	36- or 70-megabyte (formatted) Winchester disk drive expandable to 420 megabytes with 70-megabyte external drives
Average Access	30 milliseconds
Interleave Factor	One (reads entire track in one revolution of disk)
Ports	One serial and one parallel
Expansion Ports	Two SCSI for tape backup and expansion hard disk. I/O expansion board allows AppleTalk interface

The workstation PCs must each have at least 256 kilobytes of RAM and one floppy disk drive. The optional EtherStart product lets you use diskless PCs as workstations. Many popular applications programs are copy-protected and require a workstation diskette drive, so you can't run such programs if you use diskless PCs.

Network Architecture

The most economical EtherSeries configuration uses the onboard trans-ceivers and thin coaxial cable. This layout is a bus, with a T-style BNC connector hooked directly to each workstation and server, as shown in Figure 8-3. If you use standard Ethernet cable, you must connect an external transceiver unit to each workstation and server with a drop cable.

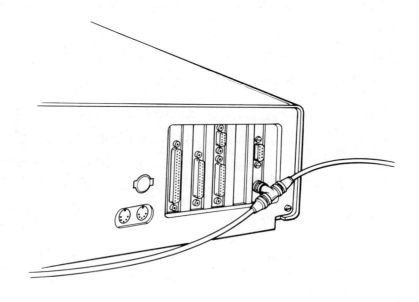

Figure 8-3.   Thin-cable Ethernet connected directly to the network nodes
             (courtesy 3Com Corporation)

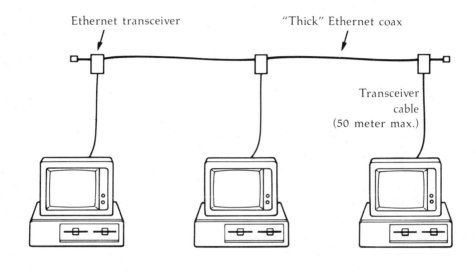

Ethernet transceiver   "Thick" Ethernet coax

Transceiver
cable
(50 meter max.)

Figure 8-4.   Bus transceivers and drop cables (courtesy 3Com Corporation)

Figure 8-4 shows the standard Ethernet hookup.

A single Ethernet setup can combine thin and standard cable. You can connect up to 100 nodes in a single segment, and you can use repeaters to connect multiple segments, as shown in Figure 8-5. The thin cable segments can be up to 1000 feet in total length, and the standard cable can be up to 3280 feet long. You cannot separate two computers with more than two repeaters.

Workstations and Servers

3Com sells network interface cards (called the EtherLink) for several different microcomputers, including the IBM PC, PC XT, and PC AT, the HP 150, and the TI Professional. These different computers can all be connected to a single Ethernet at the same time. You can have as many servers as you want on a single network, within the previously mentioned general constraints on numbers of network nodes.

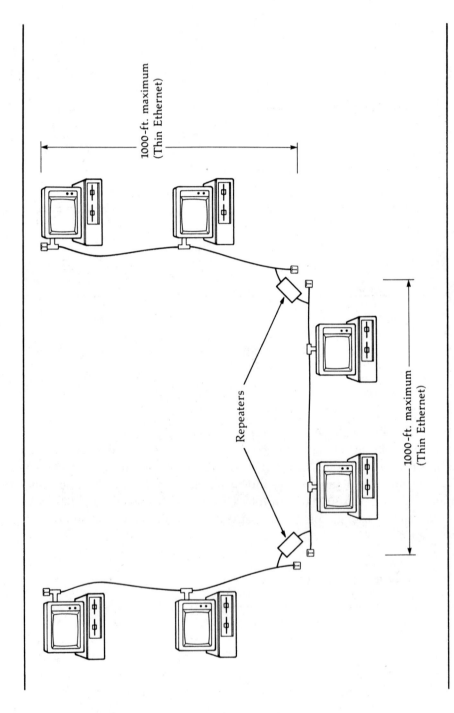

Figure 8-5.   Using repeaters to extend the network (courtesy 3Com Corporation)

The IBM PCs that you use as workstations should have at least 128 kilobytes of memory and 192 kilobytes to run the optional EtherMail software. The 3Com workstation software takes up only 8 kilobytes of RAM, so most of your PC's memory remains free for MS-DOS and applications software.

Network disk servers can be 3Com dedicated network servers, PC XTs, PC ATs, or PCs with add-on hard disks. 3Com states that most PC XT-compatible third-party hard disks should work with their software.

PC disk servers devote more memory to running the Ethernet software than do PC workstations. EtherShare, the software that lets workstations access the server's hard disk, takes up 160 kilobytes of RAM on the server. If you are using a PC as a network print server, it must have another 60 kilobytes of RAM to run the EtherPrint package. The EtherMail server software takes 32 kilobytes.

A 256-kilobyte PC XT barely holds EtherShare, EtherPrint, and MS-DOS. If you plan to use the server as a workstation concurrently, you must have additional RAM to run your applications.

Network print service can come from a PC, PC XT, PC AT, or the 3Com dedicated network server. The same machine that provides disk service can concurrently provide print service. The 3Server supports two printers, one parallel and one serial; a PC can control three printers, two parallel and one serial.

A single PC XT can be used as a workstation, disk server, and print server at the same time. However, it is unlikely that you would be satisfied with its performance as a workstation if several users were accessing it as a server. The 3Server is designed to perform the print, mail, and disk server functions concurrently, and it does these functions well.

Figure 8-6 shows 3Com's recommended number of users in several possible network use patterns. These are only guidelines, since everyone's applications are slightly different, and your idea of acceptable performance may differ from 3Com's.

The 3Com EtherLink network interface cards come preconfigured to work in most IBM PCs. You may have other hardware in your PC that conflicts with low-level IBM PC hardware features such as interrupt requests, DMA channels, and I/O port addresses. 3Com lets you configure the EtherLink cards by moving jumpers to avoid conflicts in these areas. If you change any of the jumper settings, you must run a menu-driven utility that modifies the EtherShare software to work with the new hardware configuration.

	PC XT	PC AT	3Server
Light use (disk infrequently accessed)	2-10	4-20	up to 50
Medium use (disk accessed concurrently 10% to 15% of the time)	2-4	3-8	6-25
Heavy use (disk accessed concurrently more than 50% of the time)	1-2	2-4	3-8

Figure 8-6. Number of users recommended by type of server and amount of use

3Com sells a tape backup server for the EtherSeries network that can back up the hard disks of all servers, PCs as well as 3Servers. It uses 60-megabyte tapes, enough to back up one or more network disk servers in most cases.

INSTALLATION

EtherSeries products are relatively easy to install. 3Com assigns every EtherLink card a unique network address when it is made, so you don't have to select network addresses as you do on some network products.

Ethernet cabling can be easy or only moderately difficult. Thin cable is straightforward to run and connect. Standard Ethernet cable is 0.4 inches in diameter, making it somewhat expensive as well as cumbersome to run around corners. It requires the additional expense of a transceiver box and drop cable at each station.

The 3Com software is very easy to install. It is largely menu-driven, and there are MS-DOS batch programs to aid you in copying files to server and workstation disks. Much of the system software on the 3Server is preinstalled by the manufacturer.

Planning the Hardware Installation

There are several cabling guidelines that you should be aware of when you plan for the overall layout of a 3Com Ethernet. If you use thin Ethernet cable, RG-58 A/U, or RG-58 C/U coax:

- The total length must not exceed 1000 feet per segment
- Each segment can have up to 100 nodes attached
- All nodes must be at least 3 feet apart
- The ends of the network must be terminated (as shown in Figure 8-7)
- One end of the network must be grounded (see Figure 8-8).

If you use thick or standard Ethernet cable:

- Each node can be up to 164 feet from the main cable
- The total cable length can be up to 3280 feet per segment
- All nodes must be at least 7.5 feet apart.

Each workstation is allocated four MS-DOS drive letters that are linked, or associated, with volumes on a server's hard disk when you run the net-

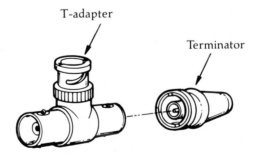

Figure 8-7.   Terminating the end of the network cable (courtesy 3Com Corporation)

Figure 8-8. One end of the network terminated and grounded (courtesy 3Com Corporation)

work. You can access many servers from a single workstation by using cross-server links, which are links to servers other than the primary one you are logged in to.

Print service should also be planned before you begin installation. You can use any server PC or a 3Server for the print service function. If you use a PC, it must run both the EtherShare software and the EtherPrint package. Your network can have many print servers. Each user's print output is kept in a separate file and printed as soon as the printer is available.

The hard disk can be backed up by use of the MS-DOS BACKUP and RESTORE commands and floppy disks or by use of the optional Ether-Backup software and the EtherSeries tape backup system attached to a 3Server.

Planning the Software Installation

Once you have decided how many servers and workstations to include in your network, you can plan the network software installation. 3Com's software is menu-driven and very straightforward. Your hardware planning largely determines the software planning, so you don't have to make as many decisions before you install this software as you do with some networks.

The principal decisions you must make are:

- Who the users of the network are
- How the hard disks are partitioned into volumes
- Where the printers will reside.

3Com also provides a user menu system called EtherMenu. Its use is optional, and it lets you create a tailored menu system for your network users. This is an alternative to the command-driven ES (EtherShare) and EP (EtherPrint) programs that otherwise are the primary interface to the network.

EtherSeries security is provided by passwords. Each user may have a password in order to connect to a server. Each volume on a server may also have a password. Server maintenance functions such as system software installation are protected by an administrative password. Users can use any workstation, with no change to their access privileges, since the privileges are associated with their user name, not their workstation.

User names are associated with a particular network server. Before using the network, you must log in to a server by typing in a user name on that server. If you need to log in to more than one server, you need different user names on each server you must access.

Every user can create volumes on a server's hard disk. Volumes are fixed-size areas of the disk that look like MS-DOS directories. There are three kinds of Ethernet volumes: private, public, and shared.

A private volume can be read or written to by one network user at a time. A public volume can be read by more than one user simultaneously, and written to by the user that created it. Shared volumes can be read and written to by more than one user simultaneously, although, to prevent data corruption, programs must be specially written to take advantage of shared volumes.

If a volume is password protected, you must supply the password before you can access the volume. If private or shared volumes do not have passwords, access is automatically restricted to the owner of the volume. Volumes can range in size from 64 kilobytes to 32 megabytes, depending on available hard disk space.

Doing the Installation

The 3Com system is easy to install and expand. The factory-assigned network card addresses simplify the hardware and software installation process. You need answer only a few questions, and most procedures are done automatically.

Physical Installation   Each PC on the network needs an EtherLink card. In most cases you just install the card into an available slot, and attach the Ethernet cable. If your configuration demands it, you may have to adjust the DMA, interrupt, or I/O port jumpers as mentioned above. If you are using thick Ethernet cable, you have to set another jumper that selects an external transceiver.

The easiest approach to wiring your network is to use precut RG-58 A/U cable terminated with female BNC connectors. These connectors attach to the T-connector at each node. Alternatively, you can purchase bulk coaxial cable and install the connectors yourself at each network node. Doing so may save on materials cost and result in use of the correct amount of cable, but you must consider the cost of cutting the cable and hooking up the coax connectors.

3Com sells terminators that connect to the end of the cable. One end is simply terminated, the other end must be terminated and grounded.

Installing the System Software   System software installation is very flexible. The order in which you do things is not rigid. You can install a server, add a workstation, add another server, bring up two more workstations, and so on.

The software you run in order to install each network node depends on the type of node and the service it performs. The EtherShare software must be installed at each node. This software is for basic network access and hard disk sharing. Print servers need the EtherPrint software, and workstations that will use print servers need the EP.COM utility.

3Com provides batch command files to ease the installation of workstation software. If you are installing the software for a diskette-based system, you run the SETUP macro. A hard disk workstation requires you to run FDSETUP. These macros copy the necessary system files, listed in Table 8-2, to a boot diskette or to your hard disk.

Each workstation must have the following line in its CONFIG.SYS file in the boot directory:

`DEVICE=ENET.SYS`

The ENET.SYS device is the driver code that lets you access the network.

Table 8-2.   EtherSeries software copied to MS-DOS disk during installation

File	Purpose
ES.COM	User interface to EtherShare software
EP.COM	User interface to EtherPrint software
CONFIG.SYS	Set up network driver software
ENET.SYS	Network driver software
LOGIN.BAT	Batch file to connect to a server
PRINT.BAS	Utility to print formatted text files

If you already have a CONFIG.SYS file, it is copied to a file named CONFIG.OLD by the installation macro. You can merge your old file with the new CONFIG.SYS files using the MS-DOS command

```
A>COPY CONFIG.SYS+CONFIG.OLD CONFIG.SYS
```

To configure a PC with a hard disk as a server, you need EtherShare/PC software. The EtherShare software can be installed once only, and it becomes permanently associated with the network address of the Ether-Link card on which it is installed. You can move the card and reinstall EtherShare on the new PC. This form of copy protection requires you to purchase as many EtherShare software packages as your network has servers.

Like the workstation installation, EtherShare is installed with a single command, INSTALL. This batch command file creates a subdirectory called \ETHERSHR on your PC's hard disk and copies the contents of two diskettes into it and the root directory. As with the workstation installation, a new CONFIG.SYS file is created in your server's boot directory, and in this case an AUTOEXEC.BAT file is also created. The AUTOEXEC.BAT file contains a series of commands that are automatically executed when you start your PC. If you had old AUTOEXEC.BAT and/or CONFIG.SYS files, they are copied to files named $AUTO.BAT and $$CONFIG.SYS before the new files are created. You can merge your old files with the 3Com files by using a procedure similar to that shown previously.

When you reboot the server, the system automatically comes up in the menu that gives you the choice of running the PC server in *dedicated mode* or *standard mode* as in Figure 8-9. In dedicated mode, the PC functions solely as a server, while in standard mode it can function simultaneously as a workstation and a server. You can switch between these modes, but you must reboot the system to do so, so nobody should be using the server when you do this.

Administrative functions are available only in dedicated mode, so you must start in this mode to register the server. The first thing you must do when configuring a server is to register it. You assign a unique eight-character name to the EtherShare server. The administration software distributes this name to all the other EtherShare servers on the net, so they must all be on-line and active when you do the registration. Thus, each server knows the names of all the other servers on the network.

From the installation menu you can install additional disk drives on the server or install optional EtherSeries applications. Software installation is simple this way. The system prompts you to put each application diskette

```
            3Com EtherSeries Network Server
                     Version 2.4


        1 - START THE DEDICATED MODE SERVER

        2 - SWITCH TO STANDARD MODE

        3 - START THE ADMINISTRATIVE FUNCTION

        4 - EXIT TO DOS WITHOUT STARTING SERVER




                  Select a menu item.

         (c)Copyright 3Com Corporation 1984, 1985
```

Figure 8-9.   Starting server menu

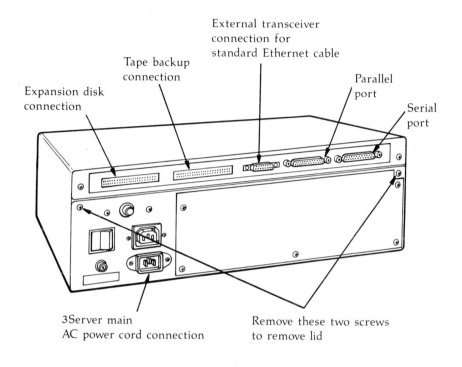

Expansion disk
connection

Tape backup
connection

External transceiver
connection for
standard Ethernet cable

Parallel
port

Serial
port

3Server main
AC power cord connection

Remove these two screws
to remove lid

Figure 8-10.   Back panel of 3Server (courtesy 3Com Corporation)

in drive A: and press RETURN. The necessary files are copied from each diskette to the correct place on the server.

Installing the 3Server dedicated network server is equally easy. Figure 8-10 shows the back panel connectors available for hooking up printers, tape backup, and expansion disk drives, and you can connect all peripherals before starting the software installation. You turn on the 3Server and it runs several self-tests, reporting status on its one-line output screen. When it is ready for use, the current date and time are displayed.

You can install the 3Server from any PC on the network. The PC must already be installed as a workstation. You insert the 3Server system software diskette in drive A, and give the command

A>ECONSOLE

and press the RETURN key. The program asks for a server name and you respond with **LOAD**, the generic name for an uninstalled server. If all is well, the server administration menu appears on your PC screen. You follow the same steps in registering the server with a server name. Use the applications installation menu to install the EtherShare software, and any optional Ethernet software you may have purchased (such as EtherPrint or EtherMail).

At this point you are ready to create volumes and user names on the server. The procedure is the same for both 3Servers and PC servers, and is run from a workstation. The EtherShare program, ES, is used to create, modify, and delete user names and volumes. ES is also the main interface to EtherShare, used to log in to a server, associate volumes with local disk drive letters, and log out when you are finished. The ES program is similar to other MS.DOS programs, in that it has subcommands and arguments. A subcommand is the name of the operation you want to perform, such as LOGIN to a server or CREATE a volume. The arguments are information for the function, such as the name of the server you are logging into or the name and password of a volume you are creating.

Before you can do anything on a server, you must log in to it. For instance, to log in to the server called FINANCE, give the command:

`ES LOGIN FINANCE`

LOGIN is the subcommand, FINANCE is the name of the server. Note that the LOGIN subcommand takes a user name rather than a server name, as an argument (in this case, FINANCE is also a user name). When you register a server, a user with the same name as the server is automatically created so you can log on for the first time.

If you have successfully logged in, the system indicates that the user named FINANCE is now connected to the server named FINANCE. The first thing you must do is create a disk volume. By convention, 3COM suggests you create a volume named SYS2 and store MS-DOS and other frequently used files there. For instance,

`ES CREATE SYS2 /500KB`

creates the SYS2 volume and allocates 500 kilobytes to it. The volume is formatted when it is created; this is one of the slower operations in Ether-Series, but fortunately it has to be done only once for each volume.

EtherShare Commands:

1 - Login to the server. (LOGIN)

2 - Logout from the server. (LOGOUT)

3 - Link to an EtherShare volume. (LINK)

4 - Unlink from a volume. (UNLINK)

5 - List all volumes. (DIR)

6 - Create a new volume. (CREATE)

7 - Modify an existing volume. (MOD)

8 - Delete an existing volume. (DEL)

9 - List all users. (UDIR)

10 - Create a new user. (UCREATE)

11 - Delete an existing user. (UDEL)

12 - Modify your user password. (UMOD)

13 - List all servers. (SDIR)

14 - Receive help. (HELP)

Figure 8-11.   Prompted mode of EtherShare command

The ES command has two modes of operation. You can supply all the arguments as in the two preceding examples, and it runs without further keyboard input. You can also run ES in prompted mode. Typing **ES** by itself generates the screen shown in Figure 8-11. You can select a command by number, such as 6, to create a new volume. You are then prompted one at a time for the arguments.

If you need more help with a command, you can give the ES HELP command and get a menu of choices for more information. The ES command provides a quick, command-driven function for the experienced user as well as a menu-driven, help-assisted program for the novice or the forgetful.

A volume must be *linked* before it can be accessed. The command

```
ES LINK C: SYS2
```

links the drive letter C: to the SYS2 volume. Once you have done this,

MS-DOS and applications programs can access the files in SYS2 just as if they were on a local drive labeled C:.

When you are done using a volume, the UNLINK command deletes the temporary association between your local drive letter and that volume:

```
ES UNLINK C:
```

You must unlink a volume before you can modify its characteristics. All volumes are created as private volumes. You can make a volume public or shared with the MODIFY command.

You can change a volume to public, shared, or private as many times as you want, as long as no user is linked to it at the time you want to make the change. You cannot change the size of a volume, so you must be careful to allocate enough space when you create it.

User names are created with the UCREATE command. Each user name is associated with a particular server, and you must be logged in to that server when you run UCREATE. Passwords must be assigned with the UMODIFY command. When you are completely finished with a network session you should log out with the ES LOGOUT command.

Table 8-3 lists all the ES subcommands. Note that you can list, create, modify, and delete user names and volumes, as well as log in, link, unlink, and log out of a server.

USING 3COM ETHERNET

If you run the EtherSeries software daily you can highly automate the process. If you typically need to log in to the same server and link to the same volumes, you can add the appropriate lines to your AUTOEXEC.BAT file to accomplish this automatically. For example, the lines

```
ES LOGIN JOE (SEAGULL)
ES LINK C: SYS2
ES LINK D: MYDATA (TURTLE)
```

log in a user named JOE and supply his password SEAGULL, link drive C: to the SYS2 volume that contains MS-DOS and commonly used programs, and link drive D: to a private volume named MYDATA. MYDATA is password protected, requiring that the password TURTLE be supplied to link to it. The commands described later in this chapter to connect to a network printer can also be included in your AUTOEXEC.BAT file so they are executed when you start your PC.

Table 8-3. Subcommands of the EtherShare program

Subcommand	Purpose
CREATE	Create a new volume
DEL	Delete a volume
DIR	List existing volumes
ERASE	Delete a volume (same as DEL)
HELP	Explain ES commands
LINK	Associate a drive letter with a volume
LOGIN	Connect to a server
LOGOUT	Disconnect from a server
MODIFY	Change name, password, or type of a volume
RENAME	Same as MODIFY
SDIR	List all server names on network
UCREATE	Create a user name
UDEL	Delete a user name
UDIR	List existing user names
UERASE	Same as UDEL
UMODIFY	Change password for a user name
UNLINK	Disassociate the drive letter from a volume

If you are using a PC server concurrently as a workstation, you must log in to it just as if it were a remote server before you can write to its hard disk. The 3Com software needs to control all access to the hard disk, and it does not allow the workstation MS-DOS to write to the disk while it may also be writing to the disk on behalf of remote network users.

PRINT MANAGEMENT

PC servers can connect to as many as three printers, and 3Servers can connect one or two printers. The 3Server can have one parallel and one serial printer, and the PC server can have one serial printer and two parallel printers. You can set up more than one print server on a network, and you can use a print server on a different node from the file server you are logged into. You can also link to more than one print server at a time.

The EtherPrint software is installed by use of the applications installation option of the EtherShare menu. The EtherPrint software is started automatically when you start the server. It is copy-protected in the same way as EtherShare—it reads the network address of the PC it is installed to and reinstalls itself only to that address.

Most printers can be made operational with no further attention, but some customization is available if you need it. Associated with each printer on the server are a *name*, *printer type*, and *reset sequence*. You use the name to select the printer from a workstation, much as you use volume names to select disk volumes. The printer type selection initializes the reset sequence, which is a series of codes sent to the printer before each file is printed. These codes are printer-specific and return the printer to a standard condition (such as registered at the top of form, 10-characters-per-inch spacing, and so on). If your printer is not among the listed types, or if you want to supply a different initial setting, you can enter the exact reset sequence you desire.

The EtherPrint command, EP, is used for printing as the ES command is used for disk sharing. EP takes subcommands and arguments as ES does, and has both command line and prompt modes. Table 8-4 explains the EP subcommands.

If you are already logged into the printer server you can just give the EP LINK command. If you don't supply any arguments to EP LINK, it links your MS-DOS PRN: printer device to the first printer defined for the server you are logged into (MS.DOS treats PRN: and LPT1: as the same device). You can explicitly link LPT1:, LPT2:, or LPT3: to a network printer. When you have established the link, you can print a text file by using

Table 8-4. Subcommands of the EtherPrint program

Subcommand	Purpose
DIR	List existing network printers
HELP	Explain EP commands
LINK	Connect a printer name to a network printer
UNLINK	Disconnect a printer name from a network printer

the MS-DOS COPY command to copy the file to a printer. For instance, to print the file MYDATA.TXT, give the command:

```
COPY MYDATA.TXT PRN:
```

Most applications programs that print to LPT1: or PRN: can now print to the network printer. EtherPrint automatically spools your print output, meaning that it writes it to a disk file on the print server and sends it from that file to the printer as fast as the printer can handle it.

Many users can print to the same printer at once, because EtherPrint spools all their output to separate disk files and prints the files one at a time. This has a speed benefit, in that EtherPrint can copy your print output to disk much faster than it can print it, and you regain control of your applications program as soon as the file is created.

EtherPrint needs to know when to close the spool file and treat the data in it as a single entity to be printed contiguously. You can make this happen in several ways:

- If your program doesn't print anything for 30 seconds, EtherPrint assumes the job is finished.
- Use the EP UNLINK command to explicitly close the file.
- Use the EP LINK command to UNLINK and reLINK the printer.
- Log out from the network.

In case your application pauses for more than 30 seconds between segments of output that you want printed contiguously, you can direct Ether-Print to hold all your output until you UNLINK with the /HOLD option. The /PLOT option is like /HOLD, but it additionally suppresses the banner page that is normally printed at the beginning of a file and the trailing form feed that is printed at the end of a file.

You can completely control a network printer with the /DIRECT option on the EP LINK command. This option is useful for printing forms or single sheets when you might need to manually intervene during the printing process. While the printer is linked with the /DIRECT option, all other network users' output is spooled. If you don't print anything for 10 minutes (or the number of minutes you specify), you lose control of the printer. This prevents you from tying up the printer indefinitely.

From the administration menu on the server, you can check printer status. You see the name of each printer and a list of files that are in queue to be printed. The owner and length of each file are shown. You can delete files from the queue while you are running this program, but files in the print queue cannot be resequenced.

SECURITY

Security on a 3Com Ethernet system is principally controlled by passwords. Passwords are optional, and you can design your Ethernet system with no security if you wish. If you want to use passwords they can protect:

- User names
- Volumes
- Administrative software.

If a user name is password protected, you cannot log in to a server without knowing the password. You must know a volume's password to link to it. If the administrative software on a network server is protected, you must know the password in order to perform such system software maintenance as installing applications, deleting files from the print queue, and removing user passwords.

The ES program used on network workstations lets a user perform such functions as creating and deleting volumes and user names. Since you may want to limit people's ability to do these things, there is a limited-function version of ES called XES. XES cannot create, modify, or delete user names or volumes but it can do everything else that ES does. If you want to exclude your network users from access to these functions, you can replace ES.COM with XES.COM on their PCs.

MULTIUSER SUPPORT

3Com's Ethernet supports multiple-user access to data in two ways: files in a public volume can be read by multiple users, and files in a shared volume can be read and written by multiple users. The first approach has been discussed throughout this chapter. The second approach requires custom programming, or an application that has been programmed specifically to work with 3Com's file-locking scheme.

Unlike the software of some networks, 3Com's software does not automatically support multiple users' writing to different files in the same volume. In such a case, the last user to update the disk directory might overwrite an update placed there by a previous user. 3Com recommends that files be preallocated before they are written to by multiple users. This approach requires that you know the maximum size of a shared file ahead of time; it solves the directory update problem but puts the burden on the system manager to decide how big to make the file.

The EtherSeries software provides semaphores and a means for locking and unlocking them. The interface to the lock and unlock functions is through assembly language. Many commercial database management systems use 3Com's network semaphores.

UTILITIES

The EtherMenu package is menu-based workstation software that replaces ES and EP. EtherMenu is supplied with EtherShare and provides a menu-driven interface to common network functions as well as a customizable menu system that supports your own additions. Figure 8-12 shows one preconfigured EtherMenu screen, which controls access to some frequently used MS.DOS functions.

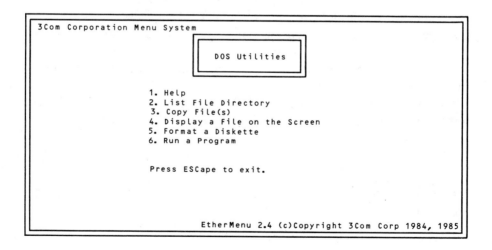

Figure 8-12.   EtherMenu MS-DOS utilities menu

You can customize the menus, supply your own batch files, and build a simple but effective interface for novice users. Since EtherMenu does not support error recovery and parameter checking, you can't build a "bullet-proof" system from EtherMenu. You may find, however, that EtherMenu helps people get accustomed to the network.

Backing Up the Server

An Ethernet hard disk server can be backed up to tape or floppy disk. Floppy disk backup is done using the standard MS-DOS BACKUP and RESTORE commands. This works just as well as it does when backing up a PC XT or PC AT hard disk, but it has the same problems: it takes a long time and many floppy disks to back up a hard disk.

A better solution is a network tape drive. 3Com sells a 60-megabyte tape backup server, enough to back up a small- to medium-size network on a single tape, so you can let the backup job run unattended at the end of the day. The process is thus much easier and less error prone.

EtherMail

3Com sells an optional application software package that provides electronic mail for EtherSeries networks. EtherMail is one of the better LAN mail systems, providing full capabilities for sending and filing short messages as well as MS-DOS disk files. A built-in help facility explains how to use the program. You can run the mail server software on any disk server and store mail for all the users who log into that server. The system can receive mail for you even if your PC is turned off, because the server holds it until you log in.

Each user has a mail folder that holds messages that are received from other users or are waiting to be sent. You can do several things to any message in your mail folder:

- Read it
- Send it (if you wrote it)
- Send a reply to it
- Forward it to another user or users
- Print it
- Save it in an MS-DOS file.

Messages are entered by means of a simple full-screen editor that supports word wrap, insertion and replacement of text, paragraph right justification, deletion of words and lines, and moving, copying, or deletion of text blocks.

You can append up to 26 MS-DOS files to a single message. Appended files are sent to all the recipients of that message. This lets you use a word processor instead of the mail text editor to create a memo and then send it by attaching it to a message. You can also send program or data files such as spreadsheet templates and databases.

Distribution lists are lists of network users. When you send a message to a distribution list it is sent automatically to every user on the list. Distribution lists are maintained by use of the message editor; they are stored as MS-DOS files and can be shared among all the users of a server if they are in a public disk volume.

DOCUMENTATION

The 3Com manuals are among the best offered with the networks in the book. They are clearly written and well organized, provide plenty of information, and are attractively laid out and illustrated. 3Com's manuals take you quickly through the setup and installation phases, providing enough information in sequential order to get your network up and running, but also giving clear pointers to additional information that is needed to handle special cases such as dealing with hardware conflicts.

3Com's documentation effort is greatly assisted by the EtherSeries software, which is straightforward and tolerant of doing things out of sequence. One of the few confusing features of the documentation is the relationship between the *User's Guide* and the *Administrator's Guide*—both must be referenced during initial setup and installation, but there is no higher-level guide that tells you which manual to follow during setup. It turns out that you can't really foul things up by starting in either place.

The manuals have some of the best troubleshooting information supplied with any of the reviewed network systems. Software test programs are also included to isolate and track down problems.

Useful appendices include glossaries of network terminology, error messages and explanations, technical specifications, and cabling guidelines for both thin and standard Ethernet.

EXPANDING THE NETWORK

Ethernet was designed to be expandable, and the ease with which you can incrementally expand the 3Com network attests to this. Adding a new server is simply a matter of running the INSTALL batch file (although recall that you must purchase a separate copy of EtherShare for each server) and registering it from the administration program. All the other

Table 8-5.   Running third-party software packages

Program	Task	Time	
Lotus 1-2-3	Load program	4.6 seconds	
	Load worksheet	3.6 seconds	
	Print portion of worksheet to spool file	2.2 seconds	
	File manager	works OK	
	Copy protection	OK with key disk in workstation disk drive	
WordStar	Load program	7.9 seconds	
	Load document	2.5 seconds	
	Position to end of document	9.1 seconds	
	Append document	23.2 seconds	
	Save document and quit program	7.2 seconds	
	Printing	works OK on network printer	
dBASE III	Load program	7.5 seconds	
	Copy protection	OK with key disk in workstation disk drive	
		ONE USER	TWO USERS (AVG.)
	Sort	20.8 seconds	22.9 seconds
	Reindex	41.2 seconds	42.1 seconds
BASICA	Sequential write	41.0 seconds	42.5 seconds
	Sequential read	29.5 seconds	29.5 seconds
	Random write	9.3 seconds	11.8 seconds
	Random read	7.5 seconds	10.8 seconds

servers must be on-line when the registration is done, and they update their records to show the new server's presence on the network. You then go to any network workstation and create user names and volumes on that server. There is no need to run any special installation software on the other servers or workstations. Adding new print servers is equally straightforward.

PERFORMANCE

The 3Server turned in a commendable performance, running the two-user tests in only slightly more time than the single-user tests. This is a good indication that the 3Server has plenty of reserves left to handle additional users, although as mentioned in Chapter 4 these benchmarks cannot predict performance at higher usage levels. The 3Com documentation indicates that the degradation with many users is small. It does suggest that the 3Server — designed to be a network server — yields more value than a general-purpose PC XT in that role.

All the tests for compatibility with third-party software, including network printing and running copy-protected software, worked successfully on Ethernet. Table 8-5 gives the results of the performance tests.

Corvus Omninet

Hardware:	IBM Transporter Local Network Interface card
	OmniDrive disk server
Software:	Constellation II Revision 4.10
Manufacturer:	Corvus Systems, Inc.
	2100 Corvus Drive
	San Jose, CA 95124
	408/559-7000
Cable type:	Twisted-pair, unshielded 20 ga. Belden 8205 VW-1 or equivalent
Max length:	1000 feet or 4000 feet with Corvus Active Junction Box every 1000 feet
Topology:	Bus
Data rate:	1 megabit per second
Protocol:	CSMA/CA with positive acknowledgement
Max nodes:	64, any combination of workstations and servers

9

CORVUS OMNINET

Corvus is one of the best-established vendors of microcomputer networks. They have delivered multiuser hard disk servers for most of the popular small computer systems over the years, and they claim more users than any other network products supplier. Their experience is evident in the simplicity of setup and use of the Corvus system. However, their poorly organized (albeit well-written) documentation sometimes makes using the Omninet seem more difficult than it really is.

The first Corvus products used networking mostly as a method of sharing expensive peripherals such as hard disk drives. You can still see this philosophy in the way that a Corvus Omninet system appears to the user. There is no direct PC-to-PC communication. Instead, PCs communicate with the network servers, such as the OmniDrive hard disk, the printer server, tape backup units, and gateways to SNA or broadband networks.

This setup should not present you with any problems. Software written by you or bought from Corvus can make the system appear to support PC-to-PC communication, although messages will make an intermediate stop in the OmniDrive.

OVERVIEW

Corvus sells networking products to support many different microcomputers. All of its major products are available in IBM PC versions. As shown in Figure 9-1, a single Omninet can host a variety of microcomputers that can share data and peripherals.

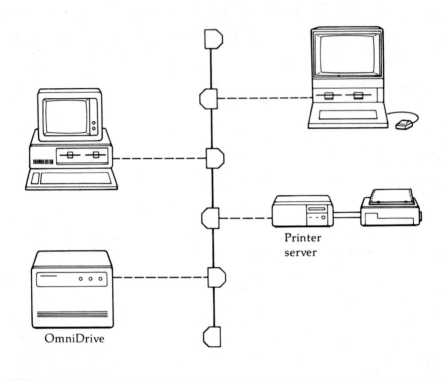

Figure 9-1.   Single Omninet LAN connecting a variety of computers

Network Architecture

Omninet's physical connection scheme is very simple. It uses unshielded twisted-pair cable in a bus arrangement. The bus can be 1000 feet long without any additional hardware and can extend up to 4000 feet if an Omninet Active Junction Box is added every 1000 feet.

The network supports 64 nodes, which can be either workstations or servers. Each node is connected to the bus via a 15-foot shielded twisted-pair cable supplied with each Omninet product.

Omninet transmits data at a rate of 1 megabit per second, making it slower than many PC LANs, although the rate is quite adequate. The network protocol is CSMA/CA with positive acknowledgment.

Workstations and Servers

You need one Omninet Transporter local network interface for every IBM PC workstation connected to the network. The Transporter card takes up one expansion slot in each PC.

For hard disk service on the network, you can choose to dedicate a PC XT or purchase an OmniDrive from Corvus. The OmniDrive comes in several sizes, ranging from a small 5 megabytes to a very respectable 126 megabytes. OmniDrive is a simple Z-80-based microcomputer with a hard disk drive and an Omninet interface in a box 14 inches long, 9.5 inches wide, and 5.5 inches high. The OmniDrive has a fan for cooling; noise level seems comparable to a PC XT. The system reviewed for this chapter was based on a 5-megabyte OmniDrive.

Like the hard disk service, printing can be done with a PC or a special dedicated server purchased from Corvus. If you use a PC it can function as a workstation when it is not running the printing program.

Corvus was one of the first manufacturers to offer hard disk backup to a home VCR (video cassette recorder). This device, the Corvus Mirror, is still available as a network storage backup device. If you don't have a VCR, or don't want to use it this way, you can buy the Corvus Bank, a fast tape backup device.

Finally, Corvus offers an SNA Gateway server that allows you to connect an Omninet to an IBM SNA mainframe network. A gateway to the IBM PC Network is promised for the future.

INSTALLATION

Installing an Omninet system is pretty straightforward, and once you have one workstation running it is even easier to set the next one up. The ease of installation is somewhat marred by the disjointed set of manuals. The first time through you many have to spend a great deal of time with the manuals. Be sure you have a complete set of manuals and that you follow the suggested order of reading. The manuals themselves are clearly written and illustrated, and the installation process is fairly simple.

Planning the Hardware
Installation

When you plan the cable layout for an Omninet system, you must bring the main cable or bus within 15 feet of each workstation. You must also observe the 1000-foot limit between Omninet Active Junction boxes, and the total network bus cable length cannot exceed 4000 feet. These simple rules are all you need to know to plan your Omninet cable layout, other than normal good practices such as not running the cable right next to possible sources of electrical interference.

Next you need to plan for the number of PCs you will be connecting to the network as workstations, keeping in mind that you can have a combined total of no more than 64 workstations and servers. You must decide whether to purchase OmniDrives or use PC XTs as network disk servers. The OmniDrive may be a less expensive solution than a PC XT since it contains less hardware and may hold more data.

You also need to plan print service for your network. You have several alternatives:

- Attach a printer to each PC workstation in the usual fashion.
- Dedicate a PC on the network to print service (network printers will be connected to this PC and it will run the DESPOOL program described later).
- Purchase the Corvus Printer Server and use it as just described.

You may choose to mix these approaches; for example, provide each workstation with a low-cost dot matrix printer and attach a laser printer to a Corvus Printer Server for shared use. As in the case of hard disk service, the Corvus Printer Server may be a less expensive way to make printers available than a dedicated PC.

Planning the Software Installation

Software installation and Omninet system management involve three major questions:

- Who are the users of the network?
- How will the hard disk or disks be allocated among users?
- What access privileges will each user have to each portion of the hard disk?

The Corvus Omninet software, called Constellation II, requires you to set up *user accounts:* pairs of user names and passwords needed to gain access to the network. The user account is the key to network control. Each

```
Volume Manager [2.5e]     DS SERVER00
Main Menu                 Drive DRIVE1
(c) Copyright 1982, 1983, 1984 Corvus Systems, Inc.
---------------------------------------------
        A - Add a volume
        R - Remove a volume
        C - Change volume attributes
        L - List volumes
        X - Extended list
        F - Free space list

        H - Help
        E - Exit
---------------------------------------------

    Enter VOLMGR function:
```

Figure 9-2.   Main menu of the volume manager

password should be known only to those people who need to know it. As
the system manager, you can specify exactly which information each user
account can access.

The Constellation II software lets more than one user gain simultaneous access to the system using the same user account, so you might find
it appropriate to designate user accounts for classes of users (such as secretary, accountant, or manager) rather than for each individual user.

You must decide how the hard disk in the system will be split up into
volumes. Volumes divide the hard disk into smaller areas (although the size
of each individual area remains fixed once it has been created). Figure 9-2
shows the main menu of the volume manager software that lets you create
and modify volumes. The questions you must answer to create a volume
are shown in Figure 9-3. If you wish you can later change the name and
accessibility of a volume, but you cannot change its size or location.

Since you cannot change the size of a volume once it is created, you
should put some real thought into this stage of the network planning process. If you forget something or your requirements change in the future,
you might have to copy all the files from the hard disk and create new
volumes from scratch.

A good general scheme is to create a *public* (shared) volume that is large
enough to hold the programs needed by the users of a single hard disk,

```
Volume Manager [2.5e]        DS SERVER00
Add a Volume               Drive DRIVE1
-----------------------------------------
Enter attributes of new volume:
                    Name: IBMMS
             Volume type: MSDOS
           Size (blocks): 3072
                Location: 2133

Do you want to initialize the volume (Y/N)? Y
       Enter MSDOS attributes:
          Cluster size (blocks): 8
               Reserved sectors: 1
              Directory entries: 256
```

Figure 9-3.   Adding a new volume to the OmniDrive

then give all the user accounts read-only access to that volume. The read-only privilege means that the users can run the programs stored in that volume, but cannot delete or add to its contents. Most programs will run satisfactorily from this volume, but some may require write access to the disk. You have to decide whether to make the public volume have write access or to put these programs in a separate volume with write access.

Each user can have one or more private (personal) volumes for storage of data or programs needed only by that user. Again, you need to plan ahead, making each private volume large enough so that your users won't run out of space too soon, but not so big that you don't have enough volumes for all your users. This is one of the hardest details of the network to plan. A useful method is to divide the disk space into equal portions, let people use the network for a while, then reformat the disk and reallocate storage when you determine the use patterns.

The designations "private" and "public" are not descriptions of a volume, but rather of the way that a volume is used. A volume meant to be used by a single account is considered private; a volume in which a number of accounts share common data is considered public.

Doing the Installation

Once you have planned your installation and acquired the necessary hardware and software, installing an Omninet system is fairly easy, especially if you avoid the few minor snags and pitfalls outlined here.

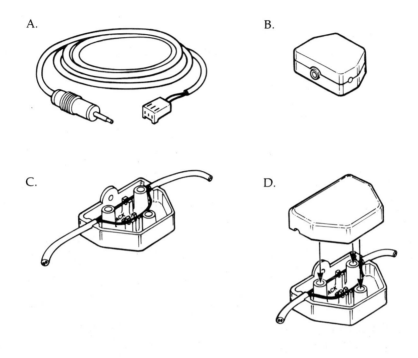

A.

B.

C.

D.

Figure 9-4. Omninet cabling: (A) tap cable; (B) tap box; (C) putting wires in a tap box; (D) closing the tap box

Physical Installation   The physical cable layout is noncritical, as long as you follow the guidelines for length discussed previously. All nodes connect to the network via "tap cables" and "tap boxes," shown in Figure 9-4. A tap cable is a 15-foot piece of twisted-pair wire; on the end that connects to the tap box there is a miniature phone plug, and on the end that connects to the workstation or server node there is a three-prong connector.

Tap boxes are small white plastic boxes that pull apart into two halves. One half has plastic wire guides, the other half has metal fingers that grasp and connect to the wires of the main network bus. Drawing C in Figure 9-4 shows how you strip a couple of inches from the outer insulation of the network bus cable, put the wires into the plastic guides, and push the two halves of the tap box back together. Some dexterity with hand tools is all that is needed. If you've never stripped insulation from a cable before, you should practice on an extra piece of wire before tackling the main network cable. Concentrate on removing the insulation without cutting the wires.

The far ends of the network bus cable are terminated with tap boxes containing resistors (supplied by Corvus). You can connect network devices to these tap boxes.

Each node on the network must have a unique address between 0 and 63, inclusive. Unlike other systems, where the node address is uniquely assigned by the manufacturer, you must choose and maintain unique addresses yourself on an Omninet system. On each device that connects to the network there is a DIP switch (a bank of eight small switches); you set the hardware address by flipping the switches to a unique pattern as explained in the manual. You may find it convenient to mark the address of each network node with a small label placed on the back panel of that device. Be sure to set the node address of the primary hard disk server (OmniDrive or PC XT) in your network to 0. This is indicated by setting all switches ON.

The orientation of the three-prong connector is another area of confusion, since the connector on the tap cables is not keyed, while the illustrations in the manuals show a keyed connector. The connector will work properly if you connect it so that the black wire is on top when it is going into a vertical connector such as the ones on the PC network interface cards, and to the right (when viewed from the rear) of a horizontal connector like the one on the OmniDrive.

The connectors on the network interface cards feel flimsy since they are anchored to the cards only by the soldered prongs of the connector itself. Although no problems were observed during testing of the Omni-Drive, it was disconcerting to see the connector bend under the considerable pressure required to plug in the tap cable.

Installing the System Software   The Corvus Constellation II software comes on six diskettes. Installing the system to an OmniDrive server involves initializing the server disk drive and loading firmware and software from the Constellation II diskettes to the disk server. (Firmware in this case is the set of code that is run by the Z-80 microprocessor contained in the Corvus OmniDrive disk server. It is not important for the user to understand anything about the firmware, and the system manager does not need to know much more than how to load the OmniDrive with firmware and any updates that might be issued by Corvus.)

```
           (c) Copyright 1982, 1983 Corvus Systems, Inc.
           DISK DIAGNOSTIC [1.2d]        Slot:  1
           Select Drive                 Server: 0
           ------------------------------------------
           Slot 1: an OMNINET interface



           Enter slot number    : 0
```

Figure 9-5.   Indicating the slot number

Loading the firmware is explained step-by-step in the *MS-DOS System Generation Guide* that comes with the OmniDrive. Don't be too concerned if the screens produced by the software do not always match the manual exactly. Most of the time, simply accepting the default choice by pressing the ENTER key produces the desired results. There are some cases, however, where a bit of intuition and an adventurous nature help. Figure 9-5 shows one step in the installation process where you must supply the "slot number," a concept that is not covered in the documentation. The default supplied, 0, is not accepted by the software. The top of the screen shows "Slot: 1," and entering 1 seems to make everything work.

After the firmware is loaded, you have to insert a different diskette in your PC and run some programs that initialize the OmniDrive. These programs are also simple to run and take about 15 minutes. Most of the work involves swapping diskettes so the installation program can copy their contents to the OmniDrive. The system software takes up 3156 of the 10,728 blocks of storage space on a 5-megabyte OmniDrive (a block holds 512 bytes).

Setting Up the Workstations   Workstations can be IBM PCs with no disk drives or diskette drives only, or XTs with a hard disk. If you are using a PC with no disk drive, the user must type a rather arcane three-line program into the PC's built-in BASIC interpreter:

```
DEF SEG = &HDF00
X = 0
CALL X
```

This starts the process of loading software from the OmniDrive server and sets the workstation up to use the Omninet just as if the software had been loaded from a diskette or hard disk drive.

It's up to you to decide whether the users of your system should have to type this in whenever they start their PCs running. It will save you some money on every PC, since you won't need a disk drive or controller. On the other hand, with a local diskette drive you can set up your Omninet so the user simply turns on the computer and everything else happens automatically.

PC workstation users must boot their computers with a Corvus boot diskette, which contains the software that is needed to access the Omninet. Creating this disk is a simple procedure. Corvus provides an MS-DOS batch program that copies all the necessary files to a diskette or, if you have an XT or AT, to the hard disk. Figure 9-6 shows the files. The boot diskette or the main directory of the hard disk must contain a CONFIG.SYS file with the following entries:

```
BUFFERS = 3
FILES = 8
DEVICE = CORDRV.BIN
DEVICE = SPLDRV.BIN
BREAK = ON
```

As MS-DOS starts running on the workstation, it reads the CONFIG.SYS file, which directs MS-DOS to load software from the workstation's disk-

```
                    FILENAME
                    --------
                    CORDRV.BIN
                    SPLDRV.BIN
                    CONFIG.SYS
                    PBOOT.DAT
                      CSD.COM
```

Figure 9-6.   Files on a boot diskette

ette or local hard disk. The "BUFFERS = 3" and "FILES = 8" lines allocate space in memory for the MS-DOS file system. The line "DEVICE= CORDRV.BIN" loads the file CORDRV.BIN. This file contains *driver* software, which is the program that allows your workstation to access the network.

The "DEVICE=SPLDRV.BIN" line loads the Corvus printer spooler program. When you run a program on your PC that sends output to the printer, MS-DOS will intercept that output intended for the printer and send it to the network print server instead. There is, however, a pitfall here that is not covered clearly in the manual: when you start a PC and SPLDRV.BIN is loaded, your printer output is sent to the network. But if you have not yet set up the necessary files to receive print output on the OmniDrive, your PC will stop working when it tries to send print output to the network.

Finally, the BREAK=ON line tells MS-DOS to look for the BREAK key and stop the running program when it is typed.

USING OMNINET

After you have a basic Omninet network installed, you should explore the basic system a bit to get the feel of the network. When you are comfortable with the system, you can tailor the network to your system requirements. This system management is the process of defining the user accounts, volumes, and access privileges for your installation.

Logging On

To log on you first turn on the OmniDrive and start up a workstation. You will see a screen on your PC similar to that in Figure 9-7. You can log on to the OmniDrive by typing **IBMUSER** and ENTER in response to the first prompt. IBMUSER is a public account with no password. As supplied by Corvus, the account gives you access to one volume on the OmniDrive called "IBMMS" (the IBM MS-DOS volume). The screen clears and a message at the top of your screen tells you where to find IBMMS:

```
Mounting Volume IBMMS    from Server SERVER00 on UNIT D
Corvus-IBM driver CORDRV [5.9] installed.
```

The last part of the first line ("on UNIT D" in this case) tells you the MS-DOS drive letter that is now associated with the volume IBMMS on

```
                           *
                         *   *

                   C O R V U S   S Y S T E M S


                       CONSTELLATION    II


        Please enter your name: IBMUSER

        Please enter your password:
```

Figure 9-7.   Omninet log-on screen

the OmniDrive. You access the files in this volume in the same way that you access files on a local drive of your PC.

You can set up the CONFIG.SYS file so the log-on screen is skipped and the log-on process happens automatically. You must change the line in the CONFIG.SYS file to contain the user account name (this user account cannot have a password):

```
DEVICE = CORDRIV.BIN /U:IBMUSER
```

In this example, the user name IBMUSER is logged on when the CONFIG.SYS file is read. To make logging on easy for the system users, you can create boot diskettes for each user account.

If security is not much of an issue and your workstation has a hard disk, you can put the /U option in the CONFIG.SYS file on your hard disk. Simply turning on the power will connect to the network. Since anyone who can turn the system on can now access such a user account, you should be sure that no confidential files are on such a volume.

Using the OmniDrive

The files on the OmniDrive are accessible just as if they were on a local diskette or hard disk drive. For example, the MS-DOS command

```
DIR D:
```

would list the contents of volume IBMMS.

Although the files on the OmniDrive are accessed the same way as files on a local hard disk or diskette, an additional step is needed that is equivalent to swapping diskettes on your PC. Since the OmniDrive may contain many volumes, a utility program is provided that lets you select the volumes that will be accessible to you at any given time. Making a volume accessible is called *mounting* it. Mounting a volume associates it with a DOS drive letter.

When you log on to the OmniDrive, from 1 to 10 volumes may be premounted for you, depending on how the system manager has configured your user account. Corvus encourages the convention of storing the common programs that all users need in the IBBMS volume and mounting it as the first volume.

You should load the utilities supplied by CORVUS on the MS-DOS utilities diskette into IBMMS. These utilities allow each user to mount and unmount volumes and manage the print spooler. To copy the programs to the IBMMS volume on the OmniDrive, you use the MS-DOS COPY command. Put the MS-DOS utilities diskette in your PC's drive A, then give the MS-DOS command:

```
COPY A:*.* D:
```

The files in Table 9-1 will be copied onto the OmniDrive.

The MNTMGR2.EXE program is the *mount manager,* a utility program that lets you list and specify the volumes on the OmniDrive that are associated with each drive letter for each workstation. When you run it, the

Table 9-1.   Constellation II MS-DOS utilities

Utility name	Description
MNTMGR2.EXE	Mount manager program used to associate volumes with MS-DOS unit letters
SPOOL.EXE	Sends a file to the pipes area
DESPOOL.EXE	Removes files from the pipes area and sends them to a file, the console, or a printer
SHOWMT.COM	Quick listing of currently mounted and accessible disk volumes

```
MOUNT MANAGER  -  [2.21]
(c) 1983, 1984 by Corvus, Inc.


    User: IBMUSER
  Server: SERVER00
   Drive: *
------------------------------------------
C - Change Mount Status
L - List Units and Volumes
S - Select Drive
H - Help
E - Exit
------------------------------------------
Enter MOUNT MANAGER option:
```

Figure 9-8.   Running the mount manager utility

screen shown in Figure 9-8 appears. Option L (List Units and Volumes) produces the screen in Figure 9-9 when run on a newly initialized OmniDrive. It shows that the volume IBMMS is mounted on unit D, meaning simply that the MS-DOS D drive is now associated with the volume IBMMS on the OmniDrive. Note that no other units are assigned.

The third column in this screen shows whether you have write access to this volume. If you don't, you can only read the files and run the programs in that volume. If you do have write access, you can add new files to

```
Mount Unit Assignments -

                write                       res       dir   FAT
   unit  volume  acc   length   clus  sects      ents  sects  server       drive
      D  IBMMS   yes    1024      4     1         256    1    SERVER00     DRIVE1
     +E                    0      0     0           0    0
     +F                    0      0     0           0    0
     +G                    0      0     0           0    0
     +H                    0      0     0           0    0
```

Figure 9-9.   Listing units with the mount manager

```
Volumes Accessible -

                     write                res   dir   FAT
     unit   volume   acc   length   clus  sects ents  sects server        drive
      D     IBMMS    yes    1024      4     1    256    1    SERVER00      DRIVE1
```

Figure 9-10.   Volume listing from the mount manager

the volume and delete or modify existing files in the volume.

The next column shows the size of the volume on the disk. The length of 1024 means this volume holds 1024 512-byte blocks, giving it a total size of 512 kilobytes. The next four columns contain technical information about the layout of the volume on the disk, and it is unlikely you will ever be concerned with this information. The last two columns show the names of the server and drive where this volume resides. These are the default names supplied by the Constellation II software. You may change them to more descriptive names of your own choosing.

The second screen, which is displayed when you press the space bar, is shown in Figure 9-10. It lists the volumes that are accessible to you, according to the access privileges that the system manager has granted to your user account. At this point, only the IBMMS volume is accessible.

The SHOWMT command displays the names and drive letters of the currently mounted volumes. Its output looks like this:

```
--- Mounted Corvus Volumes ---
unit     access    volume    length
 D        R/W       IBMMS     1024
```

The access of each volume is indicated as R/O for read access and R/W for write access.

PRINT MANAGEMENT

As you saw earlier, you can (1) connect printers to each PC workstation, (2) use one or more dedicated PCs as print servers, or (3) purchase the Corvus Printer Server and use it for network printing. The first case is no different than using a printer in a nonnetworked environment. In both the second and the third cases, printer output from programs running on the workstations is put into a holding area called the *pipes* area on the Omni-Drive. The DESPOOL program running on the PC or the print server transfers the pipes to the appropriate printer.

Pipe Files

A pipe is an area of the disk that is used as a conduit for passing information between two programs. In the case of the print spooler, pipes are used to pass information between an applications program and the despooling program.

Before you can use pipes, you must set up a special area for them on the OmniDrive. To do this, run the system management program and create a new volume named PIPES. You then select another menu option to initialize the pipes area.

Spooling to Network Printers

There are two ways to use a network printer. The first method causes printing that would normally have occurred on a workstation PC to happen instead on a network printer. The second method, using the SPOOL program, manually transfers a single file to the pipe area.

The first method is a natural way to use spooling, but it isn't appropriate for all applications. For proper spooling to take place, your application must use an MS-DOS or BIOS system call to send data to the printer. Most programs do this correctly, but a few control the printer interface hardware of your PC directly, and the spooling software can do nothing to stop these applications from printing on the local printer instead of a network printer.

You can work around these misbehaving programs if your application has a way to send printer output to a disk file instead of to the printer. Instead of printing, create a disk file that is ready to be printed, then run the Corvus SPOOL program to manually send the file to the pipes area where it can be despooled and printed on a network printer.

Table 9-2 shows the CONFIG.SYS parameters available when you start up SPLDRV.BIN. The system defaults are usually acceptable, and you probably won't need to adjust the options. If you do, it is easily done by editing your CONFIG.SYS file. For example, the line DEVICE=SPLDRV.-BIN/F:ROBERT directs the spooler to print the banner ROBERT before

Table 9-2.   Spool driver parameters

Parameter	Meaning
D	Direct print output from workstation to network or local printer
P	Set pipe name to receive print output
F	Change file name banner on print output
S	Identify server holding pipe files
C	Define control characters that indicate end-of-file for print output
T	Set length of timeout that denotes end of print output from a workstation
E	Force pipes to close manually

each file printed from your workstation.

Since multiple workstations may be sending output to the print server at once, the DESPOOL program can't start printing any single pipe until the sending workstation closes it. There are three ways to close a pipe file:

- Send a special character sequence at the end of the print output.
- Don't send anything for a predetermined time; SPLDRV.BIN will "time out" and automatically close the pipe file.
- Manually close the pipe using a Corvus utility program called CSD.

Despooling to a Printer

If you are using a PC as a network print server, that PC must run the Corvus DESPOOL program whenever you want the network printer to function as such. This is an unfortunate feature of the Corvus system: the despooler takes over the whole PC when it runs.

One other technical detail could cause you some head-scratching. The CONFIG.SYS file of the print server PC must not contain the line "DEVICE=SPLDRV.BIN", because if it does it will set up an infinite loop. When the print server tries to really print something on its printer, the SPLDRV software intercepts that output and sends it to a pipe.

```
Corvus Despool Utility [3.9b]
Main Menu
-------------------------------------------
   D  - Despool a file

   C  - Change despool parameters

   H  - Help

   E  - Exit
-------------------------------------------
Please select an option:
```

Figure 9-11.   DESPOOL program's main menu

Figure 9-11 shows DESPOOL's menu choices (the Help choice was not implemented in the version reviewed here). The main choice, "Despool a file," ceaselessly looks for pipes named PRINTER and copies their contents to the PC's local printer.

The "Change despool parameters" choice provides the menu shown in Figure 9-12. The "Pipe name" option lets you specify the name of the pipe the despooler should look for (the default is PRINTER). By changing this name you can despool any file that was spooled under any pipe name.

```
Corvus Despool Utility [3.9b]
Change Parameters
-------------------------------------------
   P - Pipe name                     : PRINTER
   O - Output device                 : PRINTER
   L - Do you want <lf> after <cr>   : YES
   S - Single page printing          : NO
   T - Transparent despool of DATA   : NO
   E - Exit to main menu
-------------------------------------------
Please select an option :
```

Figure 9-12.   Changing parameters of the DESPOOL program

Another option lets you change the output device type from PRINTER to CONSOLE or FILE. CONSOLE sends the output of the despooler to the screen; FILE sends it to a disk file.

Other options let you specify whether linefeeds should be automatically sent to the printer after carriage returns, and whether to pause between pages if you are feeding single sheets.

If you are using a PC as a print server, you can despool to only one printer at a time. This means that if you want two or more network printers (such as a letter-quality printer and a high-speed draft printer), you will need two print server PCs. The Corvus Printer Server hardware supports multiple printers on a single server.

The current Corvus despooling software does not let you specify or change the order in which files get printed. If you have a high-priority print job, it will have to wait its turn. There is only marginal support for printing on forms. Control over such printing is spread over several utilities. The SPOOL program lets you set lines per page, tab stops (fixed tab length only), and formfeed character; and lets you stipulate whether to strip the eighth bit of printed text and whether to format the file contents at all. The CSD.COM program does not give you control over any of the above options, so if you need them you must send your file manually with SPOOL. Some of these limitations may soon be overcome with new software from Corvus.

SECURITY

Omninet manages network security in several ways:

- User accounts may have passwords.

- Access to each volume on a network disk server is granted by the system manager to individual user accounts; access may be write or read-only. Additionally, a disk server volume may have read-only or write access for all users.

- Only the user named IBMGR can run the access manager to grant access to volumes; this account is normally password protected.

- Each disk server has a password, so even someone who learns the IBMGR account password cannot modify access privileges to a disk server unless he or she also knows its password.

Using the Access Manager

To set passwords and access, the system manager must log on as IBMGR and select the Drive Management option from the main system menu. The principal options of the Access Manager menu are to grant, remove, or change access to a volume.

The Access Manager always operates in the context of a single user's account. You can list the volumes accessible to that user, as shown in Figure 9-13. If you want to add access to another volume, but you can't remember how it is spelled, a handy listing is found under the HELP option of the main menu. There you will find another "List Volumes" choice, which produces a complete list of volumes on the drive.

The Access Manager is also the program that determines whether a volume is automatically mounted, and where it is mounted, when that user account logs onto the network. Figure 9-14 shows the "Grant Volume Access" screen, where volume MYDATA is made accessible to user account ROWLAND, with write access, automatically mounted on unit 2. If Mount/Status (M/U) is answered U instead of M, the volume is not automatically mounted, and must be manually mounted using the MNTMGR2 program.

The unit numbers here correspond to sequential MS-DOS drive letters after the ones already on your workstation. If you have a PC with two floppy drives, they are lettered A: and B:; unit number 1 then corresponds

```
Access Manager [2.2d]        User ROWLAND
List Volumes                   DS SERVER00
                             Drive DRIVE1
--------------------------------------------
        Volume    Unit   RW     Type

   1.   IBMMS       1     x     MSDOS
   2.   MYDATA      2     x     MSDOS
   3.   YOURDATA    -     x     MSDOS

Number of volumes accessible:      3.
--------------------------------------------
Press <space> to continue, or
press F to list to a file.
```

Figure 9-13.   Listing the volumes accessible to a user account

```
Access Manager [2.2d]      User ROWLAND
Grant Volume Access          DS SERVER00
                           Drive DRIVE1
----------------------------------------
Please enter:

      Volume name: MYDATA
    Access (RO/RW): RW
Mount status (M/U): MOUNTED
        Mount unit: 2

OK to grant volume access (Y/N)?Y
Access granted.
----------------------------------------
Press <space> to continue, or
press G to grant another volume.
```

Figure 9-14.   Granting a user account access to a volume

to drive letter C:, unit 2 to drive D:, and so on. If your workstation is an XT, it already has a drive C:, so unit number 1 is drive D:, and unit 2 is drive E:.

You can remove any user account's access to a volume or change access privileges without totally removing them.

MULTIUSER SUPPORT

Print spooling and disk volumes allow users to share network resources one at a time. Omninet also provides ways to allow true concurrent access to shared data, which is required by multiuser applications that use common files.

The Constellation II software does not do any implicit file or record locking. If two users have write access to the same file in the same volume, then the data of the last one to update the file will become the final contents of the file. No warning or error message is returned in this case.

If you need to share data that more than one user can read and write to, you will need applications programs that take advantage of the file and record-locking primitives provided by the Omninet network. You may be able to find an off-the-shelf application already written for Corvus' file-sharing conventions; or you may have to use custom software.

Instead of file- and record-locking commands, Omninet provides a "semaphore" mechanism. Semaphores allow a programmer to implement file and record locking, but they require more work on the programmer's part. The only documentation provided for use of semaphores is a sample Pascal program on the CORMS24 disk. The program is direct enough so that a programmer who is experienced in using semaphores should be able to figure it out.

Omninet supports one other form of data sharing: use of the PIPES volume to share files. This feature does not allow concurrent writing to data, but it does form a sort of "mailbox" to which a user, with the SPOOL program, can send a file, and from which another user, with the DE-SPOOL program, can receive the file. This method is a bit awkward, but it works. You will probably not want to use this in a working environment, and it is no substitute for electronic mail.

RELIABILITY

Corvus's long experience with networking hardware shows in the generally solid and stable feel of their hardware and software. Their hardware has a reputation for being highly reliable.

During the review process, the software hung up occasionally, although the problems were always due to lack of error recovery rather than lack of stability. In most cases, however, error recovery worked well.

If you turn off the OmniDrive server while a workstation is attempting to access it, the workstation will freeze until the drive is restarted. In the cases tested, the application program picked up where it left off when the OmniDrive came back on-line, an impressive bit of resynchronization.

UTILITIES

You can put more than one type of microcomputer on an Omninet system sharing the same OmniDrive server. Each workstation can use only volumes formatted for its own native operating system, but pipes allow files to be transferred between different types of computers.

Making Backups

When you log on to the user account IBMBACKUP, you are prompted for your user account and password (without this protection you could make a backup of anybody's files and then restore those files to your own

```
CORVUS BACKUP-TO-FLOPPY UTILITY [1.3 ]
Copyright 1983 by Corvus Systems, Inc.
---------------------------------------------

       B   -   Backup a Volume

       R   -   Restore a Volume

       I   -   Identify a Diskette

       L   -   List Volumes

       S   -   Set Options

       E   -   Exit

---------------------------------------------

Please select option:
```

Figure 9-15.   Main menu of the system backup utility

volume). After passing the security check, you get the main BACKUP-TO-FLOPPY utility menu shown in Figure 9-15. From this menu you can copy the contents of a volume to one or more floppy diskettes, or restore the contents of a previous backup to the hard disk.

The "Set Options" choice lets you specify whether you want verification or password protection or both. Verification indicates that information is read back from the floppy after it is written to make sure it was written with no errors; this, of course, takes longer, but makes your information much less prone to error. Password protection puts a password on the backup diskettes, so only someone knowing this password can restore from those diskettes.

This backup and restore utility is slow and has limited features. You may be better off using the BACKUP and RESTORE programs supplied by IBM with PC-DOS. It takes nearly 7 minutes to write a single diskette, while IBM's BACKUP takes about 3 minutes. The Corvus utility writes the entire contents of the volume to diskette, even if most of the volume is not occupied by files. Backing up a relatively empty 3072-block IBMMS volume took 35 minutes with the Corvus utility but only 45 seconds with IBM's BACKUP command. If you are backing up a full volume, the IBM utility lets you limit the files to be backed up to those that have been modified since the last backup or those modified since a given date, or lets you simply use a template and back up selectively by filename.

Corvus sells two systems for tape backup. The Mirror writes to a video cassette recorder (VCR), while the Bank is self-contained and uses magnetic tape data cartridges (neither was tested during preparation of this book). They both have a good reputation for reliability, and speed is less of an issue with a tape backup system as long as you can back up your entire drive to a single tape. The Bank can be accessed like a disk drive, a feature not found in many tape drives.

DOCUMENTATION

The Omninet manuals are very clearly written. They are printed in two colors with an appealing open layout and large type. The style is direct and concise without omitting information.

Unfortunately, the manuals do not always reflect the current product. In most cases the differences are not troublesome and are even hinted at in the text with wording like "the screen will appear similar to this." However, there are some cases where screen differences require the system manager to guess at information that must be entered, which can easily cause error. There is also a need for a programmer's manual, since taking advantage of the system for a multiuser situation requires programming to the Omninet conventions.

MANAGING THE NETWORK

Managing an Omninet system is mostly a task of adding or modifying user accounts, volumes, and access privileges, as well as installing an occasional firmware update from Corvus. Basically, the system manager logs on as IBMGR and is greeted with a screen of choices.

An Omninet can also be upgraded to have multiple disk servers. To add a new server, you must go through all the steps you used to set up the first server, and you must also merge the user tables. This process combines all the user account information from the existing drives on the network into a single master table and writes it to the new disk server. The process is clearly explained in the *Multiple Server Update Guide*.

The Omninet can be physically extended in two ways. The end of the cable can be spliced and extended, or the cable can be split and a new portion added in the middle. One advantage of twisted-pair over coaxial cable is that it is easier to splice and the tap box system described earlier makes it even simpler.

PERFORMANCE

The Omninet system performed well. The slowest part of the system is the system management software, which seemed sluggish compared to the speed of MS-DOS utilities. It seemed to take a very long time to switch between major modules in the Volume, User, and Access managers.

Table 9-3. Standard benchmarks on the Omninet

Program	Task	Time	
Lotus 1-2-3	Load program	11.3 seconds	
	Load worksheet	4.0 seconds	
	Print portion of work- sheet to spool file	4.3 seconds	
	File manager	Works OK	
	Copy protection	OK with key disk in workstation disk drive	
WordStar	Load program	6.1 seconds	
	Load document	3.0 seconds	
	Position to end of document	10.0 seconds	
	Append document	31.7 seconds	
	Save document and quit program	10.8 seconds	
	Printing	Works OK on network printer	
dBASE III	Load program	14.4 seconds	
	Run test program	5 mins. 27 seconds	
	Copy protection	OK with key disk in workstation disk drive	
		One workstation	Two workstations
BASICA	Sequential write	42 seconds	50.5 seconds
	Sequential read	34 seconds	39.5 seconds
	Random write	11 seconds	21 seconds
	Random read	7.5 seconds	15 seconds

Each workstation loses approximately 5 kilobytes of RAM for the CORDRV.BIN driver software necessary to get at the network. If you run the print spool driver, SPLDRV.BIN, you will dedicate another 4 kilobytes of RAM to this function. These are both low prices to pay for network access.

Table 9-3 shows the results of running the standard benchmarks on a one- and two-workstation Omninet system using a 5-megabyte OmniDrive server. Performance is quite reasonable, approaching normal hard disk speeds in many cases. In the multiuser case it bogged down only when running the random read test, which kept the OmniDrive busy almost constantly. Even in that test the time to run two users was only double the time to run one.

Novell NetWare/68 and S-Net

Hardware: S-Net Network Interface card
S-Net dedicated server

Software: Advanced NetWare Revision 1.0a

Manufacturer: Novell Incorporated
1170 North Industrial Park Drive
Orem, Utah 84057
801/226-8202

Cable type: Shielded twisted-pair, Belden #9302

Max length: 2000 feet from workstation to server

Topology: Star

Data rate: 600 kilobits per second, maximum cable length 500 feet
300 kilobits per second, maximum cable length 2000 feet

Protocol: Proprietary (dedicated cable per workstation)

Max nodes: 24 workstations per server
100 servers per network

10

NOVELL NETWARE

Novell has taken a unique approach to providing networks for the IBM PC. They provide network software (Novell NetWare) for PC network systems made by other manufacturers as well as their own. NetWare has an excellent reputation for performance and completeness. Many benchmarks run twice as fast under NetWare as under the hardware vendor's own software; some even run 10 times as fast.

NetWare provides a consistent user interface regardless of whether it is running on Novell hardware or another vendor's hardware. The unique features of a particular vendor's hardware are handled during installation. Although this chapter reviews NetWare on Novell hardware, most of the discussion also applies to NetWare on non-Novell hardware. Most differences between NetWare on Novell and on non-Novell hardware are in the installation steps.

NetWare lets you interconnect many dissimilar computers and PC networks. Figure 10-1 lists the hardware currently supported by NetWare. Many of these can be interconnected using Novell's Internetwork Gateway software. NetWare provides a common user and programmer interface on a system that contains more than one type of network or computer.

OVERVIEW

Novell sells two different series of network operating software. NetWare/68 runs on computers using Motorola's MC68000 series microprocessor, including Novell's proprietary network computer, S-Net. NetWare/86 is for the Intel 8086 family of microprocessors such as those used in the IBM PC family.

3Com EtherLink	Proteon ProNET
3M LAN/PC	Quadram Quadnet VI
AST PCnet II	Quadram Quadnet IX
Corvus Omninet	Santa Clara Systems
Davong MultiLink	PCnet
Gateway G-Net	Sperry USERNET
IBM PC Cluster	Standard Microsystems
IBM PC Network	ARCNET
Nestar Plan 2000	Televideo Personal Mini
Northstar Dimension	Texas Instruments
Orchid PCnet	EtherLink

Figure 10-1.   Hardware supported by NetWare

S-Net is a twisted-pair cable, star-structured network that uses Novell proprietary file servers at the hub of each star. Novell also distributes hardware, called G-Net, that runs NetWare/86. G-Net is a coaxial cable, bus-structured network that uses IBM PCs, XTs, or ATs with their own or Novell hard disks as servers. G-Net hardware is made by Gateway Communications, Inc. (it is not discussed in depth in this chapter). G-Net has much in common with other coaxial bus-structured networks, and once NetWare is installed, its user interface is identical to that described here for S-Net.

The revision of NetWare discussed in this chapter is called Advanced NetWare Version 1.0. It has many enhancements over earlier NetWare revisions, including support for multiple file servers, and remote connections via modems and phone lines between two or more Advanced NetWare systems. Unless otherwise stated, the term NetWare is used in this chapter to refer to Advanced NetWare Version 1.0.

S-Net uses a dedicated network server microcomputer that has a MC68000 microprocessor for its CPU. Rather than using a general-purpose computer like an IBM PC XT as a server, Novell designed a microcomputer specifically to perform file service and print service for a network.

The S-Net server microcomputer is a large box, 19 inches square by 7 1/2 inches high. It is built around a Novell proprietary card cage with eight slots that hold Novell printed circuit boards. The minimum configuration has three boards:

- The CPU card, with two RS-232 serial ports and the disk interface
- A memory card with at least 1 megabyte of RAM
- A LAN card for connecting from one to six workstations.

The RS-232 serial ports are for a console and a network printer. You need a 24-line by 80-column terminal to operate the server; almost any inexpensive terminal with cursor addressing can be used. The network printer port is a standard RS-232 serial port. You can add four more printer ports with an add-on card. The popular Centronics parallel printer interface is not supported.

Memory can be expanded up to 8 megabytes. You can add up to three more LAN cards to connect a total of 24 workstations to a single server. You can also connect multiple servers together on a single network. If you do so, Novell recommends running two cables between the two servers, using two LAN ports on each server.

Novell NetWare disk subsystems provide network file service. Each subsystem holds one or two disk drives, and you can connect up to eight subsystems to a single file server. Novell offers many disk drives of different capacities, and the ability to chain up to eight together lets you produce a very large file system.

The NetWare software provides true file service, not disk service. Chapter 3 describes the difference between these two in detail. In addition to an extensive set of network operating software, NetWare includes an electronic mail package, plus software to back up network disks to local disk drives, other network servers, and network tape drives.

Figure 10-2 shows an S-Net network. It contains two network servers with disk subsystems, eight IBM PC workstations, and two network printers. Each workstation on this typical network has 256 kilobytes of RAM and one floppy disk drive. Novell sells a plug-in chip called a Remote System Reset PROM for the S-Net cards that lets you use diskless IBM PCs as workstations.

Network Architecture

S-Net uses shielded twisted-pair cable. You connect each workstation with a single cable to the server, in a star configuration. Unlike most of the other PC networks discussed in this book, NetWare/86 does not have a

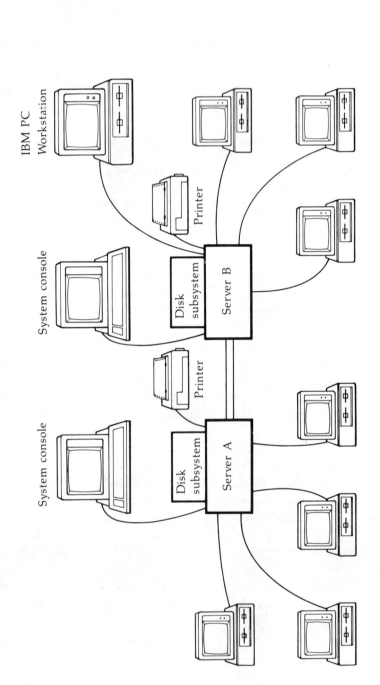

Figure 10-2. Typical Novell S-Net network

network bus; a separate cable connects the server and each workstation.

Novell calls a NetWare network with more than one server an *internetwork*. The wiring between S-Net servers is very flexible. Each workstation needs at least one path to each server it accesses, and that path can wind through multiple servers. You can connect up to 100 servers in an internetwork, and each server can have up to 24 workstations. If you connect the servers in a chain, you can have an additional workstation connected to each server at the end of the chain for a total of 2202 workstations on a very large internetwork.

Messages travel across the cables one at a time. You can analyze your network traffic pattern and find the bottlenecks, then add more cables at these points to improve performance. More cables allow more messages to pass between the servers concurrently, and thus support more network traffic in the same amount of time.

S-Net supports two different speeds. The high speed is 600 kilobits per second, while the low speed is 300 kilobits per second. High-speed cables must be no more than 500 feet long, while low-speed cables can be up to 2000 feet long. These guidelines are for connecting either workstations to servers or servers to servers.

Since every cable connects only two network nodes, no collision detection protocol is needed. If you have to wait for a network service, it is because the server is busy handling another request, not because the network cable is in use. However, if you are requesting something from a server you are not directly connected to, your request may queue up at an intermediate stop until there is a clear line to that server.

Workstations and Servers

Novell supports several different microcomputers as workstations, including the IBM PC, PC XT, PC Portable, and PC AT, as well as the Texas Instruments TI Professional and the Victor 9000. Each workstation needs a Network Interface card (also called an NIC). You must have the network interface software installed in each different type of microcomputer, but you can connect different types of workstations to the same network.

The IBM PCs you use as workstations should have at least 128 kilobytes of memory, and 192 kilobytes to run under PC-DOS 3.0 or higher revisions. You can use diskless workstations as previously described, but at least one PC on the network must have a disk drive to load the network software. NetWare/86 takes up about 23 kilobytes of memory on each workstation.

If you want to share printers on the LAN, you must connect them to an S-Net server. You can connect local printers to any workstation, but they can be accessed only by programs running on that workstation. The S-Net server comes standard with one serial printer port and has room for four more serial ports.

Novell sells a 60-megabyte tape backup that connects directly to the server and backs it up at a rate of about 2 megabytes per minute. The server must be off-line while the backup is in progress. Novell also supports the Alloy PC Backup and the Mountain Hardware tape cartridge systems for network backup. Either system must be connected to a workstation on the network.

INSTALLATION

S-Net, and Novell NetWare in general, takes longer to install than many competing products. The resulting network, however, has more features than most other PC networks. NetWare is more complex than others chiefly because it is a file server rather than a disk server. As such, NetWare has its own operating system and file structure, which must be installed first. Advanced NetWare must be entirely installed by the user; the older NetWare software is installed on the server at the factory. After the file server is installed and running, you can set up the rest of the network, establishing disk directories, user names, and passwords.

The S-Net hardware is easy to install on workstations, and somewhat complex to install on servers. The workstation network cards simply plug into an available full-size slot in a PC. Depending on how much extra hardware you have, putting the S-Net server together is similar to setting up a small microcomputer system that has multiple plug-in cards and connectors.

S-Net cabling can quickly become expensive, since you need a separate cable from each workstation to its server. The wiring job itself is easy.

Planning the Hardware
Installation

When you plan an S-Net network, you should keep in mind that each LAN card can connect up to six workstations and that each server can have four LAN cards (workstations use one port each, and Novell recommends that servers use two ports to connect to each adjacent server). If your system has more than one server, you must decide how to interconnect them. Figure 10-3 shows several possible server-connection schemes. The ring

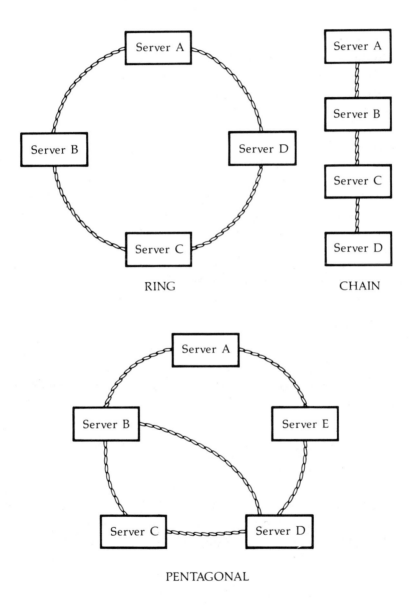

RING

CHAIN

PENTAGONAL

Figure 10-3.   Possible server connections

and chain configurations are general-purpose setups guaranteed to allow every workstation access to every server. The pentagonal configuration adds two cables between servers B and D to speed up network traffic between them. This configuration would be appropriate if, for example, you determine that workstations connected to server D need frequent access to files stored on server B.

You can add cables at any time, and the network learns about the new connection within 30 seconds. This is an extremely handy feature, since you can experiment with improving the system performance without reconfiguring the network software.

The number of servers that you need depends on your network applications and data storage requirements. For instance, if you can partition your users on many servers, you may be able to improve performance.

If you need a great deal of network file storage, you must decide how many disk subsystems to buy and where to connect them. Each subsystem can hold two disk drives, and you can connect up to eight subsystems to a single server. There is a cost/performance trade-off, however, since you must access all these disk drives through a single server. Better network performance may be had by using more servers and connecting fewer drives to each. You are better off starting with one or two disk subsystems and expanding, if you need the space and the server can handle its current load.

You should also plan the location of network printers. Any printers that are going to be shared must be connected to S-Net servers (the cable can be up to 50 feet long). Local printers can be installed on workstation PCs in the usual way.

Planning the Software Installation

After you decide how to position and wire your workstations, printers, and servers, you can start planning the network software installation. NetWare has many options, including one of the most comprehensive security systems of any PC network. Coming up with the right setup for your needs can take quite a bit of study and planning. On the other hand, you can change many individual selections without having to reinstall the entire network. Also, you don't have to decide in advance how much disk space to allocate to each user, since NetWare allocates disk space on a first-come first-served basis.

The most complex part of NetWare is the security system. It uses concepts similar to minicomputer and mainframe operating systems, such as groups of users with the same privileges; access rights at the user, directory, and file levels; password protection on user names; and rules for passing access rights from one user to another. If you need tight or selective control over the security of data in your network, Novell's security is among the best. But if security is not important, you can choose to operate with no passwords and give everyone access to everything.

NetWare is a file server with its own operating system. The S-Net server's hard disk contains this file system, and it looks very much like MS-DOS's hierarchical directory structure with several extensions. Each workstation user can map directories on any server to any one of 26 MS-DOS drive letters. For example, the file server may be mapped to drive C on your workstation. Each disk drive connected to a server must have at least one volume. Novell recommends that you create one volume per drive. You can control user access to files completely at the directory level, so there is no need to create different volumes for security.

You can assign access control individually to each directory on a file server. Nobody but the SUPERVISOR, a special user, can get around this access control. Table 10-1 lists the privileges that can be offered or denied to every user for every directory. *Parental rights* include the ability to create, rename, and delete subdirectories in a directory, and to set access control information in this directory and its subdirectories.

Table 10-1.   Directory access rights

Access	Meaning
R	Read open files in the directory
W	Write open files in the directory
O	Open existing files
C	Create and open new files
D	Delete existing files
P	Parental rights to the directory
S	Search for files in the directory
M	Modify the attributes of files in the directory

Table 10-2.   File attributes

Access	Meaning
Normal	Equivalent to nonshareable, read/write
Shareable	May be accessed by more than one user at a time
Nonshareable	May be accessed by only one user at a time
Read/write	May be read, written, and deleted
Read-only	Can only be read

If you are using password protection in your installation, you must assign rights to users or groups of users for each directory created on the file server. No user can access a directory until the supervisor gives that user, or the group the user belongs to, privileges in the directory.

If several users need the same access rights to several files, you can create a group for those users. For example, you might create a group called SECRETARIES, and make all the secretaries members. You can then add or delete access rights for the entire group of secretaries at once.

If the directory's access control restricts certain actions, such as deleting files, no one but the supervisor can perform those actions in that directory even if the user's privileges allow them. Finally, associated with each file in a directory are certain attributes, listed in Table 10-2. Many other PC networks allow this level of control only at the volume level.

NetWare lets you have shareable and nonshareable files in the same directory. If a file is read-only, then no one can modify or delete it, even if that user has the rights to do so in the directory. Read/write files can be written or deleted as well as read, as long as the user has the proper access rights to the directory.

A user can have the same or different names on multiple servers. Before you can access files on a server, you must log in to that server with the LOGIN command. If your system is password-protected, you have to supply the password associated with your user name when you log in.

Doing the Installation

You should carefully read the Novell documentation before starting the installation. NetWare is a complete operating system and employs many concepts unique to it. It is helpful if you have experience with operating systems other than MS-DOS. The NetWare concepts are not difficult, but in comparison to a network that is purely an extension to MS-DOS, Net-Ware presents a lot more to learn.

Physical Installation You can start the installation at the S-Net server. If you have ordered additional memory or LAN cards, you must open the server and install them. The documentation for this is not clear, although the process is straightforward if you have done similar work on other micros. If you have never opened a computer, you should have your dealer or a consultant install the boards for you.

If any of your cables are longer than 500 feet, you must purchase pre-modified LAN boards or modify the LAN boards yourself to run at slow speed. This involves cutting a trace on the printed circuit board and soldering in a jumper wire. You should be comfortable with doing this kind of work before you try it on a LAN card.

Associated with each new LAN card you install is a bank of six nine-pin DIN connectors, as you can see in the drawing of the server's back panel in Figure 10-4. Four screws hold each assembly of six connectors in place,

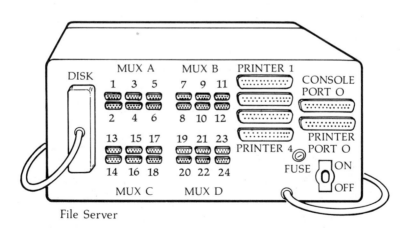

Figure 10-4.   Back panel of S-Net server (courtesy Novell, Inc.)

and a ribbon cable carries the signals from the LAN card to the connector bank. The details of how to do this are not described in the documentation, although by examining the LAN card already installed in the server you can determine how to proceed. The LAN cards are manufactured for a particular group of port addresses, so you must connect the card to the correct group.

Next you can install the disk subsystems. Novell supplies a 3-foot cable that connects the back panel of the S-Net server to the back panel of the disk subsystem. Because of the length of this cable, the disk subsystem must be either on top of or next to the file server.

If you have more than one disk subsystem, you must chain them together, connecting each to the adjacent one with the 3-foot cables. Figure 10-5 shows such a configuration for three disk subsystems. Each disk subsystem is manufactured to occupy a particular position in the chain, and the system numbered "zero" should be at the end of the chain furthest from the server. Novell recommends that higher-numbered systems be positioned in ascending order as they get closer to the server.

Each file server must have a console, or terminal, attached to it. Novell provides an 8-foot cable, or you can build one up to 50 feet long if necessary. The console port on the server is a standard DB25 RS-232 connector. Many brands of terminals will work as the console.

Next you connect any shared printers to the server. The server has one RS-232 serial port for network printers, and you can add an expansion card that gives you four more serial ports.

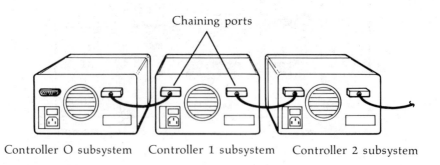

Chaining ports

Controller O subsystem   Controller 1 subsystem   Controller 2 subsystem

Figure 10-5.   Chaining three disk subsystems (courtesy Novell, Inc.)

If your system has more than one file server, Novell recommends that they be connected together by at least two cables each. You can add more cables later, even while the system is running, to improve performance. The system determines the shortest path by which to send a message to another server, and it also learns how many cables connect it to each server, then uses them all.

Each workstation PC on the network must have a Network Interface card. The cards require very little configuration. You must set a jumper if you are running at low speed, and install the Remote Reset PROM chip if your workstation has no diskette drive.

The final step of installing the hardware is to wire the workstations to the server. The recommended cable is Belden #9302, shielded twisted-pair, terminated with nine-pin DIN connectors. You can purchase ready-made cables from Novell or build your own. The wiring at the workstation end differs from that at the server end. If you use Novell's ready-made cables, be sure to observe the marking on each end that specifies whether it is the workstation or server end, and orient it appropriately before installing it.

Installing the System Software   There are many steps in installing the S-Net software, and although the manual is very thorough, you should plan on spending at least several hours, depending on the size and complexity of your S-Net. There are three main steps:

- Initializing the servers
- Initializing the workstations
- Creating users, directories, and groups.

If you wish to run under Advanced Netware, the software reviewed in this chapter, the first step is time-consuming but straightforward: you must generate the operating system that runs on the file server. The manual provides a reasonable explanation of each question and how to answer it, and default values are usually offered by the software. If you are using the simpler NetWare software, this installation step has been done for you by Novell. You only need do it if you want to change the system parameters.

Configuring the workstations is very simple. If you have diskless workstations there is nothing to do. If you have a disk drive, you need to make sure that two programs can be run so that you can access the network.

Creating users, directories, and groups requires the most planning, but you can modify your initial settings later. The major source of complexity is security; if security is not important, you won't have to think much about it. If security is important and you have a diverse user community with many different access levels, you should spend extra planning time in this area.

Server file system initialization is similar to a hard disk installation in an IBM PC or PC XT. The disk drive is formatted at the factory, so you will rarely have to perform this step. Most of the work gets done by the SYS-GEN.I program; it creates volumes on the disk drive, divides memory among various server functions, and defines peripherals attached to the server such as disk drives, printers, and the console.

Since there is no floppy disk drive on the server, you need to have a PC connected via the network to load the system software. This workstation PC can be connected to any one of the first six LAN ports. During installation you need to have access to both the PC and the server console, so you may want to temporarily locate a PC near the server.

When you turn on the file server, it displays the Novell copyright banner and then displays the question whether it should load from the PC.

Press the L key on the console and the server responds

```
Loading...
```

and waits for you to run the LOAD program on the PC. You must insert the Installation Utilities diskette in a PC drive and give the command

```
LOAD SYSGEN.I
```

SYSGEN.I begins executing on the server, and you interact with it through the server's console. It asks you a series of questions related to the configuration of the server. Allowable answers are usually provided with the question, and the manual explains what the different answers mean. The first set of answers tells NetWare:

- The number and types of disk subsystems attached to the server
- The number of printers attached and their communication parameters
- How to control the server's console, including how to position the cursor and clear the screen.

You next tell NetWare how to allocate the server's memory. A portion of server memory can be used for *cache* (disk information) that has been recently accessed. Novell provides a great deal of flexibility here. You can make the cache blocks 512, 1024, 2048, or 4096 bytes long. Larger cache blocks mean fewer total blocks can be kept in memory. If your applications access many small pieces of data that are widely separated in a file or in different files, a smaller block size may yield higher performance. Since this is a performance tuning mechanism, you can experiment with this setting.

Another question asks how many *routing buffers* to reserve. A routing buffer holds messages that come from workstations and are destined for other servers. Novell recommends 50 buffers minimum plus 10 for each line connected to another server.

The final questions asked by the SYSGEN.I program refer to creating disk volumes. Novell's security mechanism gives you control over disk data at the directory level, and unless you have a compelling need to do otherwise, you should allocate all the disk space to a single volume. The volume named SYS is automatically created for you by SYSGEN, and it holds all the NetWare operating software. Several directories are automatically created in SYS. Table 10-3 lists them and describes their contents.

You next run LOAD on your PC again and load the file named NET$OS.SYS from the "System Files" diskette. This is the NetWare operating system. After the loading finishes, the operating system starts running and prompts you for the date and time on the server console.

The file server prompt appears on the console and the server is ready to accept console commands. Table 10-4 lists some of the commands that are used to control the server.

Next you complete the server installation process by loading the NetWare utility files from the PC. To do so you log onto the network from the PC workstation and copy files from a diskette to the server. This process parallels the everyday use of the network from a workstation.

You first run either ANET20S or ANET30S to install the network shell software on the workstation. This software is called a *shell* because it sits

Table 10-3.   Directories created by SYSGEN.I

Directory	Contents
SYSTEM	NetWare operating system and supervisor utilities
LOGIN	LOGIN program and SLIST (lists all servers)
PUBLIC	User commands and common programs

Table 10-4.   Server console commands

Command	Purpose
BROADCAST	Send message to all workstations
CLEAR MESSAGE	Clear message line on console
CLEAR STATION	Force log-out of a workstation
DISABLE LOGIN	Prevent any more workstations from logging in
DOWN	Shut down the server
ENABLE LOGIN	Allow workstations to log in to the server
NAME	Display the name of the file server
SEND	Send a message to workstations
SET TIME	Set server time and date
TIME	Display server time and date

between your applications programs and the operating system like a shell around the operating system. You use ANET20S if your workstation is running MS-DOS version 2.0, 2.10, or 2.11 or use ANET30S if you are running MS-DOS Version 3.0 or higher. If everything is working, when you type ANET30S on your PC, the system responds with the familiar "A>" prompt. (The "A>" prompt comes from MS-DOS on your PC, *not* the server.)

When the NetWare shell sees a request that needs to go to the network, such as a request to read from a network file or print to a network printer, it intercepts that request and sends it down the net. This software must be loaded whenever you start your workstation, and the appropriate command (ANET20S or ANET30S) should be added to your AUTOEXEC.BAT file.

Even though the workstation interface software is now loaded and running, you cannot access files on the server until you identify yourself to the server. This is done with the LOGIN command. LOGIN establishes the connection between your workstation and the server. Since you are still setting up the network software, you should log in as the supervisor:

`LOGIN SUPERVISOR`

The LOGIN command requires that a password be supplied as well as a user name. When you first install the system software, SUPERVISOR does not have a password. You should assign one as soon as possible, since unauthorized users who log in as supervisors can access anything on the network. You must also be very careful not to lose the supervisor's password. If you do, you may have to rebuild your entire network from scratch. You can have more than one supervisor on a network, and this multiplicity of passwords is a good way to prevent such a catastrophe from happening.

After you have logged in, your PC displays something like this:

```
Good afternoon, SUPERVISOR.
Drive A     maps to a local disk.
Drive B     maps to a local disk.
Drive C := SERVER00/SYS:SYSTEM
Drive D := SERVER00/SYS:LOGIN
Drive Z := SERVER00/SYS:PUBLIC
           -----
SEARCH1 := Z:. [SERVER00/SYS:PUBLIC]

A>
```

This greeting tells you how the MS-DOS drive letters are mapped to local and network directories. In this case, the workstation has two local diskette drives A and B, and they continue to be referred to by those names. Two network directories are assigned to MS-DOS drives C and D. The SYS:PUBLIC directory on this server (named SERVER00) is assigned to drive Z. Z is used instead of E because Z is a *search directory.*

A search directory is automatically searched whenever the NetWare software can't find a file in the current MS-DOS directory. Search directories are lettered in reverse order from Z to K. You can have up to 16 search directories at one time. In the preceding example, the SYS:PUBLIC directory is set up as the only search directory. This is where you might store programs and files that all users need to access.

Next copy the NetWare software onto the file server. Put the System Files diskette into the PC's drive A and copy its files to the SYS:SYSTEM directory using the MS-DOS copy command:

```
COPY A:*.* C:
```

Since drive C has been mapped to SYS:SYSTEM, all the files from drive A are copied to SYS:SYSTEM. You also use the copy command to copy the contents of the "Login Files" diskette to D, the SYS:LOGIN directory, and the several "Public Files" diskettes to Z, the SYS:PUBLIC directory.

Since anyone can access the PUBLIC directory (unless you change this default setup), you should protect those files from modification. The Net-Ware FLAG command protects the files. Make the directory the current MS-DOS directory by typing **Z:** at the MS-DOS prompt, then type

```
FLAG *.* SRO
```

This makes all the files shareable, meaning that more than one user can access them at a time, and read-only, meaning that no user can modify or delete them. You should do this to all the files you loaded in SYS:SYSTEM and SYS:LOGIN.

At this point you have a basic working S-Net system. For it to be useful for your applications, you need to set up user names, groups, and directories with the SYSCON command. This is a menu-driven, full-screen utility that uses pop-up windows to display information and interact with you. Only supervisors can run SYSCON.

From the main screen of SYSCON, you can create, display, modify, and delete user names, group names, and directories on the file server, and list the names of network servers. This screen is shown in Figure 10-6. The first thing you should do is create the directories to hold your applications and data files. When you select a directory, you can specify the

- Users who can access the directory.
- Maximum allowed access to the directory.
- Date and time of creation (modifying that automatically supplied by the system).
- Owner of the directory.

SYSCON provides a consistent response to commands and makes good use of the PC keyboard. If there is more than one window on the screen, as is often the case, the active window's border is brighter than the inactive window's. SYSCON's ease of use puts some fun into what might otherwise be a tedious activity.

When you are finished creating directories, you should create users and groups. Pressing INS causes the box in Figure 10-7 to pop up, and you type in the name of the new user. SYSCON blanks the screen and displays the menu of access details you can set up about this new user. You first establish a password. Next you should set up security equivalences—

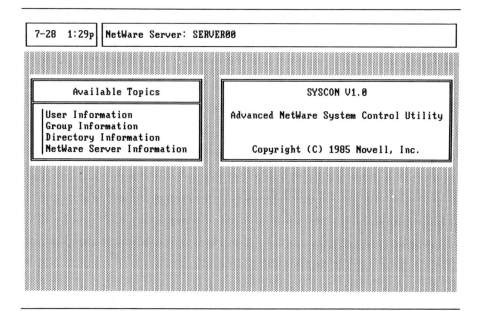

Figure 10-6.   Main screen of SYSCON

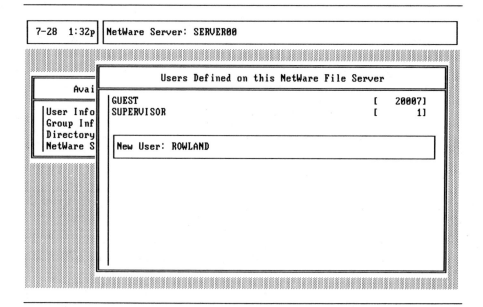

Figure 10-7.   Adding a new user

names of users or groups that this user is equivalent to. Trustee assignments are the directories that this user can access. For each such assignment, you can specify exactly which rights the user has. The Full Name entry lets you store more information about the user, such as his or her full name. The next selection, Groups Belonged To, lets you add this user to a group or groups. By doing so, this user gets all the rights assigned to that group. By default, all users are assigned to the group EVERYONE. This default may save you some time in assigning access rights if most network users need a common set of privileges.

Next you should establish user groups. The Group Information selection from the main screen gives you the list of groups currently defined. You can select an existing group, such as EVERYONE, or define a new group.

A restricted version of SYSCON, called MYCON, is available for non-supervisors. It lets you view and modify most of the information (except for sensitive information such as passwords) that SYSCON does. It allows users to modify directory structures in the directories they have access to, and to grant access rights in them to other users.

USING NETWARE/68 AND S-NET

Much of the mechanics of your daily starting up and accessing the network has already been covered, since you need to do both during the installation of system software. In summary, the daily startup process is:

1. Turn on the server and disk subsystem and press the Reset button
2. Enter the date and time when prompted on the server console
3. Boot MS-DOS on your workstation and give the ANET20S or ANET30S command
4. LOGIN with your user name and password.

Steps 3 and 4 can be automated by including them in an AUTOEXEC.BAT file. At this point you have access to a pre-determined set of directories on the server. You can use most MS-DOS commands to run programs and access files in these directories. Table 10-5 lists commands that either don't work on network disks and printers or have restrictions. These commands function as before on local disks and printers. For all these commands Novell provides functional equivalents that can take full advantage of the

Table 10-5.   MS-DOS commands restricted on the network

MS-DOS Command	Restriction
BACKUP	Can't handle multiple disk subsystems on a file server
CD	Works within a single server
CHKDSK	Doesn't work at all
COPY	Works within a single volume
DIR	Works within a single volume
PRINT	Prints to local printer
RESTORE	Same as BACKUP

enhanced network environment. The set of new commands available is listed in Table 10-6.

The MAP command may be used to change the assignment of MS-DOS drive letter to file server directory. MAP lets you set each of the 26 letters A: through Z: to a different directory, on up to eight different servers at once. You can also establish up to 16 search directories, as described earlier in the chapter.

Further automation of your initial environment is possible with the SETLOGIN command. A SETLOGIN script is equivalent to an MS-DOS AUTOEXEC batch file, except that it is run only when a user logs in. It is commonly used to MAP the directories you frequently use, although the scope of commands available, shown in Table 10-7, suggests many other possibilities, including running programs and connecting to other servers.

PRINT MANAGEMENT

Network print service on Novell's S-Net is provided by printers attached to the server. You cannot share printers attached to workstations. A server can have from one to five serial printers attached.

Using the network printers is very simple. From a workstation, execute the SPOOL command. SPOOL maps LPT1: to the specified network printer. Any application that uses MS-DOS system calls to print to LPT1: can

Table 10-6.   NetWare user commands

Command	Function
ATTACH	Connect to a server on an internetwork
CASTOFF	Disable messages from other workstations or the console
CASTON	Enable messages from other workstations and the console
CHKVOL	Like MS-DOS CHKDSK command
FLAG	Modify file attributes
LISTDIR	List subdirectories and access rights
NCOPY	Copy files within internetwork directories
NSNIPES	Network maze game
PURGE	Permanently erase files marked for deletion
Q(ueue)	Display print server information
RIGHTS	Display your privileges in a directory
SALVAGE	Recover accidentally erased files
SEND	Send messages to other workstations or the console
SETPASS	Set your password
SHOWDIR	Display directory structure of a volume, drive, or directory
SYSTIME	Show file server's date and time
UDIR	Search in a directory and its subdirectories for a file
USERLIST	Show names of users currently logged on
VOLINFO	Display free disk space for all volumes of a server
WHOAMI	Show your user name and security data

now print automatically to the network printer. Print output is saved in a file until the ENDSPOOL command is issued. At that time, the spool file output is placed in the network server's print queue and is printed as soon as the printer is available.

Another way to print a file is with the NPRINT command. NPRINT takes most of the options of the SPOOL command, but it specifies a file or list of files to print. NPRINT does not remap LPT1:, and it does not require you to issue the ENDSPOOL command to start printing.

Table 10-7.   SETLOGIN script commands

Command	Function
ATTACH	Log in to an inter-network server
MAP	Map an MS-DOS drive letter to a server directory
COMSPEC	Tell MS-DOS where to find COMMAND.COM
INCLUDE	Execute another log-in script
DRIVE	Make a new drive the MS-DOS default
WRITE	Send messages to the workstation
IF...THEN	Conditionally execute part of a log-in script
#	Run an MS-DOS program
EXIT	Terminate the script and optionally execute a command
BREAK	Enable or disable interruption of the script from the workstation keyboard
DOS BREAK	Activate or disable MS-DOS's check for keyboard interruption of executing programs
DISPLAY	Show the contents of a text file on the screen
FDISPLAY	Like DISPLAY, plus filter out non-ASCII characters
REMARK	Insert a comment in a script file
FIRE PHASERS	Generate a beeping noise at the workstation

LOGIN, LOGOUT, SPOOL, and NPRINT perform an automatic ENDSPOOL command. Thus, if your workstation hangs up or crashes, when you LOGIN to the server again, your print output on the server is printed. Applications programs can also send the equivalent of an END-SPOOL, so custom programs setup for NetWare can use network printers without user intervention.

You can have up to five printers on a server, and you can NPRINT files to more than one server at a time. You cannot establish spooled connections to more than one printer at a time, since NetWare does not handle more than one logical printer at the workstation. In other words, you cannot establish that LPT1: is a printer on one server and LPT2: is a printer on another server.

Many commands can be executed from the server console to control network printers. NetWare provides an extensive set of commands, including some that are unusual on PC networks, such as a command for changing the order in which queued files are printed.

SECURITY

NetWare's security system is among the most comprehensive and selective available on any PC network. Many systems rely on passwords as the principal means of protection. With NetWare, the password is only the key to get in the first door. You cannot access any file unless the system administrator has explicitly granted you access to its parent directory. The type of access you may have is also controlled more selectively than in most competing systems. Any combination of reading, writing, opening, creating, and deleting files, modifying file attributes, searching directories, and parental rights (ownership) to directories may be specified.

There can even be blanket restrictions on access to directories themselves. The maximum rights mask, specified with the SYSCON utility, may prevent all users from having any combination of the above privileges, regardless of the general access rights granted to any individual user.

The concepts of groups and granting of access privileges from one user to another is also unusual in a PC network. Once a group has been given an appropriate set of privileges, a single user can be given those privileges simply by being made a member of that group. You can temporarily give another user access to your files by the same means. This method is far simpler than having to specify all the privileges individually for each user needing them. Users can pass their privileges to other users with the MYCON utility program.

MULTIUSER SUPPORT

Novell's NetWare provides one of the best multiuser support systems in PC networks. Since it is a true file server, rather than a disk server, the operating system running on the file server mediates access to data.

What this means in practice is that NetWare prevents many more accidental data-update collisions between users and applications programs than a disk server possibly can. The best solution is still to use software written for a network environment, but if you have to run single-user software, you are less likely to accidentally overwrite important information with a file server system such as NetWare.

Files can be fully shared with NetWare. Two users can run applications that write to different parts of the same file, as long as their applications are programmed to do this properly. Users can always write to different files in the same directory, assuming they have the proper access rights. If a file is marked nonshareable, then NetWare prevents two or more users from accidentally attempting to modify it at the same time. For example, suppose you have a large text file that many people in your department must update. You should mark it nonshareable so that only one user can modify it at a time.

Novell provides an extensive set of software interfaces to enable programmers to write network applications. Several unusual locking mechanisms are available. The read-only lock can be applied to a range of bytes in a file. More than one user can lock the same range for read-only access, since there is no harm in letting several users read the same information. As long as at least one user has the range locked in this way, no program can lock that same range for read/write access.

Only one program can hold a read/write lock on a given range of a file. Read/write is an exclusive lock; the read-only lock is a shared lock. Both kinds of locks can be requested with timeouts. If the requested lock is not available, control returns to the applications program after the specified time has elapsed.

In addition to these locking mechanisms, a general-purpose semaphore is provided. The semaphore is not given a specific meaning by the system, whereas the record locks are used to lock part of a file. Thus, the semaphore is a general-purpose synchronization mechanism that allows applications or systems programs to coordinate access to any shared network resource. Whatever program defines the semaphore is the one that establishes its meaning; NetWare simply provides the mechanism.

UTILITIES

NetWare includes an excellent electronic mail system. In addition to sending memos to other users or lists of users, you can mail files or groups of files. Mail can be forwarded to other users, and express mail notifies the recipient immediately with a message on the 25th line of the screen. The mail system is command driven but includes a help facility. The commands are fairly easy to remember. Thanks to the security of the system, it is easy to protect your mail from access by other users.

Another excellent feature of NetWare is Remote Workstation access to a network. All the software you need is provided to access a remote NetWare network by modem over the telephone lines. You must have a modem at each end of the phone line, and the appropriate interface cards for connecting the modems to your PCs. A workstation must be dedicated to this function at the server side of the connection.

Table 10-8.   Supervisor utilities

Utility	Function
CPMOFF	Don't automatically open closed files
CPMON	Automatically open closed files
EOJOFF	Don't automatically close files when program ends
EOJON	Automatically close files when program ends
HIDEFILE	Make a file invisible
SHOWFILE	Make a hidden file visible

A very useful HELP program is provided with NetWare/68. It has a full-screen display and uses many of the same keyboard conventions as SYSCON.

Table 10-8 lists the utilities available for system supervisors. The CPMOFF and CPMON utilities adapt an S-Net system to an oddity of the CP/M operating system that was implemented in MS-DOS as well: application programs can access a file after closing it without first reopening it. By contrast, NetWare really closes the file, and your program cannot access the file unless it is reopened. The CPMON command tells NetWare to emulate the CP/M convention. EOJON and EOJOFF have related functions. NetWare normally closes all files in use by a program when it terminates. These commands let you activate or disable this feature.

```
 ┌─ANetWare/S V1.0 (3/1/85)─┬─Percent Utilization - 20 ─┬─Disk  I/O Pending - 4 ──
 │ Stn 1: Read File          │ Stn 2: Write File          │ Stn 3: End Of Job
 │
 │ File              Stat   │ File              Stat     │ File              Stat
 │ F:68-SYS-A.SEC    PRPW   │ F86:SYS-D.SEC     PRPW      │ F:68-SYS-C.SEC    PRPW
 │ Z:WSOVLY1         R      │ Z:WSOVLY1         R         │ Z:WSOVLY1         R
 │ Z:WSMSGS.OVR      R      │ Z:WSMSGS.OVR      R         │ Z:WSMSGS.OVR      R
 │ P:NEWFIGURE       PRPW   │ C:ENTERTAI.KRI    PRPW      │ P:OLDFILES        PRPW
 ├──────────────────────────┼────────────────────────────┼──────────────────────────
 │ Stn 4:                   │ Stn 5:                     │ Stn 6:
 │ File              Stat   │ File              Stat     │ File              Stat
 │
 └──────────────────────────┴────────────────────────────┴──────────────────────────
```

Figure 10-8.   Typical MONITOR display (courtesy Novell, Inc.)

HIDEFILE and SHOWFILE let you make files invisible or visible. If a file is invisible, it does not show up when a user lists the contents of the directory. This is yet another protection mechanism.

The server console can run a system utility called MONITOR. Figure 10-8 shows a typical MONITOR display. For each workstation connected to a server, MONITOR shows the files it is using, the attributes of that file, and how the workstation is accessing the server (reading or writing, for example). It also gives an estimate of server load in percentage form, and the number of disk cache buffers in use but not yet flushed back to disk. This tool is very helpful for determining the load on a server and showing you how to balance the load if you have more than one server.

Backing up the Server

Backup of network files can be done to local disks on workstations, a different file server's hard disk, or a cartridge tape drive. A different set of commands is provided to do each network backup chore. LARCHIVE works with local floppy or hard disks. You can give a file specification or interact with the LARCHIVE command and have it query you whether to back up files matching a specification. You can skip individual files or entire directories. You can also request that LARCHIVE back up only files that have been modified since they were last backed up. LARCHIVE splits large files across multiple floppy disks if necessary. A report of the entire LARCHIVE process can be saved to disk or printed out. The LRESTORE command reads the archived disk or disks and restores the backup to the file server.

NARCHIVE has the same options as LARCHIVE but writes to a network drive instead of a local drive. Additional facilities handle locked files and inaccessible volumes. NRESTORE is the companion program for NARCHIVE.

TARCHIVE works much like LARCHIVE and NARCHIVE, but with the difference that its destination is magnetic tape. Files can be split among more than one tape if necessary. Special options let you save user and group definitions, save directory rights and trustee lists, append to the end of the tape, and skip locked files. TRESTORE reads from the archive and writes to the file server.

DOCUMENTATION

Novell's documentation is clearly written, and the organization makes sense after you get used to the system. Part of the initial difficulty with the manuals may stem from the system supervisor's needing to know much of what is presented in three of the manuals in order to properly configure the system, so some juggling and cross-referencing is inevitable. The lack of an index in any of the manuals hampers this effort, although the table of contents is helpful.

The manuals are standard small IBM PC-size, three-ring notebooks. Sections include the table of contents, a preface that overviews the manual, a very thorough glossary of terms, an overview of NetWare/68, and a discussion of system security concepts. The next section tells you how to use your workstation, assuming a supervisor has already set up the system. This is followed by an alphabetical list of user commands, presented in IBM PC-DOS manual style, giving for each command its purpose, format, remarks, and examples. The Electronic Mail system is described in the next section, followed by an appendix describing how to use the Advanced Net-Ware/68 Remote Workstation.

Given the range of hardware that is covered, it is understandable that it is sometimes difficult to find the answer to specific hardware-related questions. This orientation also makes it hard to provide a step-by-step approach, since many things must be discussed generically.

EXPANDING THE NETWORK

S-Net is easily expandable. New workstations are simply plugged into an available server. By running SYSCON, the supervisor can create a directory for the new user without having to juggle allocations of disk space among volumes as on a disk server.

Additional servers can be connected and the system automatically adjusts to their presence. Of course, you must perform the entire system software installation process on each new server, setting up volumes and directories and granting access to them via SYSCON. You do not have to update existing servers or workstation software, however.

You can add network printers, but you must change the SYSGEN information. You have to take the network down in order to do this, but you don't have to reload any network software.

PERFORMANCE

The S-Net server was designed to handle network operations, and one of its strongest traits is performance. It showed almost no performance degradation when a second user was added. Since every user has a dedicated

Table 10-9. Standard benchmarks on NetWare

Program	Task	Time	
Lotus 1-2-3	Load program	6.1 seconds	
	Load worksheet	3.7 seconds	
	Print portion of worksheet to spool file	1.4 seconds	
	File manager	works OK	
	Copy protection	OK with key disk in workstation disk drive	
WordStar	Load program	5.0 seconds	
	Load document	2.4 seconds	
	Position to end of document	8.9 seconds	
	Append document	21.9 seconds	
	Save document and quit program	6.7 seconds	
	Printing	works OK on network printer	
dBASE III	Load program	did not work	
BASICA	Sequential write	41.0 seconds	41.0 seconds
	Sequential read	32.1 seconds	32.1 seconds
	Random write	8.8 seconds	9.5 seconds
	Random read	7.2 seconds	7.2 seconds

connection to the server, there is no contention for the network cable. Novell's software also helps, as many benchmarks have shown it to be among the fastest on many vendors' hardware. The dBASE III benchmarks could not be run, since dBASE III would not run under the network shell software (the older Ashton-Tate product, dBASE II, worked fine). Ashton-Tate has announced a version of dBASE III that runs under NetWare, but it was not available in time for this review.

Table 10-9 gives the results of the benchmarks that ran successfully. Keep in mind that your software may require that you use the CPMON or EOJOFF supervisor commands. Novell or your software vendor may answer relevant questions.

Orchid PCnet

Hardware:	Orchid PCnet Network Interface card Orchid Blossom Multi-function plus network interface card
Software:	PCnet Revision 3.0
Manufacturer:	Orchid Technology, Inc. 47790 Westinghouse Drive Fremont, CA 94539 415/490-8586
Cable type:	Coaxial cable, RG 59B/U, Belden 8263 for up to 3000 feet, RG 11/U for up to 7000 feet
Max length:	7000 feet
Topology:	Bus
Data rate:	1 megabit per second baseband
Protocol:	CSMA/CD
Max nodes:	255 (see text)

11

ORCHID PCNET

Orchid was one of the first companies to manufacture a local area network for the IBM PC. Compared to other manufacturers their system has a relatively low cost per workstation connection. Orchid also offers innovative hardware such as their Blossom card, which combines the features of a multifunction card with a network interface but uses only a single PC expansion slot.

The Orchid system is called PCnet. Orchid does not sell special hardware to function as disk or print servers, but instead uses PCs on the network for these tasks. In a typical configuration, you would designate a PC XT or AT as the network disk server and a different PC, XT, or AT as the network print server. The network can handle many servers of each type. You may also use a disk or print server as a workstation, but you will notice some performance degradation in both functions.

OVERVIEW

Figure 11-1 shows a typical Orchid PCnet configuration (a PC XT with 640 kilobytes of memory is acting as the disk server). In Orchid's terminology, this XT is a "server PC," meaning the same thing as the term "server" throughout this book. Another PC (this one with 256 kilobytes) functions as a print server. Two more 640-kilobyte PCs, each having a floppy disk drive, are used as workstations. Orchid calls workstations "user PCs."

You can use diskless workstations on a PCnet by using an optional plug-in ROM supplied by Orchid. Using a diskless PC as a workstation can save a fair amount of money, especially if your network has a lot of workstations. Before buying diskless PCs, you must make sure that they will work with your applications software.

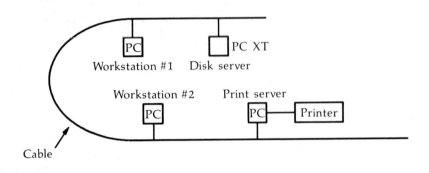

Figure 11-1.   A typical PCnet configuration

Network Architecture

PCnet uses shielded coaxial cable and BNC connectors. The network layout is a bus with a T-connector located at each PC. Figure 11-2 shows how the T-connector may be connected directly to the network card or indirectly through a drop cable.

You can connect up to 255 PCs with a single PCnet, although the network traffic load from any single PC would have to be very light to have that many PCs share a single LAN. You may use any mix of servers and workstations, although a single workstation can access a maximum of 16 servers. PCnet uses the Carrier Sense Multiple Access/Collision Detection (CSMA/CD) protocol over a baseband cable with a bandwidth of 1 megabit per second.

Workstations and Servers

Every PC on a PCnet must contain one of Orchid's network interface cards. The PCnet card provides a hookup to the network and nothing else. The PCnet Blossom card has a serial asynchronous port (for a modem or serial printer), a parallel port (for a parallel printer), a battery backed up clock/calendar, from 0 to 384 kilobytes of RAM, and a PCnet network interface.

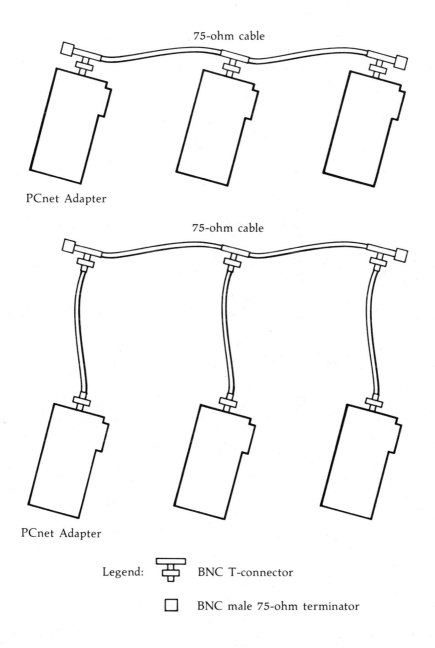

75-ohm cable

PCnet Adapter

75-ohm cable

PCnet Adapter

Legend: BNC T-connector

            BNC male 75-ohm terminator

Figure 11-2.   Connecting with a T-connector and using a drop cable

Each of these cards fits in a single PC expansion slot. The Blossom card is best if your PC configuration is short on expansion slots, and it is more cost-effective than separate network and multifunction cards.

Each workstation should have 256 kilobytes of RAM. You can configure a workstation with less memory, but Orchid strongly recommends using some memory-intensive performance-boosting software (which is discussed later in this chapter).

Orchid recommends that servers should have at least 384 kilobytes of RAM in order to increase performance. Orchid supports most XT-compatible hard disks as servers, and the manual specifically mentions support for Tallgrass, Alloy, and Iomega.

Like most network interface cards, the Orchid series uses some low-level PC hardware features such as interrupt requests, DMA (direct memory access) channels, and I/O port addresses. Although you don't need to understand what these features are, it is important that you do not configure a PC with two or more hardware cards that use these resources. Most common system configurations will not have any conflicts, but Orchid has gone out of its way to provide flexibility in its hardware and software to accommodate conflicts when they do arise. Jumpers and switches on the Orchid cards can be set to change the assignments used by the Orchid cards to nonconflicting values. The PCnet software must then be modified during the installation process to use the appropriate settings.

This complexity is not relevant to most users, but it takes up a lot of space in the installation section of the manual, and is presented in a way that assumes that the reader has technical skill. If you are evaluating PCnet by leafing through the manual, you may be needlessly intimidated. Keep in mind that the default settings provided by Orchid are probably exactly what you need, and that several competing systems just don't offer this much flexibility.

Printers can be connected to any PC on the network. In fact, a workstation can make its printer available to other workstations on the net, somewhat blurring the distinction between workstations and servers.

INSTALLATION

The installation of a PCnet system requires several steps, some of which are performed on the workstations and others on the servers. Everything must be done carefully or you will get unexpected results or even system crashes. If you follow the installation steps in the manual exactly, your system should work fine. The directions are especially critical when you add a new server or workstation, since you will reinstall software on both servers and workstations.

Planning the Hardware Installation

PCnet systems are easy to cable, using common RG 59B/U coax for a network of less than 3000 feet or thicker RG 11/U for longer runs of up to 7000 feet. You can mix and match the two cable types in a single network; for example, you may use RG 11/U coax for the main cable, or "trunk," and RG 59B/U for the drop line to each workstation, which can be up to 20 feet long. You must plan the main cable layout so the distance between the bus and each server or workstation PC is no more than 20 feet.

You must plan the network layout in terms of the numbers and placement of workstations and servers. The limit of 255 PCs on the network is not likely to cause you any problems, since performance probably becomes unacceptable before that number is reached. Still, it is worth noting that Orchid reserves 32 network node addresses (00 through 15 and 240 through 255) for future use, reducing the number of available network addresses to 223.

Your work will help determine the number of servers that you need. Each workstation can access up to 16 devices, including its own local disk drives in the total. These devices appear as MS-DOS drive letters (A:, B:, C:, and so on), and many drive letters can be assigned to a single server.

Each drive letter corresponds to a physical drive on the server or a *virtual volume.* Virtual volumes look to the workstation like normal drives but are actually large files.

PCnet has a very flexible print server scheme — even more flexible than the software installation process implies. When you run the PCNETINS program on a workstation, you are asked for the name of a single network printer that you want to access. In fact, by adding additional commands to your AUTOEXEC.BAT file, you can access up to five network and local printers.

In addition to using printers elsewhere in the network, PCnet lets you attach one or more printers to workstations and access them as you normally would with MS-DOS names LPT:, COM1:, and so on.

Orchid makes no special provisions for disk server backup, so you should use one of the commonly available tape or floppy disk backup systems. As long as the device can be attached to a PC and can be accessed with an MS-DOS drive letter, it should work with PCnet (subject to the potential hardware conflicts discussed earlier). Similarly, there is no support for communications devices or non-IBM PC microcomputers on PCnet.

Planning the Software
Installation

Orchid provides a full array of network performance-improvement software that is designed to reduce access to the network by storing data in RAM on both user and server PCs. Careful thought and experimentation will help realize the benefits of these tools, for if you don't use the tools properly, you will only waste memory.

One useful tool lets you establish *virtual disk drives* (also known as *RAM disks*) in memory on both user and server PCs. A RAM disk is simply a portion of the PC's RAM that looks to the system like a disk drive. Data on a virtual disk drive is accessed much faster than on a regular disk drive, which helps boost performance. If the power on a PC that has a virtual volume fails, however, all the data on the virtual volume is lost.

Another tool is the disk-caching utility, which is similar to a virtual disk but is easier to use. A disk cache can be established for any disk drive on a workstation or server.

PCnet also provides a print spooler, which stores print output from your applications program in memory and sends data to the printer as often as the printer is able to accept it. Since your programs can usually send information out faster than a printer can print it, the spooler speeds up your programs.

These three tools are mentioned frequently in the installation portion of the manual and add considerably to the complexity of getting started. You may be better off installing a small number of workstations and servers first, begin using them, get a feel for the network software, and then try the performance boosters one at a time until you understand their effect. When you are satisfied, you can finish the installation of the entire network taking full advantage of RAM disks, disk caches, and print spoolers.

Whether or not you use the performance tools from the start, you will have to make basic choices about who will use what network resources. Since Orchid assigns privileges to PCs and not to users, a PC should not be shared by more than one person with different access privileges. You must compensate for this lack of security in some other fashion.

The servers will hold programs and data on their hard disks. The PCnet software lets you partition the disk into virtual volumes. Each volume may be labeled "public" or "private," and it may have write or read-only access. Even though a volume is public, it must still be explicitly declared as accessible to each workstation that is to have access to it. Thus, a public volume is one that you can access from more than one PC, although it need not be accessible from every workstation.

Because public volumes can be accessed by more than one workstation, and can be written to by more than one workstation at a time, the PCnet software must do some extra work to maintain the integrity of the disk's directory information. This overhead causes extra network traffic and slower disk access. Thus, you should use public volumes only where necessary.

Doing the Installation

PCnet hardware is fairly easy to install. The software installation is a bit more complex, and it can be time-consuming if you have many workstations. Since changes in either the server or workstation configuration may require you to rerun the installation on all the network nodes, you should learn how to install the system by first practicing on a single server and one or two workstations.

Physical Installation   The PCnet interface card slides easily into a single slot in the IBM PC. The Blossom card is a "piggyback" card, with the network interface portion occupying a separate "daughter board" that plugs into the main multifunction card. This combination card also takes up a single slot, but since it is thicker than the single PCnet card, it is a tight fit in the narrower PC XT card slots. Depending on the adjacent card, the combination card may require the dedication of two slots. The PC Portable does not have any convenient slots to hold the Blossom unless you are using a half-size video card.

There are two approaches to running the main cable:

- Purchase a single long main cable, cut it near each node, and install a T-connector in the splice.

- Measure the distance between nodes, purchase precut cables terminated with female BNC-style connectors, and hook these up to the T-connector.

The first approach takes the least amount of preliminary work, but cutting and splicing the coax at each network node takes some skill in handling coaxial cable connections. The second approach makes installing faster, but requires careful measurements before you order your cable. You should add some extra length to each cable to provide a margin of error.

You may also find that you can purchase mass-produced, precut, properly terminated cable that is close enough in length to your requirements. You will have to balance the cost of custom-made cables of the correct length against mass-produced cable with some built-in waste.

The last T-connectors on each end of the main cable are terminated with 75-ohm resistors mounted in BNC connectors.

Network Addresses   Every device on the network must have a unique address, set by a DIP switch on each PCnet card. Orchid recommends that the switch values be chosen within one range for workstations and another range for servers, as shown in Figure 11-3. The ranges from 0 to 15 (00 to 0F hexadecimal) and 240 to 255 (F0 to FF hexadecimal) are reserved by Orchid for future use.

An additional restriction applies to network addresses. If any of your PCs are diskless and are equipped with Orchid's optional diskless boot ROM, the server that these workstations boot from must have address 128 (80 hexadecimal), which is the recommended first server address.

Installing the System Software   Once you have installed a server and a workstation PC, you can perform the network software installation for the pair and get the feeling of the PCnet software. Similar programs must be

Address	Purpose
00-15	Reserved
16-127	Workstations
128-239	Servers
240-255	Reserved

Figure 11-3.   Recommended network addresses in a PCnet

run for both the server and workstations. Here is an overview of the programs run during installation of each server:

- PCNETBAK backs up the distribution diskette software.

- MAKEVOL partitions the server's hard disk into virtual volumes.

- SPCGEN copies the necessary files to the server's boot disk or directory.

- PCNETINS modifies the server's AUTOEXEC.BAT and CONFIG.SYS files.

- SPCINST specifies each workstation's access to the server's volumes.

During installation of each workstation you must run:

- UPCGEN to copy network files to the workstation's boot disk or directory.

- PCNETINS to modify the workstation's AUTOEXEC.BAT and CONFIG.SYS files.

- UPCINST to specify the mapping between workstation drive letters and server physical and virtual drives.

If your PCnet has diskless PCs, you must also run MAKEBOOT, which creates a virtual boot disk on the server. This virtual disk contains the software used to start up a diskless PC and connect it to the network, the same as would be done from a local disk drive if it had one.

As with all software, you should make copies of the Orchid distribution diskettes and store the originals safely away. The MS-DOS DISKCOPY command is the simplest way to do this. Orchid also supplies a batch file called PCNETBAK, which copies the NETWORK diskette's contents onto your hard disk if you have one.

You should carefully plan the partitioning of the server disk into virtual volumes. If you need to change the partitioning, you will have to shut down the network, back up all the files, and redo much of the installation.

The PCnet software does not require that you use virtual volumes. If you wish, you could simply share entire physical drives with network users. In fact, you can even share floppy disk drives and RAM disks. If you don't use virtual volumes, each workstation will see these drives as MS-DOS disk drives. You can limit each workstation's access to be write or read-only.

However, it is likely that you will want to use virtual volumes for several reasons. By using virtual volumes you can:

- Set up public and private volumes on the same disk drive (you will probably want to put shared programs in a public volume and individual data files in a private volume).

- Control access to specific files by workstation (without virtual volumes, all users given access to a physical drive will have that same level of access to all the files on the drive).

- Give the appearance of many physical drives to a single workstation. (Many applications expect two drives: one for programs, a second for data. Virtual volumes let you simulate this setup.)

- Increase performance by using private volumes for nonshared data and programs (as explained earlier, public volumes require additional system overhead).

You must run the MAKEVOL program on the server to partition the hard disk into virtual volumes. MAKEVOL is very easy to run, although it does not let you correct mistakes made while running it. If you want to change something after running MAKEVOL, you must use the other utilities. When you are running MAKEVOL, you must supply the following information for each volume created:

- The physical server drive letter where the volume should go
- The eight-character virtual volume name
- The volume size in kilobytes (maximum allowed is 5000 kilobytes, or 5 megabytes).

When you are done you will have a screen similar to Figure 11-4, listing the volumes you have created. The server software can handle a maximum of 16 drive letters, which includes floppy disks, hard disks, and RAM disks.

One major restriction of MAKEVOL could cause you serious problems. Hard disk drives commonly have one or more *bad sectors*, which are areas on the disk with surface imperfections that can't store data. MAKEVOL must put each virtual volume in a contiguous space on the disk, that is, one with no bad sectors. Depending on the distribution of bad sectors on your disk drive, you might not be able to create virtual volumes as large as you want them.

```
ORCHID PCnet VIRTUAL DISK CREATION PROGRAM
                Version 3.0


  Virtual Disk Volume Name:      Created on Drive:     Size in Kbyte:
  -------------------------      ----------------      --------------
          MYDATA                       C:                  1024
          YOURDATA                     C:                  1024
          MASTER                       C:                  1536




              Press any key to continue or <CR> to quit:
```

Figure 11-4.   Final MAKEVOL screen

After MAKEVOL you must run SPCGEN, the Server PC Generation program. SPCGEN copies files from the backup you made of the Orchid NETWORK disk into the boot directory of the server's hard disk. It is very easy to run (you only specify the boot disk drive letter). For example, for an XT with a hard disk C:, give the command:

`SPCGEN C:`

Table 11-1 shows the files that are moved into the boot directory and their sizes.

SPCGEN also creates AUTOEXEC.BAT and CONFIG.SYS files in your boot directory. If you already have AUTOEXEC.BAT and CONFIG.SYS files, it appends the files on the Orchid NETWORK disk to them.

After running SPCGEN, you can run PCNETINS, which further modifes the AUTOEXEC.BAT and CONFIG.SYS files for the performance boosters mentioned earlier. Although each PCNETINS screen contains an explanation of the options you can install, the manual gives little explanation of the options. PCNETINS can be run only once. If you later change your AUTOEXEC.BAT and CONFIG.SYS files, you must use a text editor to do so.

Table 11-1.   Files moved into the server's boot directory by SPCGEN

Filename	Size (bytes)
SPC.COM	51660
SPCBIO.COM	1798
SPCINST.COM	17365
PRINTER.COM	4660
ORASSIGN.COM	1582
PCNETSPL.COM	6197
PCNETDRV.COM	1509
DISK13.COM	612
PCCACHE.COM	19802
DTIME.COM	2273
PCNETTLK.COM	12315
PCNETINS.COM	15643
ASK.COM	216
PCNETCLK.SYS	1337
VIRDISK.SYS	5987
CONFIG.SYS	18
AUTOEXEC.BAT	23

Figure 11-5 shows the 10 programs that PCNETINS can install by adding appropriate lines to your CONFIG.SYS and AUTOEXEC.BAT files. The first three items go in the CONFIG.SYS file. Figure 11-6 shows the opening screen of PCNETINS.

VIRDISK makes the virtual volumes on the server visible to a user working at the server itself. In other words, if your server contains the virtual volume MYDATA this volume cannot be accessed from the server unless VIRDISK is installed.

An addendum to the Orchid manual explains that you must *not* install VIRDISK on a server while it is being used by the network. Even though you can use the server to perform most normal PC functions while it simultaneously acts as a server to the network, you cannot access any programs or data in virtual volumes. Thus, a PCnet server is not really a dual-purpose PC that handles both the server and workstation functions.

In CONFIG.SYS	In AUTOEXEC.BAT
VirDisk	BootInit
PCnetdrv	PCnetspl
PCnetclk	Printer
	OrAssign
	PCcache
	Dtime
	PCnetTlk

Figure 11-5.   Programs that PCNETINS can install

The first AUTOEXEC.BAT file option is whether to install BOOTINIT, which is necessary if you have any diskless workstations or any virtual volumes on your server. The latter is likely to be true, and you will have to install BOOTINIT.

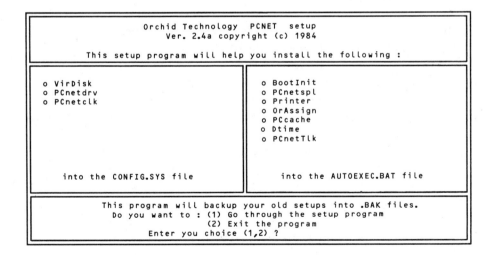

Figure 11-6.   Opening screen of the PCNETINS program

The rest of the items in the PCNETINS menu go in the AUTOEXEC.BAT file too. PCnetspl is a print spooler, which holds print output in a memory buffer and sends it to the printer when the printer is free. PCnetspl can handle all the common printer ports (LPT1:, LPT2:, COM1:, and COM2:) and it lets you reserve any amount of memory for your print spool buffer.

The PCcache program speeds up access to physical disk drives and virtual volumes. You must decide which drives are to have caches, and how many buffers to allocate for each drive.

If you have an Orchid Blossom card, you can use its battery backed up clock calendar to initialize the MS-DOS date and time. Use PCNETINS to add the PCnetclk and DTIME programs to your CONFIG.SYS and AUTOEXEC.BAT file.

You also use PCNETINS to specify how you will access other printers on the network. You must choose the device name of the printer, such as LPT2:, that will be used when you are referring to the network printer from this PC.

The final choice made in PCNETINS is whether you want to use PCnetTLK, a rudimentary electronic messaging service. PCnetTLK lets you type and send messages to other network users. If you choose to install it, you provide a name for your node that is used as your address when other users want to talk with you or send you a memo.

At this point, you still have to run the SPCINST program to complete the installation of the server. You must tell SPCINST which users can access which physical drives and virtual volumes of the server. Each workstation that can access the server must be described separately. Doing so can take quite a while if you have a large network.

You start by specifying whether you are installing a server for the first time or changing an existing configuration. You must specify a name for the server itself and a name for each disk drive on the server (virtual volumes already have names). You also specify whether each volume is public or private. Table 11-2 shows the assignments that resulted from a sample installation. Volumes A: and B: are floppy drives and C: is a hard drive; volumes D:, E:, and F: are virtual volumes; volume G: is a virtual drive that has been declared public.

The final step in server installation is supplying the network addresses of the workstations that can access a server. For each workstation, you go through the list of volumes on that server and specify whether that workstation has no access, read-only access, or read/write access. Once a workstation has been given access to a private volume, the volume will not be offered to any other workstations.

Table 11-2. Sample configuration for a network

Volume	Name	Public/private
A:	SERVERA	Private
B:	SERVERB	Private
C:	SERVERC	Private
D:	Virtual volume	
E:	Virtual volume	
F:	Virtual volume	
G:	RAMDISK	Public

SPCINST also lets you specify whether the workstation can run programs remotely on this server. This means that the workstation can send a command to the server, where it will be executed as soon as the server is available. If commands come from more than one workstation to a single server, they are queued up and executed sequentially.

A program that is run remotely must not require any keyboard input. Running remote programs is a simple yet powerful feature, especially in a program-development environment. You can compile programs on a server while you are editing on a workstation. Of course, while the server is running a remotely started program it cannot run any local programs.

Setting Up the Workstations Workstation setup is similar to server installation, and must be run separately on each workstation. The first step is to run UPCGEN, a batch file that copies the appropriate programs from your backup of the Orchid NETWORK disk to your boot drive or directory. Table 11-3 shows the files that get copied and their sizes.

Next you must run PCNETINS, which modifies the workstation's AUTOEXEC.BAT and CONFIG.SYS files to add the programs needed by PCnet.

Finally, you run UPCINST, a parallel to SPCINST for workstations. UPCINST lets you specify which drive letters your workstation will associate with the server drives it can access.

Table 11-3.   Files moved into the workstation's boot directory by UPCGEN

Filename	Size (bytes)
UPC.COM	31930
UPCBIO.COM	283
UPCINST.COM	14105
PRINTER.COM	4660
ORASSIGN.COM	1582
PCNETSPL.COM	6197
PCNETDRV.COM	1509
DISK13.COM	612
PCCACHE.COM	19802
DTIME.COM	2273
PCNETTLK.COM	12315
PCNETINS.COM	15643
ASK.COM	216
PCNETCLK.SYS	1337
VIRDISK.SYS	5987
CONFIG.SYS	18
AUTOEXEC.BAT	23

Since you can access more than one server from a workstation, the first step is to specify the address of the server you want to access. You then step through the drives and volumes on that workstation that you have access to, giving a different drive letter for each one.

Figure 11-7 shows the end result of configuring one workstation. It is a PC XT workstation with local floppy drives A: and B: and local hard disk drive C:. Drives D: and E: are virtual volumes on the server. D: corresponds to the volume named MASTER and E: is a private volume named MYDATA. Drive F: is a RAM disk on the server, where files that are accessed frequently are stored for high performance.

When you are finished running UPCINST, a file named UPC.COM on the workstation is modified and the system is rebooted. If UPC.COM is ever deleted, UPCINST must be rerun on a backed up copy.

```
╔══════════════════════════════════════════════════════════════╗
║ ┌──────────────────────────────────────────────────────────┐ ║
║ │                   VOLUME CONFIGURATION:                    │ ║
║ └──────────────────────────────────────────────────────────┘ ║
╠══════════════════════════════════════════════════════════════╣
║ ┌──────────────────────────────────────────────────────────┐ ║
║ │     Volume A: local drive "A"                              │ ║
║ │     Volume B: local drive "B"                              │ ║
║ │     Volume C: local drive "C"                              │ ║
║ │     Volume D: remote volume "MASTER"       sPC # 80        │ ║
║ │     Volume E: remote volume "MYDATA"       sPC # 80        │ ║
║ │     Volume F: remote volume "RAMDISK"      sPC # 80        │ ║
║ │                                                            │ ║
║ │                                                            │ ║
║ │                                                            │ ║
║ │                                                            │ ║
║ │                                                            │ ║
║ └──────────────────────────────────────────────────────────┘ ║
╠══════════════════════════════════════════════════════════════╣
║ ┌──────────────────────────────────────────────────────────┐ ║
║ │              Is this correct?  (y/n):                      │ ║
║ └──────────────────────────────────────────────────────────┘ ║
╚══════════════════════════════════════════════════════════════╝
```

Figure 11-7.   Final configuration of server

USING PCnet

The installation of PCnet is somewhat complicated, but once it's completed the system performs reliably and as expected. Many PC applications packages can be run from the server disk drive.

A typical startup of the network is very simple. You turn on the server PC, and everything it needs to do to become a server on the network happens automatically from the AUTOEXEC.BAT and CONFIG.SYS files. The workstations load their network connect software through the same methods. At that point, most MS-DOS commands and applications can act on the network drives the same as they act on local drives. For example:

```
DIR D:
```

would display the directory of the MASTER drive on the server disk.

The mapping of drive letters on the workstation to volumes on the server is determined when you run UPCINST, and there is no way to change these without rerunning UPCINST and rebooting the workstation. There is no utility program that lets you change these assignments without having to reboot.

PRINT MANAGEMENT

The PCnet software lets each node on the network access up to five print-ers anywhere on the network. Orchid recommends that you not put print-ers on the same PC that is acting as a disk server for performance reasons. PCs that act as network print servers perform that function in the back-ground, meaning that they are not tied up with printing and can be per-forming other tasks concurrently.

To use network print service, the PRINTER command must be run first, usually from your AUTOEXEC.BAT file. It has no arguments and simply loads the software that enables network printer access.

The ORASSIGN command establishes the translation of local printer names to network printers. For example, the command

```
ORASSIGN LPT2: TO PC 11 LPT1:
```

will cause all print output to LPT2: to be redirected to the LPT1: port of the network node with address 11. PCnet can redirect print output only from applications that follow the rules of MS-DOS programming and use MS-DOS system calls to do their printing.

The PCNETSPL command can also control print output in the ways detailed in Table 11-4. In addition to the usual settings for controlling the number of lines per page, PCNETSPL can restart the printing of the cur-rent page in case of a paper jam. PCNETSPL commands must be run on the PC attached to the printer, although the remote command execution facility described earlier lets you do this from another PC on the network.

Table 11-4. PCnetspl command's print control options

PCNETSPL option	Description
/LPP=xx	Set number of lines per page
/S	Stop printing
/C	Restart printing
/B	Save output for /R and /RP
/R	Restart print from beginning of current page
/RP	Restart print from top of previous page
/P	Purge the print buffer

SECURITY

Each workstation's configuration is defined by the server software installation and the software on the diskette that is used to start the workstation (there is no concept of a "user account"). This arrangement poses a security problem if your workstation has a hard disk and automatically connects to the network when it is turned on. In this case, anyone who can turn on a PC can have the same privileges on the network as the authorized user of the workstation.

There is no password protection at any level. Anyone who can access the server and knows how to run the SPCINST program can do so and make any volume accessible to any workstation.

Assuming that no one maliciously tries to break into a PCnet system, the security it does have is provided by the SPCINST software. This program defines each workstation's degree of access to each volume, ranging from no access to full write privileges.

MULTIUSER SUPPORT

PCnet supports multiuser access to shared network resources in several ways. If two users update different files in the same public directory, PCnet will automatically maintain the correct directory information. If two users update the same file in a single directory, only the second person's changes to the file are made. This is not what you normally want, and the PCnet software offers a couple of ways to keep this from happening.

Table 11-5 lists the commands available for workstation software to

Table 11-5.   PCnet commands to control file locking

File-locking command	Description
CHKLOCK	See if a lock is set on a file
LOCK	Lock a file
LLOCK	Repeat the LOCK command until it succeeds
LOCKDIR	List the lock table and the status of each lock
UNLOCK	Unlock a file

perform file locking. Although these commands can form the basis for a workable system, it relies on cooperation between users or applications programs. The "locks" set in this fashion do not really lock out the file as far as MS-DOS is concerned.

One user can access a file that has been "locked" as if the lock had not been set. What the locks provide is a guaranteed safe way for cooperating users or programs to make sure that only one of them accesses a file at a time. For example, if one user gives the command:

```
LOCK C:file1
```

and the file is not locked, the system will reply:

```
semaphore -> C:' file1' locked
```

A *semaphore* is a message sent from one computer process to another. When a different user (say B) tries to lock the file by giving the same LOCK command, the system will reply:

```
semaphore -> C:' file1' in use.
```

indicating that another user has already locked the file. Nothing actually prevents user B from accessing the file, but this locking mechanism tells user B that the file is already in use. The LLOCK command will keep retrying the LOCK command until it succeeds.

If the system crashes with locks in effect, some cleanup work must be done at the server to remove the locks. This can be done automatically by inserting UNLOCK commands in the AUTOEXEC.BAT file at the server.

In most cases it will not be adequate to rely on users to use the LOCK and UNLOCK commands. You should set up batch files that contain the appropriate LOCK and UNLOCK commands, or use applications programmed for PCnet that perform file locking under program control. The PCnet manual describes how to call the lock functions from an assembly language program and from IBM BASIC or BASICA. Orchid does not recommend using BASIC, however, because of the way BASIC itself keeps portions of a file in memory, defeating the idea of sharing the file.

UTILITIES

The Orchid system comes with many utility programs that run under MS-DOS. Table 11-6 lists the ones that have not already been discussed.

Table 11-6.   Miscellaneous PCnet utilities

Utility	Description
ASK	Check keyboard for "Y" or "N" in a batch file
CFLUSH	Write modified cache buffers to disk
CRESET	Clear the cache and free all buffers
CSTAT	Report on status of cache
MODEM	Share a modem on the network
MOVE	Copy a file and delete the source
NETDIR	List a workstation's drive and printer configuration
NETTEST	Test connection between PCs
SELFTEST	Test PCnet hardware in a single PC
SERIAL	Share serial ports on the network
STATUS	Give low-level details of network status

The MODEM program lets you share a modem on the network just as you can share a printer. Unfortunately, this modem will work only with communications programs that use MS-DOS calls for the modem port; this imitation rules out most of the major IBM PC communications programs.

NETTEST is a diagnostic program that sends messages between two or more PCs on the network. It is a helpful troubleshooting tool, since it operates at the hardware level and tells you if the basic networking function is working. Even if you have not completed the configuration of servers and workstations, you can use NETTEST for a confidence check of the network.

The SELFTEST program troubleshoots a single PC on the network and tells you whether the PCnet hardware appears to be functioning.

Backing Up the Server

Orchid supplies no special software to facilitate making a backup of the network hard disk (or disks). You can use the MS-DOS BACKUP command and save the contents of the disk to floppy disks. Most third-party tape drive systems that work in conjunction with an IBM PC XT should be able to back up the hard disk. It is very important that the backup software not ignore hidden files, since it is in that form that virtual volumes are stored.

DOCUMENTATION

The Orchid manual is reasonably well organized. Most of the information needed to install a system is grouped sensibly together, except for the information about setting the network addresses on the PCnet hardware, which is buried in an appendix.

All the PCnet commands are explained in a reference section in the middle of the manual. The documentation for each command follows the IBM PC-DOS manual format. Most commands are illustrated with one or more examples.

There is a brief discussion of the best ways to run several popular third-party software packages on PCnet. Orchid recommends keeping your data files on a server and running the programs themselves off a RAM disk at the workstation. This will certainly provide adequate speed if you have enough memory to do so.

There is also a list of multiuser database management systems that work with PCnet. These provide a good starting point if you need true multiuser read/write capability to a shared database.

A section for advanced users describes the programming interface to PCnet. In addition to demonstrating how to use the lock and unlock calls, the manual describes packet-level interface.

The manual provides plenty of information, but becomes very technical very quickly. There is not much hand-holding for the inexperienced PC user. You should have at least one person available during the installation who is very familiar with PC-DOS text editing and AUTOEXEC.BAT and CONFIG.SYS files.

EXPANDING THE NETWORK

You can add servers and workstations to the network in the future. You must bring the network down, since you need to cut the main cable to introduce the new node. In most cases, you must rerun at least the SPCINST and UPCINST programs. In several cases you must rerun SPCINST and UPCINST on all servers and workstations.

PERFORMANCE

PCnet ran all the benchmarks successfully, including handling the copy-protection schemes and printing to the network printer. Performance was quite good on the small configurations tested. Table 11-7 shows the benchmark results.

Table 11-7. Running third-party software packages

Program	Task	Time	
Lotus 1-2-3	Load program	15.9 seconds	
	Load worksheet	4.5 seconds	
	Print portion of worksheet to spool file	1.9 seconds	
	File manager	Works OK	
	Copy protection	OK with key disk in workstation disk drive	
WordStar	Load program	7.1 seconds	
	Load document	3.1 seconds	
	Position to end of document	11.6 seconds	
	Append document	38.3 seconds	
	Save document and quit program	12.0 seconds	
	Printing	Works OK on network printer	
dBASE III	Load program	14.2 seconds	
	Run test program	5 mins. 39 seconds	
	Copy protection	OK with key disk in workstation disk drive	
		One workstation	Two workstations
BASICA	Sequential Write	43.5 seconds	54.5 seconds
	Sequential Read	35 seconds	44.5 seconds
	Random Write	17.5 seconds	32 seconds
	Random Read	11.5 seconds	19.5 seconds

For the fairest comparison to the other networks, the Orchid performance-tuning tools were not used in these benchmarks. It is important to keep in mind that these tools are available, however, since their use can help increase the maximum number of PCs that will fit on a network before data transfer becomes too slow.

The bare minimum network software uses 58 kilobytes of RAM on a server, and 36 kilobytes on a workstation. Shared print service requires an additional 11 kilobytes of memory.

GLOSSARY

Access   Read or write information from or to a computer, typically a disk or file server in the context of a LAN.

Applications software   Programs that make computer hardware and systems software perform a useful function; examples include accounting software, word processing software, and spreadsheet software.

ARCnet   A network introduced by Datapoint Corp. that uses a token-passing protocol. ARCnet has been adapted for the IBM PC by many vendors and has evolved into the IEEE 802.4 network standard.

Asynchronous communications   A communications protocol used for low-speed communications, typically ranging from 300 to 50,000 bits per second in bandwidth; commonly used with a modem to communicate with a remote computer over telephone lines, or to tie terminals to a computer in a multiuser system. *See also* RS-232-C, Serial interface, Modem.

AUTOEXEC.BAT file   An MS-DOS batch file containing commands that are executed automatically when MS-DOS starts running.

Bandwidth   The amount of information that can pass through a system (usually meaning the cable in a network) per unit time. Common LAN bandwidths range from several hundred thousand bits per second to 10 million bits per second.

Baseband   A network electrical connection scheme that limits the cable to carrying only one channel of information, in contrast to broadband. Baseband LAN cables carry data as digital signals, the kind of signal found inside a computer.

Batch file   A file containing MS-DOS commands to be run automatically when the batch file is executed.

Baud rate   A measure of the speed of data transfer, approximately equal to the number of bits transmitted per second.

Benchmark   Software run on a system to measure some aspect of system behavior, or performance. Different systems can be compared by running the same benchmark program on them.

Bit   The smallest unit of storage in a binary computer, bit stands for binary digit and can have the value 0 or 1. *See also* Byte.

Boot   To start a computer. Short for "bootstrap," the term refers to the process by which a computer system loads its operating software. Once this software is loaded, it controls the hardware it was loaded from, making the initial loading process comparable to pulling yourself up by your own bootstraps.

Bridge   An active component that connects two identical networks and usually filters network traffic so that only messages destined for another network are passed to it over the bridge.

Broadband   Network connection scheme in which the cable can carry many channels of information, analogous to a cable TV hookup carrying many TV channels. A broadband LAN cable can be used to carry video and voice information as well as computer-to-computer traffic.

Buffer   RAM (*see* Random access memory) set aside to hold information, such as blocks of disk data or program output destined for a printer.

Bus   A network cable topology characterized by a single cable that runs past all the workstations and servers, connecting to each of them either directly or through a short drop cable. The ends of the bus are electrically terminated with resistors.

Byte   A single character of information storage, such as a letter, number, or punctuation mark. A byte contains 8 bits. *See also* Bit.

Cable   *See* Twisted-pair cable and Coaxial cable.

Cache   A collection of disk buffers managed by systems software to provide increased disk performance. When applications need disk blocks that are already in the cache, they can get them at fast RAM-access speeds rather than slower disk-access speeds.

Central Processing Unit   The Central Processing Unit (CPU) is the part of a computer that can can do arithmetic and logical operations, and is the component that runs computer programs.

Cheapernet   Variant of the Ethernet standard using less-expensive cable and transceivers. Compatible with Ethernet software and runs at same speed, but total cable length must be less than with standard Ethernet cable.

Cluster Controller   A dedicated computer designed to handle information from a group, or cluster, of terminals and connect that group to another computer, usually a mainframe.

Coaxial cable   Type of cable commonly used in local area networks; consists of a center metal conductor covered by two layers of insulator with a grounding shield between them. Usually more expensive than twisted-pair cable, but with less signal loss and higher noise immunity.

Code.   *See* Software.

Collision   Event in which two nodes transmit simultaneously, rendering both messages unintelligible.

CONFIG.SYS file   Contains directives to MS-DOS used at boot time to initialize system parameters, such as maximum number of open files, and to install software device drivers to support components such as RAM disks and network interfaces.

Copy protection   Method by which software vendors control the number of working copies that can be made from the diskettes they distribute containing their software.

CSMA/CD   Carrier Sense Multiple Access/Collision Detection is a network protocol in which every network node transmits messages as soon as it needs to and finds the network cable is quiet. A collision occurs if two nodes transmit at the same time. Collisions are detected and the transmission is resent after a delay of variable length.

Data file   A named repository of information stored on a computer mass storage device such as a floppy or hard disk drive.

Database management system   An application program that lets information be stored so that it can be easily retrieved, modified, sorted, and printed out.

Dedicated server   Server on a network that functions solely as a server, as opposed to a nondedicated server that can also be used as a workstation.

Directory   Used to organize file storage under MS-DOS. A disk directory can contain files and other directories, sometimes referred to as subdirectories.

Disk drive   A computer hardware device that stores programs and data files. The information that is stored persists when power to the computer is shut off.

Disk operating system   Systems software such as MS-DOS or PC-DOS that controls a computer's hardware and provides higher-level functions so that applications software can access disk drives, video display, and other input and output devices.

Disk server   A server connected to a network to provide disk storage for workstations on the network. A disk server provides a lower-level software interface than a file server, responding to requests to read and write blocks of disk storage rather than responding to requests for blocks of a specific file.

Diskette   A removable medium used in a floppy disk drive to store programs and data files. Also called floppy disk.

Diskless workstation   Workstation node with no floppy or hard disk drives; must use a network file or disk server for all long-term data storage.

Electronic calendar   Network applications software that lets you keep track of daily appointments and schedule meetings in coordination with other network users' calendars.

Electronic mail   Network software that lets network users send messages and files to each other.

Ethernet   A baseband local area network developed by Digital Equipment Corp., Intel Corp., and Xerox Corp. Ethernet uses the CSMA/CD protocol and has a bandwidth of 10 megabits (that is, 10 million bits) per second.

Expansion card   A printed circuit card that plugs into an expansion slot in an IBM PC family computer to provide additional functionality, such as a connection to the network.

Expansion slot   Space in an IBM PC family computer that accepts an expansion card that adds more capability to the PC. Network transceiver cards are one example of an expansion card.

Fiber optic cable   Cable using light instead of electricity to transfer information; used in some networks, has high bandwidth, high immunity to noise. Generally more expensive than coaxial cable or twisted-pair.

File   *See* Data file.

File locking   *See* Locking.

File server   A server connected to a network that provides file storage for workstations on the network; provides a higher-level software interface than a disk server, and can make it easier for network systems software to allow concurrent shared access to a single file.

File sharing   Feature of most networks that allows a single file to be opened and accessed by more than one workstation at a time. Applications software must use the appropriate locks (*see also* Locking) for this feature to work properly.

Fixed disk   *See* Hard disk.

Floppy disk   *See* Diskette.

Floppy disk drive   Computer hardware used to store programs and data files on diskettes. IBM PC floppy disks usually hold 360 thousand bytes (that is, 360 kilobytes) of information.

Frequency translator   Hardware used in a broadband network to convert network transmissions from a receiving frequency to a sending frequency.

Gateway   A server that connects two dissimilar networks so messages can be passed back and forth; contains network systems software to perform varying levels of translation on the traffic between the two networks.

Hard disk   A disk drive that stores information on a rapidly spinning hard platter, which provides fast access and dense storage; usually holds at least 10 million bytes (that is, 10 megabytes) of data. *See also* Disk drive.

Hardware   The physical devices that make up a computer system. Examples of hardware include disk drives, central processing units (CPUs), keyboards, and video displays.

IBM PC family   The IBM Personal Computer family includes the PC, a floppy-disk-based microcomputer, the PC XT, which adds hard disk storage to a PC, and the PC AT, which has a faster central processor and optionally a faster hard disk than the PC or PC XT.

IEEE 802   The Institute for Electrical and Electronic Engineers standards committee number 802 is responsible for developing networking standards. The 802.3 subcommittee works on a standard derived from Ethernet, 802.4 is based on the ARCnet token-passing bus, and 802.5 is used in the IBM Token-Ring Network.

ISO   The International Standards Organization, responsible for the OSI network model.

Kilobyte   One-thousand bytes of information storage.

LAN   *See* Local area network.

Local area network   A system that connects computers together within a restricted geographical area, usually a mile or so, to allow sharing of information and hardware resources; also called LAN.

Locking   Function provided by network systems software to control access to a single file by more than one network user. In its most general implementation, a lock may be used to control any network resource, not just a file.

Log off   To execute the process of telling the network systems software that you are finished using the network for now; usually consists of typing a command such as LOGOFF.

Log on   To perform the process of identifying yourself to the network systems software to gain access to network resources. Usually consists of typing in your user name and password.

Loss   Refers to the amount by which a signal is attenuated over a certain distance. Generally, more expensive cable has a lower rate of loss.

Mainframe computer   A very large computer system often used to process information for a medium-to-large corporation, or for scientific computations requiring very fast CPUs.

Mainframe link   Connection from a PC or a LAN to a mainframe computer to support message and file transfer between them; may also support emulation of a terminal and submission of work to be processed on the mainframe.

Master-slave system   Network architecture in which one node controls cable access or data transfer to a greater extent than do other nodes; in a star network, for example, the central hub is the master and the other nodes are slaves.

Megabyte   One million bytes of information storage.

Microcomputer   A small computer system, usually dedicated to a specific task or use by a single person. IBM PC family computers are microcomputers.

Minicomputer   A medium-size computer often used as a multiuser time-sharing system, for industrial process control, or as a server in a network.

Modem   A device (the term abbreviates modulator/demodulator) that translates serial data into tones that can be transmitted over a voice communications medium such as a phone line and translated back into serial data by another modem at the other end of the line; allows information exchange between two computers via asynchronous communications.

MS-DOS   Microsoft's disk operating system, a systems software package that provides basic control of a computer's hardware. Runs on the IBM PC and compatible computers.

Multifunction card   Printed circuit card containing more than one function to expand the capabilities of a microcomputer. For example, it may contain RAM (random access memory) and a network interface.

Multiuser system   Computer system that lets more than one user share a single computer using video display terminals; also called a multiuser time-shared computer system.

NETBIOS   ISO session-level interface (short for *Network Basic Input Output System*) to the IBM PC Network and the IBM Token-Ring Network; is becoming a de facto standard adapted by other computer vendors and programmed to by network applications software vendors.

Network   *See* Local area network and Wide area network.

Network architecture   The technical design of a network; usually refers to the network's topology, protocol, and workstation/server relationship (peer-to-peer or master-slave).

Network interface card   *See* Transceiver card.

Network manager   Person responsible for network setup and maintenance work, including configuring the network, allocating resources, and granting data-access privileges to network users.

Node   A device connected to a network cable; usually refers to a workstation or server, but occasionally refers to a repeater or a passive network junction box.

Noise   Interference with an electrical signal; may come from other electrical equipment such as fluorescent light fixtures or motors. Coaxial cable generally has greater noise immunity than twisted-pair.

Nondedicated server   Network server that can be used simultaneously as a workstation.

Optical fiber   *See* Fiber optic cable.

OSI model   The Open Systems Interconnect (OSI) model, a seven-layer model developed by the International Standards Organization and used to describe network systems architecture.

Parallel interface   Hardware commonly used to connect printers to personal computers, also called a Centronics-compatible port or a parallel port.

Password   Combination of characters supplied by network users to prove their identity and gain access to authorized network resources.

PBX   Private branch exchange, a local telephone switchboard; usually handles the telephones for a single building or complex. Some networks can use the same wiring as that installed for a PBX.

PC, PC XT, PC AT   *See* IBM PC family.

PC-DOS   IBM's version of MS-DOS.

Peer-to-peer system   Network architecture in which all network nodes have equal status and capabilities in controlling the network bus and communicating to each other. In a peer-to-peer system, a network node can communicate directly with another node, without going through an intermediate controlling node.

Peripheral   Hardware connected to a computer—for example, a disk drive, printer, or modem.

Physical connection layout   *See* Topology.

Print queue   A list of files waiting to be printed containing output from various network users. The print server software manages this file queue. *See also* Print spooling.

Print server   Network server that lets workstations access one or more shared printers; usually provides print spooling as well as sharing.

Print spooling   Method of accepting print output from applications programs as fast as they can generate it, saving the output in memory or on disk, and sending it to the printer as fast as it can print it. Also called print buffering.

Printer   A computer hardware device that prints information sent by the computer onto paper (the printout is also called hard copy).

Private branch exchange   *See* PBX.

Private storage   Network disk or file storage that can be accessed only by a single user.

Program   *See* Software.

Protocol   Method followed by network hardware and systems software to transmit data over the network. Governs the order in which things happen to ensure accurate and orderly information transfer. *See also* Token-passing and CSMA/CD.

Public network   A common-carrier network accessed via the phone system or leased lines to cover a wide geographical area. *See also* Wide area network.

Public storage   Network disk or file storage that can be accessed by more than one user, often by any network user.

RAM disk   Portion of a computer's memory set aside along with some systems software to manage it so that it emulates a disk drive. Data can be accessed from a RAM disk much faster than from a floppy disk, and usually even faster than from a hard disk.

Random access memory (RAM)   Storage within a computer that holds programs and data. Any individual storage location can be directly accessed by the CPU.

Read-only storage   Network disk or file storage that can be read but not written to, modified, or deleted.

Read/write storage   Network disk or file storage that can be read and modified, and usually also deleted.

Repeater   An active network connection component that boosts the electrical signal so that cable of greater length can be used.

Ring   A loop of cable with workstations and servers connected to it; similar to a bus but with the ends tied together instead of terminated.

RS-232 C   Standard low-level protocol used by most asynchronous communications devices; also called serial communications.

Security   That part of a network's systems software dedicated to preventing unauthorized access to programs and data stored on the network. In most cases, users must supply a password to prove their identity, and once their identity is confirmed the network systems software allows them to access to a prearranged subset of the network's resources.

Serial interface   Computer hardware that provides an RS-232C standard interface to connect devices such as modems, printers, and plotters to personal computers. Some low-speed LANs are based on serial interfaces. *See also* Asynchronous communications and RS-232C.

Server   A computer on a network that provides a resource to workstations connected to the network. Typical resources include printers, disk drives, electronic mail, and connections to other networks.

Server software   Networking systems software that runs on a server and makes its resources available to network workstations. Server software controls the sharing of a single server resource, such as a printer, by multiple network users.

Session level   Layer 5 of the OSI model; software operating at this level establishes a connection between two networked devices that can be resumed in case of network failure.

Shared file   *See* Shared storage.

Shared storage   Network disk or file storage that can be accessed by more than one user at a time.

Single-user software   Programs written for a single-user machine, such as a nonnetworked PC; may require modification to work properly on a network — almost certainly requires modification to allow more than one user to run the program at the same time using the same data file.

Site licensing   Method of licensing software for use by everyone at a certain site for a single fixed fee (as opposed to requiring that each user have a license for his or her individual copy of the software).

SNA   IBM's *Systems Network Architecture;* covers a wide range of proprietary communications hardware and software. It is most often associated with systems used to connect large numbers of terminals through cluster controllers to mainframe computers.

Software   Sequence of instructions written in a programming language that directs computer hardware to perform a certain function; also called programs or code.

Spooling   *See* Print spooling.

Spreadsheet   An applications program that lets you store rows and columns of numbers and formulas. When you change a number, the spreadsheet can automatically recalculate results based on the formulas stored in it.

Star   A network topology with a central hub and radiating spokes. The hub is usually a server or a gateway or a bridge, and workstations are at the ends of the spokes. Multiuser systems typically use star cabling configurations, with the computer at the hub and terminals at the ends of the spokes.

System manager   Person responsible for installing systems software, allocating network resources, and granting network access privileges to users.

Systems software   Software that controls computer hardware and provides a set of functions for applications software to use so that the computer hardware does not have to be programmed directly.

Tape drive   Device that stores data on magnetic tapes (usually on reels or in cartridges). Frequently used to back up hard disk storage so that data can be restored if the hard disk copy is damaged.

Terminal   Video display tube and keyboard combination that lets you type information into a computer and see computer output on the screen.

Time-sharing   System in which more than one terminal user shares a single computer, its resources being devoted to each user in turn for very brief intervals.

Token-passing   Network protocol in which traffic passes from one node to the other. Each node removes messages intended for it and adds any new messages. The maximum time required to send a message between any two nodes can be guaranteed.

Token-ring   A network using the token-passing protocol and a ring topology.

Topology   The layout of the connecting cable in a network. *See also* Bus, Ring, and Star.

Transceiver card   A printed circuit card that provides an electrical interface between a network cable and a workstation or server. May also contain a microprocessor and network systems software that provides a higher-level interface to the network, usually no higher than the ISO session layer.

Transport level   OSI model layer 4, responsible for breaking long messages into packets of a size the network can handle, and for restoring them on the receiving end. Also handles retransmission of messages if an error is detected.

Tree   Network topology with a single master node at the root and with every other node having a single father node and one or more son nodes. Each node's father is the node closer to the root or the root itself, and each node's sons are any nodes connected to it and further away from the root. There are no loops in this connection scheme.

Twisted-pair cable   Type of cable commonly used in local area networks. Consists of two insulated wires twisted together, sometimes surrounded by a grounding shield, and covered with an insulating sleeve. Usually less expensive than coaxial cable, but with higher degree of signal loss and lower noise immunity.

Unshared file   *See* Unshared storage.

Unshared storage   Network disk or file storage that can be accessed only by a single user at a time.

User   Someone who uses a computer — typically a workstation, in the context of this book.

User account   Collection of network use privileges granted to an individual. User accounts typically have user names and passwords associated with them that must be provided to gain access to the authorized network resources.

User name   Name provided by workstation users to identify themselves to the network systems software.

User profile   Information about the privileges and preferences of a network user; may include such particulars as volumes that the user can access and batch programs to run when the user first logs on to the network.

Utilities   Software used to perform some function that is ancillary to the main problem-solving application of the computer. For example, the MS-DOS FORMAT program that prepares floppy disks for use is a utility program.

Virtual disk   *See* RAM disk.

Volume   A portion of a disk or file server's storage that can be treated as a unit for purposes of security; for designating it shared or unshared, or read/write or read-only; and for associating it with a workstation's MS-DOS drive letter.

Wide area network   A system for connecting computers together over a large geographical area so that they can share information and hardware resources. May span the globe using satellite, microwave, and telephone links.

Winchester disk   *See* Hard disk.

Word processor   An applications program that lets you create textual data files that can be easily modified and printed out.

Workstation   A computer on a network used primarily to run applications software that may or may not access network resources. Typically has a video display screen and keyboard so a person can interact with it. Workstations on IBM PC local area networks are IBM PC family computers or compatibles.

Workstation software   Systems and applications software that runs on a workstation. Includes the software that normally runs on a nonnetworked computer, plus the software that lets the workstation access the network's resources.

Trademarks

ARCNET®	Datapoint Corporation
Blossom®	Orchid Technology, Inc.
Constellation®	Corvus Systems, Inc.
CP/M®	Digital Research
dBASE III™	Ashton-Tate
Ethernet®	Xerox Corporation
IBM®	International Business Machines Corporation
MS-DOS®	Microsoft Corporation
MS-NET®	Microsoft Corporation
NetWare®	Novell, Inc.
Novell®	Novell, Inc.
Omninet®	Corvus Systems, Inc.
1-2-3™	Lotus Development Corporation
PCnet®	Orchid Technology, Inc.
S-Net™	Novell, Inc.
StarLAN®	American Telephone and Telegraph (AT&T)
3Com®	3Com Corporation
3Server™	3Com Corporation
WordStar®	MicroPro International Corporation
Xerox®	Xerox Corporation

INDEX

■ Other related Osborne **McGraw-Hill** titles include:

Micro-to-Mainframe Links
Ronald F. Kopeck

Here's a book that sorts out all the complex issues involved in linking microcomputers to mainframes for sophisticated, high-powered applications. *With Micro-to-Mainframe Links*, data processing and communications professionals can fully understand the three major considerations behind PC-to-mainframe integration: needs assessment, implementation, and monitoring. A concise, detailed text thoroughly explains the planning and evaluation process used in determining how PC-to-mainframe linking fits into your office environment. Data transfer, security, and use of existing networks are also discussed. When Kopeck describes implementation, you'll find out about link products and the real and hidden costs of linking, as well as maintenance and service. Monitoring focuses on safe ways to begin the PC-to-mainframe link by establishing and evaluating tests and measurements. Kopeck, a widely-known consultant and editor of *Micro-to-Mainframe Link News*, draws on his extensive knowledge of this field to bring you the most comprehensive coverage possible.

$18.95p
0-07-881228-3, 300 pp., 7³/₈ x 9¹/₄

Your IBM®PC: A Guide to the IBM PC (DOS 2.0) and XT
by Lyle Graham & Tim Field

"Excellent reference for the IBM PC with PC-DOS version 1.0, 1.05 and 1.1. Provides a clear overview of IBM PC hardware and software, step-by-step operating instructions, and an introduction to BASIC programming, color graphics, and sounds. Also includes a chapter on trouble-shooting and IBM's PDP (Problem Definition Procedure). Rating: A"
(Computer Book Review)

$18.95p
0-07-881120-1, 592 pp., 6⁷/₈ x 9¹/₄

PC Secrets: Tips for Power Performance
by James E. Kelley

Power performance is at your command with these secrets for mastering the PC. This collection of shortcuts and solutions to frustrating and frequently encountered problems gives users of the IBM®PC and PC compatibles the inside edge. James Kelly, author of numerous books on the IBM PC, discloses his secrets for controlling hardware, peripherals, DOS, and applications software. You'll learn tips for keyboard harmonics, display enhancements, controlling fixed disks, managing the printer, and manipulating DOS routines that include batch files, directories and subdirectories, as well as system menus. You'll also find programs that help you use WordStar® and Lotus™ 1-2-3™ to greater advantage. With *PC Secrets*, you don't need to be a technical expert to become a PC power user.

$16.95p
0-07-881210-0, 224 pp., 7³/₈ x 9¹/₄

PC-DOS Tips & Traps
by Dick Andersen

Solve immediate problems and quickly perform specific business tasks on your IBM®PC or PC-compatible with *PC-DOS Tips & Traps*. Written for everyone using PC-DOS 2.1 or MS-DOS 2.11, Andersen provides an array of tips and discusses frequently encountered traps with their solutions. You'll find a broad range of helpful information from initializing your system and formatting disks, to controlling peripherals, and managing the DOS environment. Throughout the book Andersen shows you how to use the DOS Batch files to design your own commands and automate certain tasks. Tips for using DOS utilities including EDLIN for text editing and DEBUG for programming are also discussed. You'll save time and minimize the change for error with Andersen's insights on the PC- and MS-DOS® operating systems.

$16.95p
0-07-881194-5, 250 pp., 7³/₈ x 9¹/₄

Data Base Management Systems — MS-DOS®: Evaluating MS-DOS® Database Software
by David Kruglinski

David Kruglinski, well-known author of *Data Base Management Systems (CP/M)* and *The Osborne/McGraw-Hill Guide to IBM PC Communications*, lends his expertise to another subject: Data Base Management Systems—MS-DOS® In this book, he covers popular database programs for IBM PC and compatibles: Lotus 1-2-3, Symphony, Framework, R:Base 4000, R:Base 5000, Knowledgeman and others. After a brief introduction to databases, Kruglinski explains how to select a database to suit individual needs. In this comprehensive guide, he covers such topics as file management systems, integrated packages containing database card index simulations, relational databases, application development tools, networks and more.

$18.95p
0-07-881180-5, 400 pp., 7³/₈ x 9¹/₄

Using SuperProject Plus™
Joan Knutson and Len Glauber

Using SuperProject Plus™ gives you all the inside tips you need to successfully manage your important business projects with this new version of the top-selling software for the IBM® PC and compatible computers. The exceptional SuperProject Plus™ project management software lets you schedule and track resources, time, and all costs of even the most complicated venture. In this user guide, authors Knutson and Glauber discuss the capabilities and features of SuperProject Plus: building a work flowchart, determining task sequencing, drawing a network diagram, assigning talent to tasks, deriving time estimates, isolating a critical path, and more. You'll also learn how to implement SuperProject Plus for building, modeling, simulating, and optimizing a project plan. Written with the support of the manufacturer, Computer Associates International, *Using SuperProject Plus™* is for both experienced and beginning users.

$17.95p
0-07-881231-3, 250 pp., 7³/₈ x 9¹/₄

Project Management Using Microcomputers
Harvey A. Levine

Business professionals in all fields can make informed decisions about the best project management software available for their specific needs with the essential information in this guide. Levine, a project manager for General Electric, discusses state-of-the-art project management techniques that can be applied to every business and to most computer systems. Beginning with an overview of project management, Levine considers the role of the microcomputer in this application. Various capabilities of project management software are then discussed: resource and cost planning, reporting and graphing, scheduling, and tracking. To give you a better idea of how project management software can be used, Levine divides applications into elementary, intermediate, custom-designed, and mass-market categories. Every category offers project management examples, each contributed by an industry expert who discusses the reasons and methods behind the application.

$18.95p
0-07-881221-6, 350 pp., 7³/₈ x 9¹/₄

The Osborne/McGraw-Hill Guide to Using Lotus™ 1-2-3™ Second Edition, Covers Release 2
Edward M. Baras

Your investment in Lotus™ 1-2-3™ can yield the most productive returns possible with the tips and practical information in *The Osborne/McGraw-Hill Guide*

to *Using Lotus™ 1-2-3™* Now the second edition of this acclaimed bestseller helps you take full advantage of Lotus' new 1-2-3 upgrade, Release 2. This comprehensive guide offers a thorough presentation of the worksheet, database, and graphics functions. In addition, the revised, expanded text shows you how to create and use macros, string functions, and many other sophisticated 1-2-3 features. Step by step, you'll learn to implement 1-2-3 techniques as you follow application models for financial forecasting, stock portfolio tracking, and forms-oriented database management. For both beginners and experienced users, this tutorial quickly leads you from fundamental procedures to advanced applications.

$18.95p
0-07-881230-5, 432 pp., 7³/₈ x 9¹/₄

Financial Modeling Using Lotus™ 1-2-3,™ Covers Release 2
Charles W. Kyd

Readers of Kyd's monthly "Accounting" column in *Lotus™* magazine already know how helpful his 1-2-3™ tips can be. Now his *Financial Modeling Using Lotus™ 1-2-3™* shows experienced users how to set up a data bank that can be used by everyone in the office to make more effective use of numerous financial applications. Kyd provides models for managing the balance sheet, controlling growth, handling income statements and management accounting, using Z scores for business forecasts, and more. Each model features a summary of 1-2-3 techniques, including helpful information for using the new Release 2, and explains the financial theories behind the application. You'll also find out how data for many of these financial models can be shared in the office data bank, creating an even greater resource for business productivity.

$16.95p
0-07-881213-5, 225 pp., 7³/₈ x 9¹/₄

The Advanced Guide to Lotus™ 1-2-3,™ Covers RELEASE 2
Edward M. Baras

Edward Baras, Lotus expert and author of *The Symphony™ Book, Symphony™ Master,* and *The Jazz™ Book,* now has a sequel to his bestselling *Osborne/McGraw-Hill Guide to Using Lotus™ 12-3.™* For experienced users, *The Advanced Guide to Lotus 1-2-3* delves into more powerful and complex techniques using the newest software upgrade, Release 2. Added enhancements to 1-2-3's macro language, as well as many new functions and commands, are described and thoroughly illustrated in business applications. Baras shows you how to take advantage of Release 2's macro capabilities by programming

1-2-3 to simulate Symphony's keystroke-recording features and by processing ASCII files automatically. You'll also learn to set up your own command menus; use depreciation functions, matric manipulation, and regression analysis; and convert text files to the 1-2-3 worksheet format.

$18.95 p
0-07-881237-2, 325 pp., 7³/₈ x 9¹/₄

The Complete Book of 1-2-3™ Macros
by Robert Flast and Lauren Flast

If you're spending too much computing time with Lotus™ 1-2-3,™ this collection of labor-saving macros can shorten your work load. A macro is a keystroke that automatically activates a series of computing steps to perform a specific task. Pre-program your computer with these and you'll never have to repeat tedious routines again. The Flasts provide five categories of macros that cover: data base handling— transaction histories, accumulation analysis; statistics and math applications—iteration; text processing; business applications—project management, critical path, networking; and macros utilities—printing, sorting, backup, and keyboards. With the information that the Flasts provide in *The Complete Book of 1-2-3™ Macros*, you can easily adapt the examples to suit your business needs...or program your own.

$16.95 p
0-07-881199-6, 200 pp., 7³/₈ x 9¹/₄

The Symphony™ Book
by Edward M. Baras

Successful business management is easier than 1-2-3 with this comprehensive guide from Edward Baras, financial analyst for Standard & Poor's. The author of the popular *Osborne/McGraw-Hill Guide to Using Lotus™ 1-2-3™* teaches you how to integrate and capitalize on the spreadsheet, database, graphics, and word processing functions of the powerful Symphony software. Baras uses step-by-step instructions and skill-building applications to help you set up a smooth-running Symphony program. Aimed at both beginning and intermediate Symphony users, *The Symphony™ Book* will show you how to make the most of this dynamic all-in-one software system.

$18.95 p
0-07-881160-0, 300 pp., 8¹/₈ x 10⁷/₈

Symphony™ Master: The Expert's Guide
by Edward M. Baras

Business professionals, maximize the power of your Symphony software. Edward Baras, software instructor and a financial analyst for Standard & Poor's,

shows you how to become an expert user of Symphony's command language, spreadsheet, and database unctions. Advanced techniques like file consolidation and windowing, macro and menu design, sensitivity analysis, and database statistics are explained in a clear, concise style, and then put to use in many practical applications. Baras also introduces you to another part of the Symphectrum—communications—with other Symphony users and with external mainframes. *Symphony™ Master*—an authoritative compendium designed to give you optimal performance from Symphony.

$19.95 p
0-07-881170-8, 352 pp., 8¹/₈ x 10⁷/₈

The Complete Book of Symphony™ Macros
by Don Nicholas, Judy Quick, and Lighthouse Publishing Services, Ltd.

If you're already conducting business with Symphony,™ now you can save computing time while maximizing the power of this integrated software with *The Complete Book of Symphony™ Macros*. Macros, individual keystrokes that automatically activate a series of computing steps which perform a specific task, can speed up such routine functions as printing a worksheet, setting column widths, saving a file, or even dialing a telephone. In *Symphony™ Macros*, you learn how to build macros step-by-step and how to use macro commands to create a powerful programming language. Sample macros for worksheet design and formatting, formula generation, data entry, data and file manipulation, printing, and telecommunications can be implemented immediately. Menu building with macros and combining macros and menus for graphics, database, word processing, and telecommunications applications are also discussed.

$16.95 p
0-07-881204-6, 160 pp., 6³/₈ x 9¹/₄

DisplayWrite 3 Made Easy
by Gail Todd

Whether you're a beginning IBM® PC/XT user or unfamiliar with word processing software, *DisplayWrite 3 Made Easy* quickly shows you how to effectively use this best-selling, sophisticated word processor from IBM. Each tutorial chapter shows you how to implement new commands and functions that you can apply immediately to your office paperwork. With the easy exercises that accompany each tutorial you can practice the techniques while you gain speed and confidence. Divided into three sections, the book covers all three operations of DisplayWrite 2 and 3: writing and editing, math and tables, and finally, merging files. If you're caught in an "upgrade," Todd also provides information on file exchange between Display-

Writer, the first version of this software, and Display-Write 2 and 3. It's all here in this guide, and "made easy," too.

$17.95p
0-07-881174-0, 300 pp., 7³⁄₈ x 9¹⁄₄

Using dBASE III™
by Edward Jones

Learn how to profit from the greater speed, efficiency, and file capacity of dBASE III with this comprehensive user's guide from Edward Jones. Beginning with an explanation of data base design considerations and installation procedures, *Using dBASE III™* then teaches you how to design customized business application programs. Payroll preparation, inventory analysis, file management, and creating menu-driven mailing lists to promote your product or service are just a few of the business functions simplified by *Using dBASE III™*. You'll also learn how to interface dBASE III with other popular software programs, such as Lotus™1-2-3™ WordStar,® and dBASE II™. An excellent, nontechnical teaching guide, *Using dBASE III™* will give both the beginner and experienced computer user all the vital information needed to master this remarkable software package.

$17.95p
0-07-881162-7, 200 pp., 7³⁄₈ x 9¹⁄₄

Advanced dBASE III®: Programming & Techniques
Miriam Liskin

Experienced dBASE® programmers can improve their skills with this complete guide to designing and implementing more effective dBASE III® business applications. Nationally known columnist and consultant Miriam Liskin addresses the "real world" business environment so you can make the most of dBASE III modes of operation. Follow the development of an accounts receivable system from start to finish while Liskin outlines the strategy for planning, testing, and refining this practical financial application. You'll proceed through all the critical steps: defining your needs, establishing data files, modeling the application at command level, determining user control, writing the programs, and evaluating and documenting the system. Database managers, system designers, and other professionals can use Liskin's expertise and insights to achieve optimal dBASE III performance.

$19.95p
0-07-881196-1, 630 pp., 7³⁄₈ x 9¹⁄₄

dBASE III® Tips & Traps
Dick Andersen, Cynthia Cooper, and Bill Dempsey

Take some tips from Dick Andersen and his co-authors and you'll save computing time and avoid troublesome dBASE traps with this helpful collection of creative shortcuts. *dBASE III® Tips & Traps*, another in Andersen's *Tips & Traps* series, is written for all dBASE III® users, beginning and experienced. You'll find hundreds of tips and trap solutions for planning an application system and establishing a database, entering and updating data, ordering and retrieving data, relating databases, customizing screen displays, generating reports, interfacing with other software, and converting files from dBASE II® All tip and trap entries are illustrated and follow a concise "how-to" format.

$17.95p
0-07-881195-3, 300 pp., 7³⁄₈ x 9¹⁄₄

Available at fine bookstores and computer stores everywhere.

For a complimentary catalog of all our current publications contact:
   Osborne **McGraw-Hill**, 2600 Tenth Street, Berkeley, CA 94710

Phone inquiries may be made using our toll-free number.
   Call **800-227-0900** or **800-772-2531** (in California).
   TWX 910-366-7277.

Prices subject to change without notice.